Gender and Work

SUNY Series in Religion, Culture, and Society
Wade Clark Roof, editor

Gender and Work
The Case of the Clergy

Edward C. Lehman, Jr.

STATE UNIVERSITY OF NEW YORK PRESS

Published by
State University of New York Press, Albany

For information, address State University of New York
Press, State University Plaza, Albany, NY 12246

Production by Christine Lynch
Marketing by Fran Keneston

Library of Congress Cataloging-in-Publication Data

Lehman, Edward C.
    Gender and work : the case of the clergy / by Edward C. Lehman,
Jr.
       p. cm. — (SUNY series in religion, culture, and society)
    Includes bibliographical references and index.
    ISBN 0–7914–1591–0 (CH : acid-free). : ISBN 0–7914–1592–9 (PB :
acid-free)
    1. Clergy—United States—Sex differences. 2. Clergy—Office.
I. Title. II. Series.
BR526.L44 1993
305.6——dc20   92–30543
                                                  CIP

Contents

To the pastors, those men and women:
who are called,
who have prepared,
who struggle with sin and grace,
who serve with love,
who are loved in return.

Preface

THIS BOOK REPORTS the results of an exploratory sociological study of the ways in which men and women deal with the world of work. In cases where women and men are occupied with similar jobs or careers, do they define and approach their vocational responsibilities in the same way? Do they exhibit similar work styles, or are there modes of approaching work that tend to be gender specific? As shown in the opening chapter, recent discussions of this question manifest widespread disagreements over virtually every aspect of the issue. Virtually all we are very clear about is that both men and women indeed spend large portions of their waking lives working very hard, and that occupations traditionally defined as "men's work" increasingly have become fields of labor for women as well. That much is known. The rest is unclear.

The research reported here focuses on workers in a particular occupation, that is, ordained clergy serving as pastors of local Protestant congregations—ministers, clerics, preachers, parsons—whatever term applies. There is still a great deal we do not know about this vocation. One trend is obvious, a shift that is central to this study. Since about the early 1960s, increasing numbers of women in "mainline" Protestant denominations have entered theological seminaries to prepare for the pastoral role. While in seminary and especially when seeking placement in pastoral positions after graduation, these women have experienced prejudice and discrimination in the form of sex stereotyping, refusal to take their call to ministry seriously, denominational hesitancy to press their cause forcefully, and efforts by lay search committees (church members) to avoid giving them equal access to pastoral openings. Traditional masculine definitions of the ministry and the system of patriarchy permeating the denominations have consistently thwarted women's efforts to broaden their roles in organized religious life. In the face of these realities, religious feminists had to create strategies to overcome institutional religious sexism.

By the 1980s significant numbers of church women sought to legitimate their efforts to expand the role of women in organized religion by pointing to what they considered gender-specific approaches to enacting the role of clergy. That is, some persons involved in the women-in-ministry movement argued that the churches should be receptive to the entry of women into the ranks of ordained clergy, because men and women typically approach the Christian ministry in different ways, and that "a woman's way" is more desirable than traditional masculine ministry styles. However, other Christian feminists disagreed, replying that the ministry is really androgynous, and insisting that overemphasis in sex differences would only serve to further marginalize women. *Which is the case? Who is right? Which portrait (if either) of male and female clergy most closely resembles reality? That is what this book is about.*

Social scientists continually remind us that "things are not what they seem." They are not what they seem to ordinary people trying to make sense out of their everyday lives. And they are not what they seem, even to people propounding social and cultural changes. Things that affect our fate turn out to have many "layers" of meaning, rather like an onion. As we peel back each successive layer, the perceptions derived from each new level sometimes dramatically change our understanding of the thing we're trying to figure out.

The analysis reported in this volume sheds some light on the extent to which various assertions about "difference" and "sameness" in men's and women's ministry styles are in fact "what they seem." It reveals several layers of meaning concerning sex differences in approach to the ministry. It's a complicated system, this world of religious leaders and followers. Neither those emphasizing "difference" nor those emphasizing "sameness" were completely supported in the results, an outcome they probably would not expect, predict, or welcome. Nevertheless, uncovering such patterns is always more desirable than being ignorant of them.

I have identified the study as an "exploratory" venture. The undertaking was exploratory in the sense of being the first piece of research to examine *both* women and men as concerns their approach to work as pastors of congregations. A few other studies have investigated the ministry styles of women alone (e.g., Ice 1987; Stevens 1989; Weidman 1985). Yet others have examined patterns among seminary students (Eckhardt and Goldsmith 1984). Comparisons of men's and women's orientations have been a peripheral component of work focusing on other issues (e.g., Carroll, Hargrove, and Lummis 1983). In much of the theological and polemical literature on masculine and feminine approaches to ministry, statements about male and female pastoral styles were either conjectural or somewhat dogmatic. *This research is the first attempt to make direct empirical comparisons between clergywomen and clergymen concerning several dimensions of ministry style, using a national sample of men and women serving as pastors in the denominations participating in the project.* It is in that sense that I hope the work will make a contribution.

This research monograph is designed to be of use to a wide range of publics. The work deals with concepts and theories likely to be of interest to social and behavioral scientists studying religion, gender, sex roles, complex organizations, patterns of work, and social psychology. Within religious organizations, the issues are relevant to male and female clergy, denominational administrators, seminary faculty and students, even lay church members. Accordingly, I have chosen to write the report in a way that would communicate to both academics (social scientists) and educated readers in religious organizations (especially clergy and denominational administrators). The descriptions and explanations, therefore, will probably contain more material than academics would want to see and a bit less than church leaders would prefer to have. Since I opted to err on the side of completeness, academic readers will probably find themselves able to merely scan some sections included primarily for the benefit of nonacademics. Occasional repetition is an unavoidable artifact of writing for a diverse audience. My apologies if you find that tedious.

In analyzing data involving people of different social and cultural backgrounds and those serving in divergent ministry situations, it is necessary to categorize them clearly if the comparisons discussed are to be understood. Some people resent being categorized in any way, and as a result they can be offended by seeing such references to themselves in social science research. I am sensitive to this possibility. The situation brings to mind the jingle most of us learned in childhood— "Sticks and stones can break my bones, but names will never hurt me!" If social psychology has taught us nothing else, it has demon-

strated that while the saying may be a good ego defense against the
cruel jibes of neighborhood playmates, the thrust of the assertion simply isn't true. Names can and do hurt, and the injuries resulting from
caustic labelling can be debilitating.

I have had to make choices of "labels"—"names"—in reporting
differences in ministry style among the clergy. The criteria used in
deciding on labels for those attributes were firstly, *clarity of communication,* secondly, usage that is *familiar and customary,* and finally, terminology that is *as inoffensive as possible.* The major distinctions involving
these concerns were those delineating race and ethnicity, prestige of
one's position, and differences between the sexes.

1. Race and Ethnicity

American society is highly stratified. People differ in terms
of the prestige, power, privilege, and life chances. A persistent
factor in this aspect of social life is race and ethnicity. Racial/
ethnic groups have been dealt with in terms of "majority versus
minority" groups, "dominant versus subordinate" groups, "white
versus nonwhite" groups, and so forth. None of these sets of
terms enjoys universal acceptance. Some persons prefer one set
of distinctions, while others prefer different ones. For the sake
of clarity and consistency in this report, I have used the term
racial-ethnic to refer to racial and cultural minorities who are
typically in subordinate positions in society. For the same reason, I have used the term *white* to refer to members of the dominant white majority. In using these labels I intend no invidious
distinctions. The terms are intended simply to make clear analytical distinctions that are important in examining the evidence.

2. Prestige of Position

Another way in which clergy are "stratified" is in terms of
the size of the congregation they serve. Many ministers will
deny it, claiming that all servants of the Lord are equal, but
there is ample evidence that some servants are "more equal
than others." Lay church members recognize it, people outside
of the churches perceive it, and the clergy themselves act as
though it were true (e.g., Lehman 1990). A major distinction
made in the analysis of ministry style is whether the clergyman
or clergywoman is serving alone as pastor to a congregation or
appointed as the "senior" minister (head pastor, pastor in
charge, first in team, etc.) in a local church served by more than

one clergyperson. Those serving as the only ordained minister for a congregation are identifed as "solo" pastors. Persons serving as incumbents of the superordinate position on a team are called "seniors" or "senior pastors."

3. Sex Differences

Sex and sex differences are not favorite topics of public discourse in religious organizations. Some religious leaders rarely speak the word for fear of offending someone. Yet sex differences—variations in the ways in which men and women approach the pastorate—are central to this inquiry. We cannot avoid the word. So we shall speak of "sex differences," "sex-linked patterns," "sex of clergy," and so on throughout the analysis. Each time the text makes such a reference, the concept involved is simply the difference between being male or female as clergy. One might argue that the term *gender* is a better one to use. Unfortunately, 'gender' is also a concept that appears in the text, but it is not used to refer to being biologically female or male. 'Gender,' instead, refers to the social constructions society has created for people who happen to be female or male—the gender-related terms being *feminine* or *masculine*. Indeed the central question in the undertaking is whether clergy who are biologically males (sex) tend to have masculine ministry styles (gender) and whether biological females tend to manifest feminine approaches to ministry. So we have to talk about "sex differences."

While my name alone appears as author of this work, that fact does not also mean that I was the only one involved in the study. As most scholars know, research is a very social enterprise. Accordingly, I wish to acknowledge others who contributed to the success of the study in one way or another. The first form of contribution involves underwriting the study. Research costs money, and several organizations were very generous in providing funds to cover research costs. The Religious Research Association provided a grant to cover research expenses. The four denominations participating in the project also provided funds—The American Baptist Churches, The United Methodist Church, the Presbyterian Church (USA), and the United Church of Christ. Without their generous support, the study would not have gotten off the ground. Thank you!

Several professionals, graduate students, and upper-level undergraduate students conducted the telephone interviews to gather the data from the clergy we studied. These persons worked days, evenings, and weekends to collect the data within a specific time period. They did an excellent job. Working at the State University of New York, College at Brockport, were (Ms.) Johnnie Lehman, Stephen Vigliotti, Christine Cummings, and Barbara French. Conducting interviews from other locations were Rev. Ms. Christina Del Piero, Shannon Carr, and Rev. Mr. John Lowe. These three persons worked in New York City and Northern Indiana, and their work was underwritten by the Research Unit of the United Church of Christ with funds over and above those provided in the initial research support referred to above.

Several denominational administrators served as consultants to the project from its inception. These persons included Dr. Bonna Sue Himes of the American Baptist Churches, Dr. Sheila Kelly and Dr. Marjorie Royle of the United Church of Christ, Rev. Ms. Kathy Nickerson and Rev. Ms. M. Lynn Scott of the United Methodist Church, and Rev. Ms. Ann DuBois and Rev. Ms. Rebecca Tollefson of the Presbyterian Church (USA). Rev. Ms. Charlotte Still and Rev. Mr. David Holden of the United Church of Christ also provided important assistance. Dr. Elizabeth Verdesi, Staff Associate of the Women-in-Ministry Office of the National Council of Churches, coordinated that group and added her own important insights into the several discusssions we had. These individuals provided an important "insider sounding board" for ideas in the project throughout its entirety, and I am deeply grateful for their cooperation, patience, and insights.

Associates and co-workers usually play an important role in organizing and executing sociological research. They give ideas to one another, critique proposals and manuscripts, and sharpen each other's thinking in formal and informal conversation. At least seven of my valued colleagues provided this form of assistance to me in this study. They are Dr. Adair Lummis, Prof. Nancy Nason-Clark, Prof. Martha Ice, Prof. Victoria Erickson, Prof. Joy Charlton, Prof. Stephen Warner, Prof. Cheryl Townsend Gilkes, and Prof. Gary Bouma. They generously gave of their time to critique the data-collection instrument and the first draft of this report, and their comments were extremely helpful. While I gained important insights from their work on my behalf, of course, the final product is my own responsibility.

Research is also usually conducted from within a formal organizational base. In the case of this undertaking, I was fortunate to have *two* such bases of operation—my home campus of the State University of New York, College at Brockport, and the Department of Anthropology and Sociology of Monash University in Melbourne, Australia, where I spent a wonderful sabbatical year working on the manuscript. Both institutions provided important resources such as an office, access to competent secretaries, computing facilities, libraries, print shops, and mail services. At Brockport I am especially indebted to Ms. Gloria Condoluci, one of the most efficient secretaries I have ever known. Brockport also provided the services of Ms. Lauren Nicholson, of their Document Preparation Center, whose computer magic made the process of mass mailings go very smoothly. At home the patience and proof-reading skills of Johnnie Lehman were indispensable. Monash gave me access to the especially valuable services of Dr. Peter Hiller, who knows more about SPSS-PC than I will ever know, his coworker Ms. Kristin Diemer, who worked part time with me as a research assistant, and Ms. Juliet Yee, the department administrative assistant. Finally, of course, my work in Melbourne would have been much more difficult were it not for the assistance of several competent secretaries in the persons of Helen Moore, Margaret Walker, Gaynor Thornell, Ros Shennan, Sue Stevenson, and Corrie McKee. *Thank you* to you all!

Read on. Comments welcome.

Edward C. Lehman, Jr.
Brockport, New York
July 1992

1

Differences about Differences

"WHY CAN'T A WOMAN BE MORE LIKE A MAN?" cried Henry Higgins in the musical *My Fair Lady* (Lerner 1978, 247). The misogynous Professor Higgins was confronted with the task of transforming Eliza Doolittle, a lower-class woman, into a cultured lady. He had been willing to put his money where his mouth was—a wager that he could pull off the metamorphosis—and he sensed a danger that he was about to lose his shirt. He didn't even understand women. To him women were irrational, emotional, and infuriating carbon copies of their equally exasperating mothers. Why couldn't they be like their fathers? How was he to go about changing one of them anyway?

Higgins's lament is something that virtually everyone in Western audiences can *understand*, although many listeners would not necessarily *endorse* the sentiments. The plea "why can't a woman be more like a man?" reflects a set of untested assumptions about human beings that enjoys very broad consensus, that is, that women and men by nature are different cognitively, affectively, and behaviorally. In Western European and North American societies, for instance, the traditional culture defines man as typically aggressive, dominant, power hungry, rational, analytical, independent, competitive, unexpressive, and cool under pressure. Correspondingly those cultures describe women as

1

passive, submissive, egalitarian, emotional, intuitive, dependent, non-competitive, expressive, and flappable. People in many non-Western cultures and preliterate societies also tend to think dichotomously about men and women, although the attributes they describe do not always parallel those observed in the industrial West (e.g., Mead 1935).

Alternate assumptions have arisen in the United States and other Western countries in recent years, suppositions that turn Henry Higgins's ideas upside down. Some of those revisionist definitions of the sexes would have a Professor *Henrietta* Higgins singing a different tune. When confronted with *Elmer* Doolittle, a typical Western man, she would sing, "Why can't a man be more like a woman?" As one who could not endorse Henry Higgins's complaint, she would describe men as coldly rational, over sexed, hypercompetitive, status conscious, uncaring, and so forth—and thus equally exasperating. She'd mourn that men don't grow up to be like their mothers.

Significant numbers of women would identify with those sentiments. Especially among the cultural feminists (described below), there are broadly shared perceptual norms specifying that masculine approaches to life—and especially to work—are pathological. "The patriarchal orientation," they would say, "pits one person against another in perpetual competition. This stance is hopelessly rational, rigid, legalistic, instrumental, hierarchical, authoritarian, and power-hungry. It has dominated world affairs to date, and we need to get away from it as quickly and as far as we are able."

It is clear to anyone who has been sensitized to cultural and structural sexism in Western society that Henry Higgins's definition of the sexes is the more institutionalized version there. The dissenting feminist voice grows a bit louder each year, but the macho traditions are still able to all but drown it out. The postulates of male superiority seem to be deeply embedded in most social institutions within which formal and informal social interaction between men and women takes place. Take, for example, just the concept of "dominance"—a rather ubiquitous aspect of social relations involving power and privilege. Differences in the relative dominance men and women enjoy in relation to each other appear in virtually all institutions. In its purest form, the misogynist tradition assumes that the man is regarded as the proper "head" of the family, for example. Those same assumptions lead business and industrial organizations to recruit men almost exclusively as their executive officers. Most large work organizations still do not consider women sufficiently stable and dependable to entrust the fate of the firm to female hands. In similar fashion, the most prestigious posts in higher education tend to be occupied by men, males dominate professional athletics, they hold almost all of the significant positions of political leadership, only men are to go off to war, and on and on. To many people, the apparent social inequities in such social configurations are perfectly acceptable, because they conform to what is considered "naturally" male and female. If men are naturally the more dominant, some would say, then it is "only proper" that they occupy the more dominant positions. Assumptions such as these embody the problems feminists seek to solve, that is, eradicating institutional sexism and opening up social participation to women.

While it is clear that the Henry and Henrietta Higginses of the world differ profoundly in the evaluations they place upon each other, one must not lose sight of the fact that *they actually share an important premise. They agree on the underlying assumption that men and women are endemically different cognitively, affectively, and behaviorally.* Their articulations of those differences are highly divergent, as are their estimations of the value placed on the traits they perceive. *But they both assume fundamental sex differences.* That assumption is the focus of this research.

Gender Differences in Religion

This book reports the results of an exploratory study of some gender differences said to characterize institutional religion. More specifically, the project focuses on men and women who are ordained ministers serving as pastors of local Protestant congregations. The research involves an empirical examination of a set of assertions concerning differences in the way male and female clergy approach their work. Over the last two decades, a body of literature has emerged in which authors present some version of the argument that *it is possible to identify two major approaches to carrying out the role of pastor of local congregations, one labelled "masculine" and the other called "feminine"* (e.g., Christ and Plaskow 1979; Ice 1987; Miller-McLemore 1988; Nason-Clark 1987; Weidman 1985; Stevens 1989). The masculine stance is the traditional one, and since men had a corner on the ordained ministry until recently, this approach is considered to have derived from men's preferences. The masculine religious culture also includes legitimations based on Biblical references. The feminine approach is a direct opposite of the masculine stance in many ways, and it is set forth as an innovative way of enacting the role of minister, a uniquely feminist approach deriving from the experience of being a woman (see also Hahn 1991; Ochs 1983; Franklin 1986; Ruether 1983 1985; Maitland 1983; Russell 1974; Daly 1973; Fiorenza 1976; Collins 1974; and Christ 1977).

The masculine approach—also labelled "patriarchal"—involves a ministry steeped in impersonal hierarchies, segmental relationships, hypercompetitiveness, power over lay people, authoritarian decision making, mastery over nature, rigid theology, legalistic ethics, and exclusion of women and minorities. By contrast, the feminine stance incorporates personal communities, holistic relationships, egalitarianism, empowerment of lay people, democratic decision making, cooperation with nature, open and flexible theology, existential ethics of responsible sharing, and inclusion of women and minorities (Ice 1987; Nason-Clark 1987, 332–33). Some proponents of such comparisons also label the masculine approach as "pathological," and they argue that if the church is to fulfil its proper role in society, it is necessary that ministers adopt the "healthy" feminine way of doing things (Ice 1987, 6–7).

However, as we shall see below, the proponents of a feminine approach to the ministry do not speak with one voice on the issue of male / female differences in defining the role of parish minister. (Feminism is not monolithic, and its schools of thought involve numerous crosscutting distinctions. Here we focus on but one, gender and approach to work. For discussions of various types of feminism, see Riley 1989; Ruether 1983; and Grant 1989.) Their arguments can be divided into at least two camps, that is, those who perceive significant gender differences and those who do not (e.g., Christ and Plaskow 1979, 1–17). One camp—called the "minimalists" (see also Epstein 1988, 25ff.)—would answer both Henry Higgins's question and the inverted one posed by "Henrietta" in the same way—"They can be, and they are! Men and women in ministry are far more alike than different in their work. The songs assume major divergences, but variations between male and female approaches to ministry are but superficial idiosyncrasies. Both styles appear about equally in both sexes." Their argument asserts that there are far more similarities than differences between male and female ministers, and that the arguments for significant gender differences are primarily political and are based on self-interested speculation. Harrison says, for example, that there is no such thing as a distinctively feminist ethic. To her, normative issues are the same for all, and the need is to maintain inclusive institutions. "We must begin by rejecting the notion that there is any fundamental dimorphism in human nature / being" (Robb 1985, 29; see also Ruether and McLaughlin 1979, 19).

In contrast to the minimalists, the other camp—the "maximalists"—would reply very differently. They assume real and important differences in the way men and women approach their work. To Henry Higgins they would say (exaggerating a bit), "Given what I have experienced of men in the ministry, I wouldn't want to be like them for anything in the world! Men have been taking the church down a primrose path, and we are working hard trying to undo the harm they have done!" A caricature of their answer to Henrietta would be, "They can't! Men are men, and women are women, and there's no way men can even understand, let alone implement, a feminine approach to pastoral ministry! Women should avoid like a plague any chance of being co-opted into the patriarchal way of doing things. They should strive instead to serve the Christian community on their own as only women can do it!"

Most of the religious literature dealing with this issue tends to be maximalist. It reflects assumptions of one or more male/female differences in ministry style. Given the prevalence of sexism in the churches, along with the virtually universal experience of resistance among women seeking deeper involvements in church leadership, it is not surprising to see large numbers of women adopting and arguing the maximalist position. The perceptions of superiority in feminine approaches to church life provide meaning, legitimation, and focus to women long frustrated by the churches.

It is also important to note that the ideas about male/female differences in approach to ministry (and to religion in general) found in that literature tend to be more implicit than explicit. Theological statements appear time and again that could not be made without underlying assumptions of women doing religion fundamentally differently from men. Often the assumptions appear only "between the lines" as postulates on which other assertions would have to rest. This mode of presentation gives them the flavor of *dogma* so clearly understood that it is not necessary to spell it out. They are the "of-course assumptions" of a community—"of course that's the way it is; how come you didn't know that?" They appear to be so obvious to participants in the subculture that there is no need to articulate them in any detail.

The published literature expressing doubts about consistent male/female divergences in ministry style is much more sparse. Rather than urgently pressing an argument that men and women are basically alike, persons skeptical of other feminists' claims to a uniquely feminine ministry style have tended to remain on the publishing sidelines, where they reflect on and generally reject the arguments that women manifest a uniquely feminine ministry style. They have felt less motivation to write about it. Instead they appear to go about their work while seeking greater integration in church structures and programs.

Accordingly, there is a tendency for these differences in approach to be found in divergent structural locations. As Christ and Plaskow (1979, 13) put it, "Those feminists who work within the Biblical traditions tend to call for equality in religious rituals and symbolisms, while those whose theological or spiritual reflection is primarily rooted in the women's movement...more often call for at least temporary ascendancy of women and the female principle." The maximalists are in a position to "grind their axes" without concern for extraneous organizational consequences. The minimalists, by contrast, tend to be persons who feel responsible for some segments of existing religious structures, which makes it much more difficult for them to espouse separatist ideologies, actions that would compromise prior commitments and weaken their structural base.

In any case, in this study *we focus primarily on the arguments of the maximalists*. Can we document empirically the existence of male/female differences in ministry style? Who is right, the maximalists or the minimalists? Some empirical research implies that men and women do approach the ministry differently (e.g., Ice 1987; and Stevens 1989). Other studies suggest that descriptions of such sex differences may have been overblown (e.g., Charlton 1987; Carroll, Hargrove, and Lummis 1983; Nason-Clark 1987; Ekhardt and Goldsmith 1984; Hale, King, and Jones 1980). Which set of assumptions about how women and men take and define the role of parish minister is actually "out there" among clergy? In somewhat simplified terms, that is the question this undertaking seeks to address.

The Secular Background

These positions concerning masculine and feminine approaches to the pastoral ministry did not emerge in a vacuum. Behind the feminist challenges to patriarchal forms of ministry lay the secular feminist movement. The debates in the churches resonate well with those in the larger society, and shifts in the secular feminist movement have also seen their parallels in the religious feminist dialogue. And if there is any causal connection between the two, it is probably the events in the secular arena that are the more causally antecedent.

There is a relatively broad consensus concerning the sequence of major shifts in the position of women in discussions of social and cultural life in the United States. Until about the middle of the twentieth century, women tended to be the "residual" category in Western culture. The general cultural bias was that the interesting things in life— things that were important to study and think about—were men's things. Histories, novels, theater, economics, politics, biography, religion—all tended to be by and about men. The general assumption was that it truly was a man's world. Women were "there," of course, but they were not nearly as interesting as the men. After all, how much impact did they have on the world anyway? "Normal" life was that involving men's activities; it needed little explanation. Where women's life departed from those patterns, the analytical problem was easily defined away merely by relegating women to the status of deviant cases. In this sense, women "needed to be explained." Nevertheless, in fact most of the time women were simply ignored.

This pattern was clearly evident in scholarship about human beings prior to about the last two or three decades. Most work in the social and behavioral sciences and the humanities was "womanless." In psychology, for example, males were used disproportionately as research subjects, the results of that work were presumed to be generalizable to women, and gender was generally ignored as an important category of social reality. The research in question was done almost exclusively by men who assumed that men's activities were the ones most central to human life (Crawford and Marecek 1989, 149).

In roughly the late 1960s, this picture began to change. Social and behavioral sciences began to study women systematically. The emergence of this new scholarship didn't flow "naturally" from sophisticated perceptions of interesting research directions and questions. Instead the new focus on the feminine derived from the political agenda of the women's liberation movement (Epstein 1988, 24). The call was to "bring women in." As a result, the research tended to focus exclusively on women.

One approach to "bringing women in" was to focus on *exceptional* women. In history it involved rediscovering important female figures generally expunged from the record—Joan of Arc, Catherine the Great, Marie Curie, and Eleanor Roosevelt. In psychology it was an examination of the works of Anna Freud, Karen Horney, and others. This approach served to bring to mind the work of noteworthy women and to militate against assumptions that females are not capable of significant achievement. Nevertheless, there was also a "down side" to that focus, that is, it "may convey an underlying message that only exceptional women are...worthy of serving as role models [and]...it may reinforce the belief that success is solely the product of individual ability, determination or effort" (Crawford and Maracek 1989, 150–51). It could backfire and be used by conservatives in their arguments against structural and programmatic change to benefit women.

A second approach some observers took in moving away from the "womanless" picture of society has been described by Crawford and Marecek (1989, 151–55) as the "woman-as-problem" stance. It has also been called the "female deficiency" approach. According to this perspective, women are seen as presenting researchers with a series of anomalies that beg for explanation. Individual "deficits" included under this conceptual umbrella include dependency, eating disorders, fear of success, math anxiety, and so forth. The central question was why women differed from men in these ways. The woman-as-problem approach does succeed in focusing attention on women and thus moving away from the "womanless" paradigm of old. Nevertheless, Crawford and Maracek (1989, 153) also point out that examining women as "problems" for society gives conservatives further ammunition in their effort to exclude women from positions of responsibility. If women suffer deficiencies such as these, then won't some conservatives ask why women should be given opportunities to move into strategic positions they may not be able to handle adequately? Furthermore, the stance also still uses men as the standard by which women are to be assessed. And, of course, it is a classic example of "blaming the victim." So from a feminist perspective, the women-as-problem approach solves only the matter of female invisibility, and in the process it creates or continues other problems for the effort to "bring women back in."

A third approach to solving the "woman problem" was the development of the concept of 'androgyny' (Bem 1974). In simple form, the concept of 'androgyny' refers to a blending of supposedly masculine and feminine personality traits within a single individual, whether male or female. Discussions of androgyny assert that there are masculine and feminine traits in everyone. Sex role socialization encourages males to develop predominantly in one direction and females in another, but the potential for internalizing both masculine and feminine characteristics is said to be present in everyone.

Reflecting a political tone again, androgyny was also promoted as a *desirable* trait for everyone. The assumption spread broadly that it was "not good" for men to be purely masculine or for women to be purely feminine. The argument stated that men would be more healthy, for example, if they developed an ability to express emotions they'd otherwise "naturally" repress, such as in the act of crying. Women would be more healthy—and more acceptable in the world of business and public affairs—if they could be more assertive and analytical instead of retiring and intuitive. A spate of "therapies" burst onto the social scene to help women—especially with things like "consciousness raising," "image management," and "assertiveness training"—to help them become more androgynous. "Even more than the fear of success, [*androgyny*] became a buzz word for the public." (Mednick 1989, 1119). Still today, in certain pop circles, you are considered "with it" if you can manifest androgynous personality traits, or at least convince people that you think androgynous personality is desirable.

The major contribution that the discussions of androgyny made was in refocusing discussions of gender differences away from women alone. They dealt with both men and women largely on an equal plane, presenting any variations in personality as the result of sex role socialization rather than artifacts of biological functioning. Yet the entire discussion rests on a basic assumption of gender *differences*, and its scientific merit has been seriously questioned recently (Mednick 1989, 1119).

The most recent theories about gender differences to have gained widespread popularity are those of Gilligan (1982). Gilligan's thesis is a direct challenge to Kohlberg (Kohlberg and Kramer 1969), dealing with the issue of "moral development" in children and adults. Kohlberg had developed a scheme of stages through which people are said to develop, each stage being characterized by different criteria for making moral choices. The "lowest" stages are basically matters of crude self-interest and coercion, orientations that tend to characterize young children. The "highest" stages involve appeals to universalistic moral principles revolving around the concept of "justice." The initial application of Kohlberg's concepts tended to portray women as typically manifesting lower stages of moral development than men.

Gilligan studied groups of women confronting difficult moral dilemmas that were unique to women. She developed a scheme for describing stages of moral development that revolved not around the concept of justice but around that of 'responsible caring'. Using such conceptualization, Gilligan argued that moral development in men and women differs most centrally, in terms not of stages (which any person can go through, male or female) but of developmental schemes involving gender-specific criteria. Morality in men and women, according to Gilligan, differs not in degree but in *kind*. For men it is a matter of justice; for women it involves responsible caring. Men and women speak with "different voices" (Gilligan 1982).

Gilligan's arguments took the discussions of gender differences another step away from "women-as-problem." They asserted at least implicitly that women's morality was not only unique but also more desirable. "Women's way" was not only different but also better. Social life governed by appeals to "justice" were cold and unforgiving. It would be much better to have moral criteria of empathetic benevolence or warm parental caring. "This idea has been widely and enthusiastically accepted by many feminist scholars in numerous disciplines, as well as by many writers, politicians, journalists, and the public. It is no doubt a conceptual bandwagon" (Mednick 1989, 1119).

Unfortunately, scholarship following up on the Kohlberg/Gilligan debate has tended *not* to support Gilligan's perspective. Studies involving both schemes have indicated few, if any, differences between men and women, whether using Kohlberg's measure or moral dilemmas that reflect Gilligan's ideas (see Thoma 1986; and Friedman, Robinson, and Friedman 1987). Yet the belief in a "different voice" is still around among journalists and politicians. "It appears to be a symbol for a cluster of widely held social beliefs that argue for women's difference, for reasons that are quite independent of scientific merit....The 'different voice' is part of a currently popular category of theories, sometimes referred to as cultural feminism..., that argue for women's special, and even superior, nature" (Mednick 1989, 1120).

A Focus on "Gender"

By the late 1970s, many feminist scholars came to perceive that focusing on women to the exclusion of men would further neither their scholarly goals nor their political agendas. They needed an empirically verifiable approach that would retain a focus on women as significant players in the drama of human existence but, at the same time, would not backfire politically as a weapon to be used against women's interests. The move was to "shift the focus of inquiry from woman to gender, and from gender as difference to gender as social relations. That is, gender came to be conceived as a principle of social organization, which structures the relations, especially the power relations, between women and men" (Crawford and Marecek 1989, 155). Previous dichotomous divisions of the world by sex were rejected as simplistic, and in their place a new breed of feminists posited the idea that any such perceptions were merely social constructions deriving from the fact (experience) of hierarchy (Epstein 1988, 15–16). This position generally reflects the argument of the "minimalists."

According to Mednick (1989), minimalist views assert that "women's behavior is a function of much more than a supposedly universal trait. The latter way of thinking by some political feminists... [involves] a false universalism that leads to the incorrect perception of the situation of *all* women as the same" (1120). One of the generalizations that minimalists are first to reject is the assumption that all women manifest similar personality traits. On the contrary, race, ethnicity, occupation, education all tend to predict variations in women's sense of identity, values, behavior patterns, and so forth. Careful analyses of women in those various social locations indicate that such social and cultural circumstances significantly affect the characteristics of the players functioning within them. Men and women in similar positions of power and authority (or the lack of it), for example, think and act more like each other than do women or men in positions that differ in that regard. The implication of those patterns is that cognitive, affective, and behavioral differences perceived in men and women are not artifacts of unique personality traits within them but epiphenomena of those external circumstances.

Summary

The relative absence of reflection in the "womanless" period and the discussions of significant women, androgyny, women as problem, male and female moralities, and so on, since the late 1960s may be subsumed within the category of "maximalists." People thinking in these ways either accept without question or develop arguments for the existence of important gender differences in adults. Those who reconstruct the concept of 'gender' in terms of social interaction, especially that involving power relations, represent the "minimalists." For them variations in thought, emotions, and actions between males and females do not represent different personality traits associated with sex or gender but instead reflect the influence of external constraints and opportunities that *happen to be* associated more with one sex than the other.

Gender and Social Policy

These two camps, the maximalists and minimalists, represent two poles in a broad spectrum of points of view concerning the existence and explanation of gender differences. The research from any of the points of view along that continuum is of interest in and of itself. At the same time, as so often happens in social science research, it is difficult to divorce most of that discussion from political goals. "Gender research is replete with ideological overlays, reflecting the values of the scholar and of the social group" (Epstein 1988, xii). The assumptions of both the minimalists and the maximalists provide not only intellectual structure for inquiry but also normative goals and political strategy for realizing them (see also Bacchi 1990). In the 1970s, the ideal toward which most feminist writers were pressing was integration and equality for women. In the 1980s many feminists repudiated that agenda and instead were pressing for evidence of female superiority and for either ways of gaining feminist power and influence or ways of withdrawing from social participation in the masculine society altogether. In both cases, the predominant assumption has been one of significant gender differences. The primary strategy in the 1970s was to find ways to *play down* those differences in order to remove barriers to the entry of women into fuller participation in the political, economic, and social life of the society. The strategy that gained a greater following in the 1980s, on the other hand, was to *play up* gender differences in an effort to demonstrate the superiority of female approaches to life and to move toward replacing masculine structures with feminine ones, either for women alone or for the entire society (e.g., Daly 1978).

The political objectives of the minimalist feminists are actually not very different from the basic objectives of some maximalists, particularly those predominating in the 1970s, that is, removing social and cultural impediments to open participation of women in all aspects of social life. Here also the analytical arguments are laden with normative agendas. "The political is not easily separated from the intellectual, even for those who feel that they ought to be—and of course may believe they are the same thing" (Epstein 1988, xiii).

A major way in which the political agenda is worked out among the minimalists is to analyze the negative political consequences of the arguments of the maximalists. The minimalists argue that those emphasizing differences between the sexes are prone to jump on ideological bandwagons without thinking through the social and political implications of their actions. In the most general sense, feminist scholars who argue that "men and women live in two cultures, two domains, that they are in effect two species" actually support the traditionalists. This accrues whether they argue for a separate-but-equal situation or for female superiority. To insist on gender differences is to keep alive old beliefs and doubts about women's competence. Reinforcing those traditional assumptions bolsters the social conspiracy against women (Epstein 1988, 223–39).

Hare-Mustin and Marecek make a similar point, expressing it in terms of "paradoxes" involved in thinking about gender.

> Paradoxes arise because every representation conceals at the same time as it reveals....The issue of gender differences has been a divisive one for feminist scholars. Some believe that differences affirm women's value and special nature; others are concerned that focusing on differences reinforces the status quo and supports inequality, given that the power to define remains with men. A paradox is that efforts to affirm the special value of women's experience and their 'inner life' turn attention away from efforts to change the material conditions of women's lives and alleviate institutional sexism.... Another paradox arises from the assertion of a female way of knowing, involving intuition and experiential understanding, rather than logical abstraction. This assertion implies that all other thought is a male way of knowing, and if taken to an extreme, can be used to support the view that

women are incapable of rational thought and of acquiring the knowledge of the culture....Moreover, feminist separatism, the attempt to avoid male influence by separating from men, leaves intact the larger system of male control in the society....There is yet another paradox. Qualities such as caring, expressiveness, and concern for relationships are extolled as women's superior virtues and the wellspring of public regeneration. At the same time, however, they are seen as arising from women's subordination....When we extol such qualities, do we necessarily also extol women's subordination...? If subordination makes women 'better people,' then perpetuation of women's 'goodness' would seem to require the perpetuation of inequality. (Hare-Mustin and Marecek 1988, 462)

In summary, the minimalist argument is that some maximalists, in their enthusiasm to demonstrate unique qualities women can bring to social arenas that have traditionally been the provinces of men, may have promoted strategies that could be used to the detriment of the very women they wish to assist.

The Pattern in the Churches

The basic rationales that structure the discussions within the secular women's movement can also be seen in the literature dealing with religious feminism (e.g., Christ 1977). Prior to about mid-twentieth century, there was little discussion of significant leadership roles for women in local congregations. Even though women constituted the core of lay workers who kept the churches running from week to week, "everyone" assumed that the ordained ministry was properly reserved to men, and the men in top positions in the hierarchies did little to disabuse members of those views. A few congregations had ordained women and called them as pastors, primarily among groups with a congregational polity located in New England, however, women tended to be "invisible" in discussions of professional church leadership. Well known evangelists such as Amy Semple McPherson and Evangeline Booth were noteworthy in their day primarily because they were departures from that norm. They accomplished a great deal as religious leaders in spite of the fact that they were women. Women didn't attain any significant visibility in the ordained ministry in terms of numbers until about the 1970s.

Warner points out, however, that the current movement of women into the ministry did not emerge from a historical vacuum. The frontier spontaneity and charismatic appeals that defined the revivalism of the "Second Great Awakening" of the nineteenth century established norms of individual religious empowerment. Church members didn't require the approval or endorsement of religious leaders in existing hierarchies in order to act in what they considered to be a response to the call of God. Charismatic appeals to religious vocation and activity became sufficient criteria for assuming leadership roles in local evangelical communities. Women used those norms of empowerment to "carve out space" for themselves in religious organizations. In so doing they were able to separate themselves from the direct control of male church leaders, and they were able to define their own agendas. "From the 1830's on, women formed extraparochial associations, many of which became essential to the church's mission. Because of the power of the purse and of their personal presence, association women gained rights of representation on various church boards. Persistent pressure from various local and regional assemblies (representing lay women) and from staff of specialized agencies (representing religious professionals) eventually wore down the resistance of male elders and bishops in the years after World War II" (Warner 1989, 29). By the 1970s, large numbers of women were pursuing theological education, ordination, and eventual placement as pastors of local congregations in most mainline Protestant denominations. Women ministers were no longer "invisible."

As was the case in the secular women's movement, up through the 1970s supporters of women's ordination typically emphasized gender equality and down-played sex differences in taking the role of ordained minister. The predominant goals were to reform sexist practices, reconstruct (reinterpret) biblical traditions, and promote an androgynous ministry. All of these specific objectives were designed to open the ordained ministry to women—to "bring women in." The predominant assertion was that women could perform clergy roles just as well as men. The argument at the heart of this movement was that there were no relevant differences between men and women in terms of their capacity to serve congregations as religious leaders—a "minimalist" argument. Accordingly, the actions the churches were called upon to take were clear and simple—barriers to women's ordination and placement should be removed (e.g., Christ and Plaskow 1979; Carroll, Hargrove, and Lummis 1983; and Robb 1985).

In form the movement resembled the approach of the "integrationist" wing of the civil rights movement—an appeal to equality and a press for assimilation. The approach has been called "structural feminism" and closely resembles a broader school of thought in secular feminism referred to as "liberal" feminism (see Riley 1989; Ruether 1983; and Grant 1989). According to this perspective, the thing that is considered "the problem" is the *structure* of the church as a social system. Individuals wishing to participate in the system had unequal access to it regardless of their individual abilities to perform system roles. To those of this persuasion, it followed logically that the system—the churches—must change the rules and let women in. The problem was simply to assemble the appropriate argument and evidence, the power of which would then persuade the church leadership to recant and open up church structures to women.

However, the normative structures of social and cultural systems do not readily bow to such appeals to empirical evidence and logic. They function according to their own "*socio*-logic." Since cultural definitions, values, and normative patterns of thought and action tend to be integrated—if you change one thing, you also risk changing others as well—the religious systems did not readily concede the demands of the integrationist wing of the women-in-ministry movement. People at both the denominational and the congregational levels resisted the incorporation of women into the leadership of the church. In most mainline Protestant denominations, this resistance took the form of "not wishing to rush things"—"let's wait and see"—"let's not upset the balance of things"—"don't do anything to create a schism." These forms of resistance to increasing women's roles in religious organizations still continue today.

In the face of this resistance, many integrationist/structural feminists kept pressing and are still holding to the same strategy today. Others, however, simply gave up on the church. The classic expression of church members "throwing over the traces" is illustrated by Mary Daly (1975), who gave up all hope that the church would ever renounce its misogynistic ideology and policies. In about the 1980s, however, many religious feminists tended to take a less extreme stance than Daly, but one that nevertheless represented a major departure from the integrationist approach that had dominated the previous decade.

Standing in dynamic tension with the integrationist (and minimalist) approach, the new stance emphasizes gender differences and a tendency for rejecting the existing system and replacing it with a feminist ideology and structure. It has been referred to as "cultural" religious feminism (also called "radical" feminism by some (Riley 1989; Ruether 1983; Grant 1989). Disenchanted with the foibles and exclusions of the patriarchal system, the cultural feminist agenda emphasizes the "temporary or permanent ascendancy of women and the female principle" (Christ and Plaskow 1979, 13). The approach postulates the immaleable sexism of received traditions. Disabused of reform, its proponents call for replacing extant sexist religious systems with new feminist thought forms and structures—a new "culture."

Out of this view has come the "women-church" movement and "Christian goddess" worship (Ruether 1985; Royle 1991).

In this way, cultural feminism resembles the "black power" sector of the civil rights movement—equality (if not superiority) is to be secured, but within newly created social institutions. In both cases the prime mover—the aspect of the situation that defines the core agenda—is the experience of oppression (Neitz 1990). Blacks and women share a common history of exclusion from full participation in society in terms of access to sufficient power and authority to control their economic, political, and social lives. In each case some of them have felt it necessary to condemn existing institutions, to withdraw from participation within their structures, and to establish their own set of values and organizational structures for realizing them. This is the situation with religious cultural feminists (e.g., Daly 1975, 1978).

The Research Question

The cultural feminist orientation involves not only an ideology but also *a set of empirical assertions about unique characteristics of women's approach to ministry*. This study focuses on those postulates. The cultural feminist argument constitutes another example of the "maximalist" position on gender differences. It assumes that *there are important systematic differences between men and women and that these gender differences result in predictable variations in the way male and female clergy approach their work.*

Martha Ice (1987) summarizes the basic assumptions cultural (maximalist) feminists hold concerning differences between men and women in their approach to ministry. While the assertions are many (see also Christ 1977), with no single proponent accepting all of them, the proposed differences scattered throughout the literature can be grouped into several categories as shown in Table 1.1 (following Ice 1987).

It is important to remember that not all men and women resemble these types; individuals differ. Of equal importance is the caveat that no individual of either sex will manifest *all* of these characteristics. The paradigm involves a "summary" of various assumptions which in caricature asserts, first of all, that male and female clergy relate to other people—especially to those in their congregation—in radically and predictably different ways. Men relate to others with aloofness and manipulativeness. They feel a need to control the social situation, and they assume that social relationships within congregations make no

Table 1.1. Summary of Masculine and Feminine Approaches to Ministry

	Masculine	*Feminine*
Interpersonal Style	Impersonal, detached	Personal, intimate
	Directive	Compliant
	Suspicious	Trusting
	Agency	Communion
	Instrumental	Expressive
	Authoritarian	Egalitarian
	Closed, guarded	Open, vulnerable
Theology	Transcendent God	Immanent God
	Power over people	Power within people
	Justice	Love and mercy
	God atop a hierarchy	God a partner
	God as "imposer"	God as "infuser"
	God as abstract being	God as embodied
Career Goals	Extrinsic success	Intrinsic rewards
	Social status	Social inclusion
	Material wealth	Benevolence
	Goal attainment	Nurturance
Thought Forms	Rationality	Intuition
	Analytical thinking	Integrative thinking
	Rigidity	Flexibility
	Scientism	Holistic thought
Power & Authority	Seek power	Eschew power
	Impose order	Develop consensus
	Hierarchy	Egalitarianism
	Formal legitimation	Charismatic trust
	Of position	From results
	Like power over	Seek to empower within
	Chain of command	Free discussion; equals
	Formal authority	Charismatic authority
	Speak down to laity	Speak as one with laity
	Formal structure	Informal structure
	Clear guidelines	Crescive actions
	World mastery	World partnership
Ethics	Legalistic	Existential
	Rigid	Flexible
	Personal morality	Social ethics
	Avoidance of evil	Love & reconciliation
	Rules for living	Responsible freedom

sense unless they are directed toward specific instrumental goals. Women, on the other hand, relate to others primarily for the sake of those relationships themselves. Their interpersonal style is egalitarian, non-threatening, open, and personal.

The scheme also postulates gender differences in theological orientation. Men tend to view God in transcendental, authoritarian, autocratic terms. Theirs is a God to be feared and obeyed. The God of women, by contrast, operates from within individuals as a benevolent partner to be loved and trusted.

According to religious cultural feminism, the career goals of men and women manifest divergent assumptions as to what the ministry is all about. Men see it in extrinsic terms, as an arena within which one strives for success, status, and material wealth. Women view ministry more intrinsically—as a position from which to interact with other church members and to take satisfaction in seeing them develop as mature Christians.

Men and women go about their work employing divergent cognitive styles. Men tend to insist on being analytical, logical, and scientific, while women's style is more flexible, intuitive, integrative, and holistic.

Perhaps the point of variation between men and women that receives the most frequent and intense discussion among cultural feminists is the matter of authority and power (Lips 1991; Verdesi 1976). This arena is often the starting and ending point in conversation about gender differences in ministry, perhaps because most organizational power in the churches is still manipulated by men. Men are described as power-hungry autocrats who function most effectively in rigid hierarchical structures from which they can impose their will on others and control the directions of church life. Women, on the other hand, want little to do with authority and power over others. They wish to be able to control their *own* life, but they have little desire to impose their will on others. Indeed, their goal is to empower others. They shy away from rigid organizational structures, and their ideal is to create an egalitarian church in which all are free to participate as equal players in policy formation and program development.

Finally, the model states that men and women differ in their approach to determining what is good and bad, right and wrong, virtue and sin—their ethics. In this scheme men are by nature legalistic and rigid. They approach moral decisions by bringing with them a set of abstract rules to apply to concrete situations. They are much more interested in personal sin than social evil. By contrast women are existential and flexible. They approach ethical matters by looking for freedom to act responsibly. They are concerned about social issues and social problems, not just individual foibles.

The reader may object to the pejorative mode of describing masculine approaches to ministry in contrast to the flattering and constructive images of the feminine stance as presented above. Fair enough. Nevertheless, I have presented them in this mode, because that is precisely the "flavor" one encounters in most discussions of those differences. The patterns are only supposed empirical generalizations on the surface, but it is nearly impossible to divorce those descriptive statements from normative evaluations one encounters in the literature where they are discussed. (Unflattering terminology describing *feminine* approaches to work will appear occasionally in later chapters.)

Once again trying to bracket the political dimension, we see that the question for this research is not whether the *agendas* of the structural or cultural feminists are right or wrong; it is not whether one strategy is to be preferred over another. Those are ideological issues, broadly conceived as questions of social ethics. Considered narrowly they are matters of theology. Instead, the study focuses on two *empirical* questions:

1. whether the above differences in approach to ministry *actually cohere* as identifiable "masculine" and "feminine" types, and

2. whether female and male clergy *actually differ* in the extent to which each type is empirically associated with them.

Is there a demonstrable feminine style of ministry (in contrast to a masculine approach) among clergy, and do we in fact observe this orientation to ministry more among women than among men?

The results of a recent meta-analysis of research dealing with gender and leadership style in a variety of settings (Eagly and Johnson 1990) support some of these assertions but not others. Eagly and Johnson's synthesis indicates that the assertions concerning *power* tend to be supported. Women tend to favor *democratic* leadership styles, while men are more inclined toward *autocratic* or *directive* styles. And these tendencies emerged from studies of leadership style in all types of settings—laboratory experiments, assessment studies, and organizational studies. However, suppositions that female leaders would be *interpersonally* oriented while male leaders would be *task* oriented were *not* supported in organizational studies, that is, studies in settings where women and men were selected and trained for leadership in work organizations. Do these patterns also emerge among women and men in positions of pastoral leadership over congregations?

Using data from *both* women and men in the pastoral ministry, the question of comparisons of the leadership style of the sexes has never been asked before. There is some partial evidence of the existence of feminine forms of ministry. Ice (1987) perceived the approach among a highly selected sample of influential clergy. Likewise Stevens (1989) also documented feminine forms of ministry in the self-images of women in nontraditional forms of Anglican ministry in Canada. The problems with this evidence, while it is clearly relevant and interesting, are that it was obtained from highly selected and atypical samples of clergywomen and, more importantly, that it comes from the studies that *did not include samples of men*.

A few studies involving both female and male ministerial aspirants have touched on these issues tangentially. Carroll, Hargrove, and Lummis (1983) found little evidence of different motivations in ministry among men and women seeking ordination in several mainline Protestant denominations. The women, for example, manifested little desire to transform the church. And they found no difference between men and women on leadership style, competence in selected clergy roles, and ease of relating to lay church members. Charlton (1987), in a review of research on seminary students, concluded that there were very few motivational differences attributable to gender. Ekhardt and Goldsmith (1984; also Goldsmith and Ekhardt 1984), in one of those undertakings, found that male and female seminary students were more alike than different in their motivational profiles. There were no significant differences between men and women on measures of masculinity and femininity, but both the male and female seminarians differed from males and females in the broader college population. They also found that the male seminary students were higher than general college males on nurturance, succorance, and desirability and lower on autonomy. Similarly the female seminary students outscored the general college females on affiliation, dominance, exhibition, understanding, and desirability, while scoring lower on aggression and change. Their conclusion was that the seminary students tended to be highly androgynous, converging toward one another in personality profiles, and that it would be a mistake to assume major differences between male and female clergy once those students were in positions of church leadership.

Finally, there is considerable evidence that clergywomen tend to *differ widely among themselves* on various characteristics. They deviate from one another in terms of background characteristics, marital status, theological training, ideology, placement strategies, length of tenure, and level of success in various forms of ministry (Carroll, Hargrove, and Lummis 1983; Lehman 1985; Royle 1984; Ice 1987; Cardwell 1982). There is little evidence that "the woman minister" is at all monolithic. With clergywomen often accused of being "too masculine" and male clergy sometimes caricatured as the "third sex," the recent arguments for systematic role-related differences between male and female clergy clearly remains an open question empirically. That is the analytical problem this undertaking seeks to address.

Summary

In the world of scholarship dealing with the role gender plays in social life, there are at least two camps vying for position in their efforts to determine how we will think about the issue. One school of thought—the "maximalists"—asserts that through some interaction between biology, socialization, and individual experience, women and men are fundamentally different cognitively, emotionally, and behaviorally. The argument goes on to say that these divergent orientations to life are also manifested in people's approaches to work. As women enter occupations formerly considered as the exclusive province of men, they relate to that work differently—"as women"—and in the process the long-term effect will be that they transform the ways in which that work will be done.

The opposite stance is called the "minimalist" position. It argues that any perceived gender differences in thought, feeling, and action are spurious. Rather than attribute observed variations in these things to endemic qualities of gender, the minimalists state that such patterns are artifacts of the actor's position in social structure, including divergent experiences of subordination and exclusion from full participation in social life.

This debate pervades feminist discussions of the ministry just as it does the dialogue devoted to secular society. Some religious feminist authors argue that women and men "by nature" approach the ministry in radically different ways. They describe the traditional "masculine" approach as pathological, involving excessive rationality, scientism, legalism, authoritarianism, status seeking, rigidity, exclusivity, and power over people. By way of contrast, they prescribe a "feminine" approach as a way out. The feminine approach involves intuitiveness, holistic thought, responsible ethics, egalitarianism, intrinsic rewards from work, flexibility, inclusiveness, and the empowerment of people.

The study asks a simple descriptive question, that is, are these descriptions of male and female approaches to pastoral ministry accurate? Can we gather evidence to substantiate the existence of two styles of ministry? If so, do we observe the masculine style mostly among men and the feminine style mainly among women?

The next chapter will describe the structure of the research and will chronicle the steps taken in the research process. Then subsequent chapters will present the results of the analysis of the data and then speculate on their possible implications.

2

Getting the Evidence

THE CENTRAL OBJECTIVE of the study is to determine whether assertions about gender differences in approach to the ministry can be supported empirically. The basic research design employed to accomplish that objective was a survey of a national sample of female and male pastors in four "mainline" Protestant denominations in the United States, that is, the American Baptist Churches, the United Methodist Church, the Presbyterian Church (USA), and the United Church of Christ. These bodies were included on the basis of several criteria: (1) each one had endorsed the ordination of women to the ministry on an equal status with men for thirty years or more, (2) increasing numbers of women had been placed as solo or senior pastors of some of their congregations, as well as in other forms of ministry, (3) each denomination had participated in previous studies involving the general issue of women in ministry, and (4) each group was willing to participate in the undertaking by serving in an advisory role (especially in the research-design stage) and by contributing funds to help cover the cost of data collection among their clergy and members.

Other funding for the research was provided through the generosity of the Religious Research Association and the Brockport campus of the State University of New York. Each organization provided its portion of

23

the "shoestring" on which the study was conducted, and once the entire shoestring was in place, the project moved along to completion.

The Study Population

The ministry in most Christian denominations is not a monolithic entity. Accordingly, it is necessary to specify what we mean (and do *not* mean) by "ministers." First, the focus is on *ordained clergy*. Many religious devotees argue that the ministry involves more than the professional clergy. Both clergy and laypersons alike assert that the work they do in the name of their Christian faith constitutes a "ministry" to others. Types of local church ministry in which lay members are frequently involved include teaching, preaching, serving on church boards, committees, and task forces. Laypersons working in other fields, such as religious television, radio, and publishing, are also likely to define their work as a "ministry." Many lay members in evangelical groups pride themselves in being "soul winners" for the Lord. Many pastors, in fact, insist that the work of the church cannot proceed without the ministries of lay members. (At the bizarre end of the spectrum, there was even a woman who claimed to be "stripping for Jesus" in California, land of recent "religious innovation.")

Nevertheless, in this study we concentrated on *ordained clergy*. (The study design in fact included lay members in the project, but in a different way, which will be considered below.) We focused on the ordained ministry for very good reasons. First, when people think of "the ministry," it is usually the position and work of ordained clergy that they have in mind. They are usually *not* thinking about the work of the laity. Furthermore, the assertions about gender differences in approach to the ministry outlined in chapter one also really focus on the activity of professional church leaders. Even though one dimension of that discussion sometimes involves a decrying of the "professional" ministry, urging that it be "deprofessionalized," virtually all of the discussion of masculine and feminine approaches to ministry are really dealing with what *ordained* clergy do. Accordingly, it is on the full-time vocational clergy that we concentrate.

A second distinction involves the work setting. Especially in contemporary, industrialized societies, professional clergy work in many different surroundings. Some have responsibilities chiefly to local congregations either as pastor or minister in charge of some other function in the life of the church. But many others are in roles having little or nothing to do with local congregations. Ministers are found working vocationally in administrative positions in denominational hierarchies, hospitals, children's homes, retirement facilities, nursing homes, colleges, elementary and secondary schools, social service organizations, publishing houses, radio and television stations, newspapers and magazines, counselling centers, seminaries, and on and on. And women ministers especially have found placement in literally all of these settings and more. For some such women, the choice of one of these other work settings is made on the basis of feeling excluded from ministry in local churches. Others *prefer* nonchurch types of work and would not want to work in the context of the local congregation.

Nevertheless, again we chose not to try to study the work styles of all of these forms of ministry. We focused instead on the minister serving the local congregation. Once again it is primarily the work of clergy in local-church settings that is the subject of most purported gender differences in approach to the ministry. Discussions of interpersonal style, preaching, dogmatism, authoritarianism, and so forth, apply mostly to ministers working in a congregational context.

One final distinction remains. Just as there are many organizational milieus in which men and women work in ministry, there are many forms of ministry in just the local church. Some ministers in local churches work as a solo or senior pastor of a local congregation. Others have the title of minister of religious education, minister of music, church administrator, minister for counselling, minister for youth, associate pastor, assistant pastor, or others.

Here again, we took the narrow focus. Most of the assertions of the cultural feminists summarized in the previous chapter deal primarily (if not exclusively) with the work of clergy who are solo or senior pastors of local congregations. That position is the workplace that has generated most of the discussion. *That job—local pastor—is what we studied.*

The Sample

The central offices of each participating denomination provided lists containing the names, addresses, and telephone numbers of men and women listed as solo pastor, senior pastor, or co-pastor of local congregations. While there is some level of turnover of persons on those lists at any point in time, the lists nevertheless comprised adequate sampling frames from which to draw representative samples of clergy men and women. Where the list was found to be in error by listing someone who was no longer serving a church, that person was replaced by taking the next name down on the list. (Unfortunately, there was no practical way of getting names that had been left off the list.) In any case, the percentage of error detected was generally less than 5 percent, so the frames were judged to be adequate. We have no reason to believe that any differences in approach to ministry would be systematically related to inclusion on or exclusion from the lists.

The initial goal was to obtain a representative sample of four hundred clergy from whom to collect data. That sample was to contain one hundred persons from each of the four denominations, one-half of them men and one-half women. Two of the denominations supplied the principal investigator with separate lists of their entire population of clergy, one for the men and the other for the women. We then drew systematic samples of fifty men and fifty women from each denominational listing. The other two denominations found it easier to draw the sample themselves, following the steps done in the sampling process described above. They did the sampling according to instructions supplied by the principal investigator and sent the resulting lists to him. The problem of list errors was handled in these two cases by also obtaining from them lists of twenty-five additional ministers for use in sampling replacement. These samples of one hundred ministers from each denomination constitute the basic source of data for examining differences in approach to ministry.

We supplemented the basic sample of four hundred ministers in two ways. First, we drew an additional sample of one hundred ministers who were members of racial or ethnic groups—blacks, Hispanics, Asians, and American Indians. The supplement included twenty-five racial/ethnic clergy from each denomination, with twelve or thirteen being males and the rest females. The decision to oversample racial/ethnic groups was based on the expectation that as a group they would emerge in very small numbers in the systematic sample described above. This pattern was indeed the case. The supplementary samples were drawn following the same procedures as were involved in the basic sample.

The second sample supplement involved women placed as senior ministers in relatively large churches with multiple staff. For purposes of the discussions that follow, we shall refer to them as "seniors." According to traditional criteria of "success" in the ministry, these women were defined as high achievers and significant role models for other women in the denomination. The goal was to identify ten such seniors in each group.

The "ideal" sample, then, would most likely be composed of persons with the characteristics shown in table 2.1. There should be about one-half men and one-half women derived from the basic sample and the supplementary racial/ethnic sample, and about ten additional women included as "seniors." As will be shown below in greater detail, the actual sample departed from this somewhat. In general, however, the sampling plan was satisfactory, and the evidence of non-response bias was minimal. More on this later.

Table 2.1. Expected Distributions of Numbers of Clergy in the Sample

Denomination	White Clergy		Racial/Ethnic Clergy		Senior Women*
	Males	*Females*	*Males*	*Females*	*Females*
Baptist	50	50	12	13	10
Methodist	50	50	12	13	10
Presbyterian	50	50	12	13	10
United Church	50	50	12	13	10

*In addition to the totals in the other columns.

Data Collection

We collected data from the clergy in the sample by conducting structured telephone interviews with them. Beginning in January 1990, each minister in the sample received a letter on university stationery conveying the following information:

1. the purpose of the study,
2. the sampling plan and why that person was included in the sample,
3. a statement that an interviewer would be calling within one or two weeks, and
4. an invitation to the minister to telephone collect if he/she had any questions about the undertaking or his/her part in it.

Also enclosed with the letter was an endorsement by the head of that denomination's department of ministry, introducing the principal investigator to the respondent and urging him/her to participate in the project.

The telephone interviewers were trained to follow standard procedures for the telephone interview process, including the proper way to go through the interview itself, what to do in case of identifiable eventualities, and how to keep records of the results of the interview contacts. The interviewers also invited comments from the respondents at the completion of the structured interviews, and they recorded those remarks as nearly word-for-word as possible. Most of the interviews were conducted from midmorning through about ten o'clock in the evening on week days. A few were conducted on the weekends, but Saturday and Sunday were normally avoided due to the unique work schedules of most parish ministers—weekends are their busiest times.

The interviews themselves appeared to go well. They lasted an average of about twenty to twenty-five minutes, especially for the white clergy. The interviews with racial/ethnic clergy took slightly longer. Virtually every contact resulted in a completed interview, that is, very few ministers cut off the interview before it was complete, and of those few who had to do that, most eventually consented to complete the portions of the interview that had not been finished earlier. The interviews were completed by the end of March 1990.

The actual distributions of clergy characteristics in the sample eventually obtained are listed in table 2.2. The basic pattern resembles the outcome for which we were striving, with two exceptions. In the white and racial/ethnic samples, we did obtain about a fifty-fifty split between men and women. A noteworthy exception to that pattern occurred among the Presbyterians, where the lists of racial/ethnic clergy were not as useful as one would hope. It was not possible to contact all of the racial/ethnic females in the sample. The addresses and phone numbers were often incorrect. (The denominational records were in transition to a new set of central offices located in another state, and they were not up to date. This situation explains some of the problem, but not all of it.)

Table 2.2.   Actual Distributions of Clergy Sample Characteristics

Denomination	White Clergy		Racial/Ethnic Clergy		Senior Women*	
	Males	Females	Males	Females	Males	Females
Baptist	51	55	13	11	17	3
Methodist	50	59	12	13	12	5
Presbyterian	45	57	10	7	8	6
United Church	46	63	13	12	9	9

*Senior women were operationally defined as women serving as pastor of a multiple-staff church where they are *not* a "co-pastor."

Note also that the figures for senior women are *included* in the totals for majority and minority clergy. E.g., three of the fifty-five Baptist majority women were *also* senior women.

The second exception to the success of the sampling procedures involves the "seniors." The goal, you will recall, was to obtain at least forty women who were serving as senior minister in multiple-staff churches, ten in each denomination. If we *excluded* from the seniors the women who were serving as *copastors*, usually with their clergy husband, we ended up falling considerably short of the sampling objective. We about reached it among the women in the United Church of Christ, but we didn't even come close in the other denominations. This result is probably an accurate reflection of reality, however. The informal perception widely shared in these bodies is that there are very few women in such senior positions. The results of the sampling would support that point of view.

In an effort to maximize communication with the Hispanic clergy, the interviews with them were conducted in Spanish. To minimize possible translator bias, two persons translated the interview schedule into Spanish and compared their results. Translations that deviated significantly from each other were discussed, and the version that appeared to involve the least amount of bias was used in the interviews of Hispanic clergy. We are not aware of any systematic bias that may have resulted from that procedure, and we are satisfied that the translations resulted in better interview data from the Hispanic clergy than we would have obtained had we assumed that they could have responded in English. Unfortunately, we did not have sufficient funds to follow the same procedure in the interviews with Asian-American and American Indian clergy. While there were some problems of clergy from all racial-ethnic groups understanding nuances of some of the questions, we are not aware of any systematic biases that resulted from the interviews with any of the racial/ethnic ministers.

The Problem of Measurement

Differences in defining social roles are not always easy to detect. Most of us have little difficulty in determining whether another person is taking one role or another as, for example, in determining whether the role is that of a lawyer or a tennis player. Not only do we have clear variations in speech and behavior associated with each role, but we also have differences in dress, physical surroundings, the social identity of other roles directly related to the one we are considering at the moment, and so forth. While it is true that some lawyers also play tennis, and that a game of tennis can serve as the context in which lawyers can score points on each other "as lawyers," the characteristics of the total scene usually enable the "opponent" to identify correctly which game is being played at a given point in time.

When the roles are less clearly differentiated by their social and cultural context, however, it can be much more difficult to identify the appropriate role of the moment. Think, for example, of the various possible outcomes of a situation in which a person must determine whether another is taking the role of a "friend" or a "lover." Depending on one's own motivations and perceptions, the result can be unbridled elation or deep resentment and embarrassment. Mistakes in these judgments often make good subject matter for drama or jokes, because the differences between the roles are simultaneously so widely known in this society and yet the cues are so subtle. Most of us can identify with the players in such situations, because we've been there ourselves.

The problem of role definition with which we are concerned in this project is different still. Here we need to be able to determine differences in the way individuals define *a single role*, that is, pastor of a congregation. In this instance there is no confusion about which position is involved. Everyone in the sample is "the minister" to a congregation. The problem is to find ways to detect variations in the way each individual approaches his/her work in that position. The differences in the total social and cultural context for role definition within each denomination are likely to be very small and subtle. Yet if we are to obtain empirical evidence for the assertions cultural feminists make about masculine and feminine approaches to the pastoral ministry, we must find a way to detect those subtle variations.

The ideal approach to this problem would be to visit each parish and take note of every detail we can perceive. It would involve several personal interviews with the minister, observation of the physical surroundings, following the pastor through several days of work to note patterns of work activity, interviews with members of the congregation and other ministers in the area, noting things about the person's home life, and so forth. Unfortunately, the financial support available did not give us the luxury of such an encyclopedic approach to data collection. We had neither enough time nor enough money to implement a comprehensive research design. We were restricted to the realities of a survey.

The problem boiled down to one of formulating questions that would obtain from the clergy indications of their approach to the pastoral ministry. In order to make controlled comparisons—"apples to apples," if you will—we needed to ask the *same* set of questions of each minister in the sample, and each question had to be put in exactly the same way to everyone. The content of those questions had to embody any possible differences between masculine and feminine approaches to ministry. Ideally the items also would present evidence of differences in defining the role of minister one might obtain by employing a more encyclopedic approach to data collection. Difficult? Perhaps so. But not impossible.

We solved the problem of measuring individual differences in approach to the pastoral ministry by starting with assertions contained in cultural feminist (maximalist) literature as a definition of specific kinds of possible differences between the "masculine" and "feminine" stances. We then formulated three types of questions to ask the ministers, items that flowed from the cultural feminists' definition of the situation: (1) whether they thought a series of statements about various dimensions of approach to the ministry characterized them personally, (2) how much time they spent in a series of specific roles of local pastors, and (3) how important each of those roles was to them personally, regardless of how much time they spent in them.

The Problem of Bias

The principal investigator in this project is a man. That simple reality could result in systematic biases in the study flowing from the fact that he perceives social and personal situations through the eyes and ears of one socialized as a man and occupying social positions to which men usually are admitted readily but women are not. These biases could enter the project at every step of the research process. To minimize the intrusion of any such masculine bias into the research, the undertaking incorporated female consultants right from the outset. Feminist colleagues in sociology reviewed and discussed the basic problem formulation and research design. Women serving as administrators of the women-in-ministry sectors of the hierarchies of the four denominations also reviewed the basic design of the undertaking, and the senior investigator discussed their reactions and recommendations in a day-long conference. We incorporated many of the ideas of both the feminist social scientists and the feminist denominational administrators into the design and structure of the undertaking.

The principal investigator constructed a data-collection instrument for use in the interviews. The interview schedule was sent to the feminist colleagues and administrators for their review and recommendations. The social scientists replied with their recommendations directly to the author, sometimes by mail and in other cases by phone or in personal conferences. The denominational administrators met with the author in a conference to "clean up" the questions going into the form. We incorporated much of this feedback into the interview schedule.

Finally, the questionnaire was subjected to a trial run in a small pilot survey of male and female clergy serving churches in the area surrounding the principal investigator's place of work. That test run led to final revisions in the instrument, resulting in the form contained in the appendix. Then the interviews were conducted by both men and women, and each interviewer was assigned interviews with both male and female clergy. *There were no significant differences between the results obtained by male and female interviewers.*

After all of this effort to minimize gender bias in the project, there may still be some male bias remaining in the design and execution of the study. This writer is not the most appropriate judge of that. But it is not likely, and it is fair to say that with the safeguards incorporated in the design and implementation of the data-collection process, the burden of proof of such criticisms is on the shoulders of the critic.

Affinities with Descriptive Statements

The text of the interview schedule is contained in the appendix. Parts 2 and 4 of that instrument comprise the items that reflect facets of either the masculine or feminine approach to the ministry. The instructions called for the interviewer to read each statement to the minister and to ask the respondent to indicate how much the statement was "like her/him," using a scale of zero to five. An answer of zero indicated that the statement was personally "not like them at all," and five signified that the statement was personally "like them completely." The range of zero to five was identified as a continuum representing various levels of affinity with the statement. The ministers in the sample generally had little difficulty in understanding the instructions or responding to the statements.

The frequencies with which the clergy responded to the individual items are contained in table 2.3. A few patterns are observable on the surface. First, on every item but one (45, in the career goals category), the clergy responses are distributed across the entire range of possible answers. The ministers *differed* in their replies to each measure. So we are dealing not with "constants" but with "variables." Not everyone involved in the project expected this pattern. During the training sessions with the interviewers, for example, a few individuals commented now and then that "no one will be willing to say that" concerning the contents of one question or another. The comments, of course, typically reflected that person's own individual opinions about the issue incorporated in the item, and the individual making the comment was so convinced of the truth of his/her position that it was difficult to conceive of anyone taking another stance. Such firm convictions parallel the very phenomena on which the study is focused, that is, the opinions of many cultural feminists that "no self-respecting women" would think or act in particular ways or that "men simply don't function like that." But as the data indicate, it is almost always a mistake to project one's own opinions on others. The clergy in the sample, in fact, were *not* all alike. They differed widely in their willingness to characterize themselves in terms of the contents of the various measures. So we succeeded in measuring variations in self-perceptions.

Table 2.3. Response Patterns (percent) to "Like-Me" Measures of Approach to Ministry

Items	*Response Categories*					
	Not like me					*Like me*
	0	*1*	*2*	*3*	*4*	*5*
Interpersonal Style						
34. I am uncomfortable when people open up and share their innermost feelings with me. (M)*	65	21	8	2	3	1
36. As a minister it is important for me to remain somewhat detached from members of my congregation. (M)	27	24	19	18	11	1
37. It is hard for me to ignore requests from my congregation even when I feel over-whelmed with work. (F)	3	5	6	18	34	34
48. I find that I must be a skilled and energetic fund-raiser to prod parishioners to give enough money to keep the church alive. (M)	12	22	28	21	12	6
53. I do not feel free to express my true feelings about things with anyone in my congregation. (M)	41	24	16	12	5	1

Table 2.3. *(Continued)*

Items	Not like me 0	1	2	3	4	Like me 5

Response Categories

Interpersonal Style

Items	Not like me 0	1	2	3	4	Like me 5
56. I know I have my congregation's confidence when they openly discuss with me thier critical assessments of my program proposals. (F)	1	1	6	17	47	29
93. I prefer to use my professional title in relating to the local community. (M)	29	16	17	17	13	8
98. I feel uneasy when members of my congregation touch me in any way physically. (M)	65	20	10	3	2	1
103. As a church leader, it is important that I reveal no points of personal weakness to the congregation. (M)	45	23	21	9	3	1
107. I prefer that church members address me only by my first name	8	5	9	24	26	27
110. A collaborative leadership style works best for me in working with the congregation. (F)	1	1	1	8	43	46

Theology

Items	Not like me 0	1	2	3	4	Like me 5
35. My sermons typically focus on theological beliefs. (M)	4	6	23	37	20	10
39. My ministry is effective, because God is within me as well as beyond me. (F)	1	1	1	7	28	62

Table 2.3. *(Continued)*

Items	Response Categories					
	Not like me					Like me
	0	1	2	3	4	5

Theology

Items	0	1	2	3	4	5
47. When I preach, I always try to remember that I speak as a representative of Almighty God. (M)	1	1	7	15	32	45

Career Goals

Items	0	1	2	3	4	5
32. I make my major contribution to my congregation through my preaching. (M)	1	1	5	41	38	15
40. Of all the things I have to do as a minister, I feel least competent at financial matters like raising the budget. (F)	15	17	20	21	19	9
44. I usually focus my preaching on the concrete concerns of my people. (F)	1	0	3	22	51	24
45. I contribute the most to my congregation by sharing in their celebration or their suffering. (F)	0	1	1	17	46	36
49. I would really feel successful as a minister if I were serving a large church. (M)	38	22	19	14	6	2
94. I think there is too much talk among ministers about salaries and promotions. (F)	9	10	19	26	21	15
99. I consider myself accountable primarly to the denominational administrators in my region. (M)	30	26	21	15	5	2

Table 2.3. *(Continued)*

Items	Response Categories					
	Not like me					*Like me*
	0	1	2	3	4	5
Career Goals						
102. I would like to be remembered as a helpful mentor to other ministers. (F)	3	4	8	19	34	33
105. The measure of success of my ministry is my positive influence on the community. (F)	5	10	21	32	25	9
109. It is more important to me to maintain congregational solidarity than to follow denominational policy. (F)	4	2	13	41	30	10
Thought Forms						
38. When dealing with difficult decisions in the church, it is usually my "gut feeling" that serves me best. (F)	3	4	2	30	32	30
46. There is no substitute for rational, analytical thought for solving congregational problems. (M)	9	13	31	30	12	5
96. I think it is more important to do the work of the church efficiently than to have a lot of people involved in it. (M)	22	21	26	18	9	4
104. I feel uncomfortable in the absence of clear organizational guide lines for ongoing church programs. (M)	12	17	22	23	19	6

Table 2.3. *(Continued)*

Items	Response Categories					
	Not like me					Like me
	0	1	2	3	4	5
Power and Authority						
33. I believe that only ordained clergy can properly administer the Lord's Supper. (M)	30	12	15	14	15	16
41. My sermons simply involve one believer speaking to another. (F)	5	7	15	23	34	17
50. Sometimes I have to drag my congregation kicking and screaming in the direction I think the church ought to go. (M)	18	18	23	21	13	7
54. I cannot be the leader I want to be if I do not have authority to implement my own decisions. (M)	12	17	20	26	18	6
55. My daily working theology has little to do with my professional ministry studies. (F)	46	29	11	9	5	1
91. I believe that lay people, not the clergy, should decide the direction in which the church will go. (F)	4	5	6	40	30	15
92. My authority as minister rests primarily on my professional training and ordination. (M)	9	10	26	29	21	5
95. When I'm really sure about what the congregation should do, I try hard to get them to take my advice. (M)	1	2	7	21	45	24

Table 2.3. *(Continued)*

Items	Response Categories					
	Not like me					Like me
	0	1	2	3	4	5
Power and Authority						
97. I think that democratic decision making is a poor basis for local church policy. (M)	40	22	17	12	6	2
100. I think ordination to the ministry places too much distance between ministers and lay people. (F)	24	24	21	20	8	2
101. I don't think congregations can function very well without guidance from the clergy. (M)	4	10	16	29	29	12
106. One of my ministry goals is to enhance the power my members have in the mission and operation of their local church. (F)	1	1	3	12	39	46
108. My ministry will be most successful if I can lead my congregation to get along without me. (F)	1	2	6	15	41	36
111. One of my goals in ministry is the eradication of social inequalities in the church. (F)	5	2	6	17	34	35
112. If I have any power in my congregation, it is based simply on the trust I have earned from the people. (F)	4	1	3	14	39	39
Ethics						
42. I try hard to get my people involved in social issues that affect their lives. (F)	1	2	9	25	35	28

Table 2.3. *(Continued)*

Items	Response Categories					
	Not like me					*Like me*
	0	1	2	3	4	5
Ethics						
43. I encourage my congregation to innovate when dealing with current issues instead of sticking with traditional patterns and programs. (F)	1	1	3	22	46	27
51. I will often bend church rules if they don't meet the needs of the congregation. (F)	11	17	16	25	21	10
52. I think today's church members need to hear the correct position on ethical issues delivered from the pulpit. (M)	11	11	19	26	21	12
57. My primary concern in concrete moral choices is applying the best rules for conducting human life. (M)	5	8	11	31	31	14

*M indicates a masculine statement; F indicates a feminine statement.

The second pattern that is immediately apparent is a clear tendency for the sample as a whole to characterize themselves in relatively *feminine* terms. This pattern is especially evident on the items dealing with "interpersonal style." While it is true that the ministers' answers range across the entire spectrum of possible responses on every interpersonal style item, the *majority* of the replies to each one tend to fall in the "feminine" category. Persons with a feminine approach to ministry, for example, will be open to people sharing feelings with them (34), will be receptive to criticisms (56), and will tend to avoid the use of professional titles (93). As a group, then, *the clergy tend to manifest feminine styles of interpersonal relations.* The same tendency for feminine answers is also evident among the "career goals" and "power and authority" questions. A few items tended to show little tendency for either masculine or feminine response patterns—that is, the answers tended to bunch in the middle of the range of possibilities.

The response patterns are a bit more mixed in the case of the "theology," "ethics," and "thought forms" questions. Here there are two items reflecting a tendency for a "masculine" definition of ministry, that is, speaking in behalf of a God with power over people (47), and being rule oriented in morality (57). Other items, such as 35, 46, 51, and 52, show the "mixed" response pattern.

Why the Feminine Response Pattern?

Overall the clear tendency is for "feminine" responses to questions about approach to ministry. Why is this so? We'll deal with this issue somewhat in the next chapter as we try to explain differences in the responses. However, at this point the most plausible answer to the question involves the matter of "social desirability" reflected in the various items. In most cases, clergy would perceive the "feminine" response categories as the ones that would be most likely to bring social approval from peers, superiors, and lay church members. Norms associated with pastoral ministry, for example, would tend to proscribe clergy detachment from their congregations, autocratic leadership styles, avoidance of the concrete concerns of members in sermons, and so on. It would be naive not to expect some such socially desirable responses in the presentations of self which were given by the ministers. This phenomenon appears frequently in research dealing with attitudes, values, motives, and behaviors, because all of those concepts involve folk notions of 'right' and 'wrong', 'good' and bad'.

This characteristic of research on normative topics does not mean that the respondents are "lying" or that the data are of no value. One must simply bear in mind the realities of the typical interview situation. The ministers in the sample had been approached by a total stranger who was asking for personal information. These clergy are highly educated individuals whose work calls upon them to have developed considerable skills in social interaction. It is highly unlikely that they would have dropped their guard and dealt with each question with reckless abandon. They were cautious, no doubt usually dealing with each item in light of their perceptions of a wide range of possible consequences of answering in one way or another. What typically takes place in such circumstances is that individuals will unconsciously "skew" or "lean" their answer in the direction of what they perceive to be the socially desirable categories if their actual feelings would appear to depart significantly from accepted definitions of what is expected by others.

Nevertheless, among a *group* or in a *sample* of many persons dealing with normatively sensitive issues, differences will still emerge in the total set of responses to those items. The response pattern will simply be "skewed" in a socially desirable direction. Variations will still appear, because the answer each person gives derives from *both* his/her own position on the item and the perception of social desirability in the response options. (Remember also that the reply involves the person's *perceptions* of what is socially desirable. People will disagree on that point as well.)

Accordingly, even though the overall response patterns appear to reflect some tendencies to give socially desirable answers, the fact that each item yielded responses across the entire range of possibilities indicates that we in fact succeeded in measuring the differences for which we were looking. On the point of predicting those differences, it appears that the cultural feminists are correct. The survey results demonstrate that *some people manifest "masculine" approaches to clergy roles, while others demonstrate "feminine" approaches.* We shall address the question of whether these differences are associated with gender in the next chapter.

Time Spent in Clergy Roles

Another arena in which we looked for differences is in how clergy spend their working time. As noted in chapter 1, the image of male clergy as depicted in the writings associated with cultural religious feminism includes the idea that men are relatively instrumental, authoritarian, oriented to power over people, status conscious, hierarchically inclined, and so forth. Women clergy, on the other hand, are described as more expressive, egalitarian, empowering of people, inclusive, given to personal autonomy and freedom, and so forth. Such gender differences reportedly lead clergy men and women to seek different kinds of opportunities and rewards—in short, to approach their work differently.

If those characterizations are accurate portrayals of clergy men and women, then one might expect persons of each gender to gravitate toward divergent kinds of activities in the ministry. This line of reasoning would lead one to predict that more men than women would seek out situations that allow them to pursue the masculine values—power, authority, status, hierarchy, and so on. Thus one would predict that more men than women would be heavily involved in preaching, teaching, local church administration, and involvement in other church structures. Those social arenas are typically hierarchically structured, instrumental, analytical, and they often involve manipulation of power and authority. Women clergy, on the other hand, might be expected to desire visitation, counselling, fellowship, community activities, and personal growth and to promote social justice. Those roles involve values of nurturance, inclusiveness, egalitarianism, intimacy, expressiveness, consensus, and so on.

To pursue this line of inquiry, we included on the interview schedule a listing of specific roles in which Protestant ministers are usually involved (see Blizzard 1958). The segment of the interview dealing with these roles is part 3 of the interview schedule (see the appendix). As may be seen there, the issue of involvement with specific roles was considered from two frames of reference, (1) how much time ministers spent in each role and (2) how important each role was to them personally.

The clergy respondents were asked to indicate *how many hours they actually spent in each role during the two weeks immediately preceding the interview*. Differences in their responses are contained in table 2.4, from which several generalizations can be drawn.

Table 2.4.   Hours Clergy Report Spending in Specific Roles

Role Activity	Lowest Hours	Highest Hours	Average Hours	SD*
Sermons	0	80	18.0	10.5
Funerals	0	48	2.2	4.6
Teaching classes	0	40	5.5	5.2
Visitation	0	70	11.5	10.0
Counselling	0	60	5.7	6.5
Church Fellowship	0	48	5.4	4.7
Administration	0	80	14.4	11.8
Other church structures	0	60	6.6	7.1
Community activities	0	80	3.8	5.6
Personal development	0	76	8.3	8.5
Social issues	0	40	2.6	4.3

*Standard Deviation.

1. The ministers claimed to spend more of their time preparing and delivering sermons than in any other role activity. An average of 18 hours was spent dealing with sermons in the last two weeks. And based on the standard deviation of that figure, proportionately more of the ministers were clustered close to that mean than was the case involving any of the other activities, that is, in a two-week period a lot of people spent the equivalent of two or more full working days working on sermons.

2. The two other activities in which the ministers spent large proportions of their time were church administration and visitation.

These patterns are consistent with those found in earlier studies (Blizzard 1958; Glock and Stark 1965, 144–50). Ministers typically spend a great deal of time in church administration, usually more than they claim to like. Likewise, the demands of the congregation for pastoral visits usually consume many working hours, although lay church members sometimes complain that the minister does not do enough of it. These data suggest that ministers engage in more visitation than many members think they do.

3. Funerals consumed the least amount of time. The average number of hours spent in funerals was only 2.2. The standard deviation of 4.6 indicates that the time clergy spent in funerals was scattered widely around that mean. Clergy have little control over their involvement in funerals, so this item doesn't necessarily indicate anything about their role preferences. Most likely the variations in time spent in this role reflect the frequency of chance occurrences of death in the community.

4. Excluding funerals, the ministers spent the least amount of time in community-wide activities and social justice issues. Unlike funerals, these activities *do* involve clergy choice and preference. The clergy either preferred to spend their time and energy in other pursuits or were so caught up in the internal demands of the congregation that they could not find time for community involvements. No doubt individuals concerned about meaningful involvement of the church in society's problems *outside* the church will find this pattern a bit disconcerting. The low degree of immersion of the clergy in community-wide activities and social justice issues suggests an isolation of professional church leaders from the community. Whether due to congregational demands or individual priorities, the low degree of involvement of clergy in matters beyond the church walls can only serve to reinforce the perceptions of some outside the church that religious concerns are irrelevant to the "real" problems of daily life. One would hope, instead, that the pastor makes such community contact through his/her l a y members who have been inspired and equipped by the minister to be the church's direct influence in the world.

Priority Placed on Roles

In part 3 of the interview, the respondents were taken through the list of clergy role activities in yet another way (see the appendix). After asking how much time each minister spent in the roles, the questioning shifted to the relative priority the ministers placed on them. The respondents were asked to indicate *how important each role was to them personally, regardless of the amount of time spent in it.* The answer categories employed in this section involved another simple scale of zero to five, with zero indicating a role was not important at all, and five signifying that a role was extremely important. As before, the clergy had little difficulty relating to the questions during the interviews.

The distributions of the responses are contained in table 2.5. A number of patterns are discernible in the results:

Table 2.5.   Importance Ministers Place on Clergy Roles (Percent)

Role Activity	Minimum 0	1	2	3	4	Maximum 5
Sermons	0.5	0	0.5	5	26	68
Funerals	1	2	3	13	32	51
Teaching classes	0.5	1	7	25	40	27
Visitation	0	1	4	24	37	34
Counselling	1	1	10	31	33	24
Church Fellowship	0	1	8	37	37	16
Administration	1	7	19	32	28	13
Other church structures	1	5	21	37	27	9
Community activities	1	4	22	35	28	9
Personal development	0	0	4	18	41	37
Social issues	1	4	12	32	31	18

The ministers tended to place relatively high value on *all* of the role activities. More than two-thirds of the cases fall within the top three response categories on every item. Very few individuals indicated that any role was actually unimportant to them. This pattern could be another artifact of social desirability ministers perceived in the responses available to them. Some of that was probably present in their answers. However, I think it would be a mistake to reduce all of the positive responses to that factor. It is equally likely that most clergy share a broad consensus that these activities do constitute important aspects of their ministerial activities, regardless of the actual amount of time they spend in them.

As a group the ministers placed greatest importance on the preacher role—preparing and delivering sermons. Fully 94 percent of the respondents selected one of the two top response categories in relating to the role of preacher. Viewing preaching as the superordinate activity is consistent with the nature of the denominations involved in the study—non-liturgical bodies with long traditions giving the pulpit a central place in church life. Placing great importance on preaching also makes sense in terms of what lay church members typically expect of ministers in these denominations. The major event in the collective life of the congregation each week is the Sunday morning worship service, and the central component of that ritual is the sermon. Preaching is also the activity on which ministers are evaluated most often. They "make a name for themselves" (or not) primarily in terms of preaching successes, and excellence in that activity offers the best promise of career mobility, which usually means a pastoral position in a larger church. As noted above, the ministers also indicated that they spend more time in this role than in any other activity included in the study, a happy consistency.

The other roles that tended to rate high in importance are funerals, personal development and growth, and visitation—in that order. While funerals are typically few and far between, they are crises of the greatest significance in most families. It is often in such critical circumstances that ministers have the chance to be of the greatest service to their members. If they are successful in that way, they usually develop close bonds with the families involved and reinforce the social solidarity of the congregation. Hence it is not surprising to note the high degree of importance they placed on their roles in funerals.

It is interesting to note that personal development and growth are very important to most ministers, even though in fact they do not get to spend as much time in it as in other activities. This is sometimes a source of frustration and resentment for pastors. They are expected to "give" continually to others, but they often do not get the time they need to maintain their own spiritual, mental, and physical health.

The high priority placed on visitation also is consistent with the amount of time the ministers reported spending in visiting members and prospects. Such visitation meets the needs of individual members, and it performs important organizational maintenance functions by retaining "old" members and attracting new ones.

The roles receiving the *lowest* priority from the ministers were church administration, involvement in church structures beyond the congregation, involvement in community activities, and working with social justice issues. The low level of interest in church administration is consistent with the findings of others (e.g., Glock and Stark 1965; and Blizzard 1958), who also noted that ministers' time often gets "eaten up" by local administrative tasks, even though they would prefer to be devoting their energies to other pursuits.

Involvement in church structures beyond the congregation receives one of the lowest priorities. This outcome is a bit surprising, because becoming integrated into denominational structures often leads to increased visibility and status. Heavy denominational involvements would be an indication of a "cosmopolitan" orientation, a perspective on ministerial work in which one's primary frame of reference is something other than the local parish, for example, the denominational hierarchy. Evidently most of these clergy have more of a "local" orientation, investing their time and energies in activities closely related to their local congregation (for more discussion of the local/cosmopolitan dichotomy, see Roof 1978; and Lehman 1990). Also in some circles it is fashionable *not* to want to "waste" time in denominational activities. Finally, women tend to receive more requests for denominational involvements than do men, due often to the simple fact that denominational administrators feel a need to have women represented on various committees (Royle 1991).

The low priority given to involvements in the wider community and to pursuing social justice issues is consistent with the relatively meager amount of time the clergy actually spent in those activities (above). It also suggests that the reason for little overt immersion in community issues is not entirely a matter of insufficient time for those things. The ministers were not only involved in them very little, but they also tended to give social issues lower priority than other matters, concerns perhaps more directly and exclusively tied to the local congregation itself.

Summary

This chapter has described the structure of the research project designed to gather evidence with which to assess the assertions that female and male clergy differ systematically in their approaches to their work as ministers. Defining "the ministry" narrowly, as involving senior or solo pastors of local congregations, the project involved conducting telephone interviews with systematic samples of men and women pastoring churches in four mainline Protestant denominations. The level of response was exceptionally high, and generally representative samples emerged from the interview process. The one exception to that level of success concerned efforts to locate female clergy serving as senior pastors in multiple-staff churches. It was not possible to locate as many such "seniors" as we had hoped for.

The project measured divergent approaches to ministry in three ways: (1) by presenting the ministers with a set of statements representing masculine and feminine ministry styles and asking them to indicate how much each statement was "like them," (2) by obtaining the number of hours each person spent in a set of common clerical role activities, and (3) by determining the relative importance each minister placed on those roles. As one would expect, the responses manifested a degree of social desirability. Nevertheless, each item revealed differences in emphasis among the respondents. Some ministers gave answers indicating a masculine approach, while others indicated feminine ministry styles. The next chapter will address the question of whether it is the men and the women who tend to manifest the masculine and feminine approaches respectively.

3

Men's and Women's Ministry: Different?

THE CENTRAL QUESTION that the study sought to address is whether women clergy tend to manifest a "feminine" approach to ministry, while men tend to be characterized by a "masculine" orientation. This chapter presents an analysis of data focusing on that basic comparison. The results of applying the measures of masculine and feminine ministry styles presented in chapter 2 are analyzed by sex in order to see whether the male/female dichotomy in fact predicts the variations observed in those items.

The basic masculine/feminine dichotomy in ministry styles, while appearing simple at first glance, is a complex concept. Previous discussions of gender differences in ministry include a wide variety of perceptions, opinions, values, attitudes, and behaviors (see chap. 1). Those descriptions portray men and women as differing in many ways, including interpersonal style, theology, career goals, thought forms, power, authority, and ethics.

The first step in approaching these issues is to determine if there are in fact divergent approaches to ministry that can be considered basically "masculine" and "feminine." The survey of clergy asked the respondents to indicate the extent to which a series of statements resembled their own self-perceptions. Those statements embodied various aspects of ministry style defined in terms of assertions found in religious cultural feminist literature, and they constituted the major mode of determining the existence of masculine and feminine approaches to ministry. The survey also measured the amount of time clergy spent in various specific role activities and asked them to indicate how much value they placed on those role segments, another way of assessing divergent approaches to ministry.

As noted in chapter 2, every item resulted in some differentiation of the clergy in terms of ministry style. The "self-perception" questions produced wide differences in response, with some ministers describing themselves in relatively "masculine" terms and others presenting more "feminine" self-definitions. Similarly, the measures of time spent in roles and value placed on them also resulted in broad differences. So we do have evidence in the preceding chapter of clergy variations in masculine and feminine approaches to ministry. *Ministers actually differ in ministry style as predicted by some cultural feminists.*

However, we still do not have any evidence that the divergent approaches to ministry are associated with sex differences. The next question then, the one that is central to the study, is *"does the sex of the minister predict those gender differences in ministry style?"* Do the "masculine" responses appear mainly among the men? Is it the women who emerge with primarily "feminine" orientations? That is the question to which we turn in this chapter.

Sex Differences on Single-Item Indicators

The first step in the analysis was to run simple cross-tabulations between each indicator of ministry style and sex, incorporating all of the cases in the analysis. The results of those comparisons are only marginally supportive of the cultural feminist argument concerning sex differences in approach to ministry. Statistically significant sex differences emerged in only thirteen (19 percent) of the total possible seventy crosstabs (see table 3.1).

Eleven of those significant correlations (*gamma*) involve "self-description" measures, while two relationships deal with the relative importance of certain role activities. *None* of the comparisons involving time spent in clergy roles were statistically significant. According to these measures, male and female clergy *do not differ significantly in terms of how they allocate their working time.*

Nevertheless, the items that involve statistically significant relationships to male/female differences show that more men than women presented themselves as:

1. essential to the proper administration of the Lord's Supper,

2. uncomfortable when people share personal feelings with them,

3. rational and analytical in relation to congregational problems,

4. viewing appointment in a large church as a symbol of true success,

Table 3.1. Correlations (Gamma) between Sex of Clergy and Indicators of Ministry Style

Item	*Correlation*
I believe that only ordained clergy can properly administer the Lord's Supper (Holy Communion).	-.19
I am uncomfortable when people open up and share their innermost feelings with me.	-.31
When dealing with difficult decisions in the church, it is usually my "gut feeling" that serves me best.	.34
My ministry is effective because God is within me, as well as beyond me.	.23
There is no substitute for rational, analytical thought for solving congregational problems.	-.30
I would really feel successful as a minister if I were serving a large church.	-.27
I think today's church members need to hear the correct position on ethical issues delivered from the pulpit.	-.30
It is more important to do the work of the church efficiently than to have a lot of people involved in it.	.26
I think democratic decision making is a poor basis for local church policy.	-.15
It is more important to me to maintain congregational solidarity than to follow denominational policy.	-.21
A collaborative leadership style works best for me in working with the congregation.	.26
High importance placed on involvement in church structures beyond the congregation.	.24
High importance placed on involvement in social issues.	.18

Note: These items are significantly correlated with sex. None of the other indicators involved statistically significant associations.

5. insisting that the correct position on ethical issues be delivered from the pulpit,

6. preferring program efficiency over member involvement, and

7. rejecting democratic decision making for local church policy.

More women than men defined themselves in terms of:

1. dealing with difficult decisions in terms of "gut feeling,"

2. God working within them to render their work successful, and

3. preferring a collaborative leadership style.

Each of these relationships is in accordance with the predictions one would make on the basis of cultural feminist assertions. However, one other significant association is in the opposite direction from those arguments, that is, more *men* than women thought that it was more important to maintain congregational solidarity than to follow denominational policy.

On the matter of the relative importance clergy place on various role activities, more *women* than men placed great importance on involvement in church structures beyond the congregation and on involvement in social justice issues. The second of these correlations is consistent with prior assertions, while the first is contrary to them. According to some cultural feminist arguments, it is the *men*, not the women, who are supposed to desire participation in the bureaucracy, the opposite of the pattern noted above.

Accordingly, it is only in 16 percent of the comparisons that we find support for the cultural feminist arguments about sex differences in approach to ministry when the analysis is approached in this mode—bivariate tables involving single indicators of ministry style and the male/female dichotomy.

Composite Indicators of Dimensions of Ministry Style

Another analytical strategy for determining whether differences in approach to ministry are related to sex differences is to combine into composite measures those items whose referents constitute various dimensions of underlying complex concepts. Once those indexes are constructed, the analysis can compare differences in index scores with sex of pastor to see if the underlying concepts are associated with sex differences. The procedure is possible with these data, because the study employed multiple items to measure differences in broad dimensions of ministry style. The step is desirable, because sometimes composite indicators of complex concepts can uncover relationships to other variables when the single items cannot capture enough variance to attain statistical significance.

The advantages of employing index scores in quantitative analysis have long been recognized (e.g., Babbie 1979, 129–33, 146, 395–96). Composite measures tend to be more inclusive of various (often subtle) dimensions of complex concepts. When dealing with unidimensional concepts, such as age, sex, group size, and so forth, a single item usually constitutes a perfectly adequate measure. However, when measuring complex (multidimensional) constructs—such as 'patriotism' or 'authoritarianism', for example—a single item (question) will usually be unable to tap the many facets of the concept. There are many ways in which a person may be said to be "patriotic," for example, as in participating in the political process, defending the country, and sharing tax burdens. No single (closed-ended) question is likely to tap those various dimensions. By combining a series of questions, each one tapping a different aspect of the concept (as in 'patriotism'), one has in hand a composite measure that incorporates more dimensions of the concept in its complexity.

A second advantage is increased validity. In using multiple-item indicators, one is not totally and exclusively dependent upon the validity of any single question. Combining several items tapping different dimensions of a concept will result in relatively valid measurement, even if the validity of one of the items composing the total set is marginal. Thus one can have more confidence one is measuring the concept in question with multiple-item indicators than with single-item measures.

A third advantage of composite measures over single items is increased reliability. One is more likely to obtain similar results with repeated applications when using several items to measure a concept than when depending on but one question.

Clergy Use of Power

Five of the "like-me" items concern differences in tendency for clergy to use some form of power—legitimated, coercive, or persuasive social influence—in dealing with individuals and groups in their congregation. Those five statements are:

48. I find that I must be a skilled and energetic fund-raiser to prod parishioners to give enough money to keep the church alive.

50. Sometimes I have to drag my congregation kicking and screaming in the direction I think the church ought to go.

95. When I'm really sure about what the congregation should do, I try hard to get them to take my advice.

101. I don't think congregations can function very well without guidance from the clergy.

112. If I have any power in my congregation, it is based simply on the trust I have earned from the people.

Clergy who see themselves as having to "prod" parishioners, "drag" them in some direction, "try hard" to persuade them to follow, "incapable of functioning" without them, and having power "independently" of earned trust are persons who at least assume the legitimacy of using power and who at most place high value on possessing it. Those attributes are contrary to the ideology reflected in much cultural feminist discussion, where the process of emergent consensus, dialogue, and group empowerment are upheld as values that are superior to power and are assumed to be pursued primarily by women.

It is not within the objectives of this study to examine all of the possible uses and conceptions of "power" employed in sociological, political, and social-psychological literature (see, e.g., Kahn and Boulding 1964; Lenski 1966; Bendix and Lipset 1953). Indeed, there are many approaches to the concept and numerous ways in which it can be useful for understanding the experiences of women in social life in general and in religious institutions in particular. Suffice it to note at this point that a concern for social power is central to most feminist discussion, including religious feminism, whether of the structural or cultural variety, and that it remains a major concern of persons involved in the women-in-ministry movement (e.g., Ice 1987; Neitz 1990; Christ and Plaskow 1979).

Power has been ascribed to men in the Judaeo-Christian tradition for centuries. It was largely in response to this cultural assumption that men should be in positions of religious power and that women should *not* be that the women-in-ministry movement arose in the first place. Profound rejection of that assumption is a major motivation behind involvement in religious feminism of all varieties. That seems clear to most observers. Nevertheless, the cultural feminist argument goes beyond power holding as an ascribed status for males. Germane to this study, the central assertion is that *male clergy, more than clergy-women, enjoy wielding power over others, seek to be in positions that allow them to possess it, and attempt to exert power over others (including their congregations) in ways considered to be contrary to Christian values of egalitarianism, the priesthood of the (lay) believer, other-centered love, and so on* (e.g., Stevens 1989, 266; Ice 1987, 88ff.; Jacobs 1988; Nason-Clark 1987, 332–33; Neitz 1990). Parallel to that argument is the point that women, by contrast, seek only sufficient power to plan and control *their own* lives and that power enters women's working with their congregations in an obverse way, that is, with women clergy (more than men) seeking primarily to *enhance* the power congregations have over their own affairs. Is there evidence that will support this argument?

We combined these five items to form a composite measure of tendency to use power in dealing with the congregation. The mode of combination was to give each respondent one "point" for each of the five questions clearly answered in a way indicating a tendency to use power and a *negative* point for each question answered in the opposite way, that is, indicating clear *rejection* of the use of power. We set the cutting points at 20 to 30 percent; that is, we defined response categories as "endorsing" an item by taking those scores that included about the top 20 to 30 percent of the cases—those 20 to 30 percent of clergy who most clearly manifested the attribute in question. For example, on item 50 ("drag the congregation kicking and screaming"), about 20 percent of the respondents answered with categories 4 or 5. Thus we gave each person one point on what we call the "power index score" if he/she answered that item with response categories 4 or 5. Similarly, we awarded negative points to respondents in the "bottom" 20 to 30 percent—in this case response category 0, which contained closest to 20 percent of the cases. (It was not always possible to adhere precisely to that criterion in the construction of every composite measure, but we applied it as closely and as consistently as the response distributions would permit.)

Sometimes *not* rating oneself very high on an item portrays the characteristic defined by the concept. In the power index, for example, replying with a *low* self-rating on item 112 ("power based on earned trust") indicates a preference for personal power, in this case showing that one's power is based not on earned trust but on something else—most likely personal attributes or behavior. On that item, then, applying the 20 to 30 percent criterion, the respondents would receive one point for their power score if they replied to the item with a rating of 3 or lower (see table 3.2). They would receive negative points for answering with response categories at the opposite extreme. Each composite measure was created using these general criteria.

Table 3.2. Cross-Tabulation (Percent) of Power Scores with Sex of Clergy

Power Score:	Males	Females
-3	9	12
-2	12	13
-1	16	21
0	22	21
1	20	17
2	11	10
3	11	6
totals	237	271

Note: Correlation (gamma) = -.15.

The resulting composite index involved scores of negative five to positive five, with negative five indicating the lowest tendency to want power and plus five standing for the highest tendency. The distribution pattern of power socres (see table 3.3) indicates that clergy have widely divergent inclinations to use power in relation to their congregation. The median power score is 0. The distribution of responses is fairly symmetrical from the midpoint. As a group the clergy appear neither to hunger for power nor to reject its use.

Table 3.3. Distribution of Power Scores

	Low Use of Power								*High Use of Power*		
Score	-5	-4	-3	-2	-1	0	1	2	3	4	5
Percent	1	3	7	13	18	21	18	11	6	30	.2

Before cross-tabulating power scores with sex, it was necessary to collapse the extreme score categories containing small numbers of cases—that is, scores of -3, -4, and -5 were combined to make one score of -3. The reason for that step was that there are so few cases in score categories -4 and -5 that the movement of but one or a few cases in a contingency table distorts the overall pattern in any relationship portrayed by the table. The same strategy was applied to the opposite end of the continuum, grouping scores of 3, 4, and 5 into one category. (This step was also taken in other score distributions discussed below.)

Table 3.4.   Distribution of Scores on the Collapsed Power Index

	Low Use of Power				High Use of Power		
score	-3	-2	-1	0	1	2	3
percent	11	13	18	21	18	11	9

If the cultural feminist argument is to be supported empirically, then low (negative) power scores should be associated with the women, while high scores should be found more among the men. The results of cross-tabulating power scores with sex are contained in table 3.2, *which supports the argument that use of power is associated with sex.* More women than men have power scores in the lower categories, while more men than women manifest scores at the high end of the spectrum. Men tend to be involved with the use of power slightly more than the women are. The relationship is not strong by any means. The correlation (gamma) in the association is but -.15 (the negative sign is an artifact of coding), a pattern also revealed by the small differences in percentage distributions of the men and women. Nevertheless, the sex differences are in the predicted direction and they are statistically significant. This aspect of the cultural feminist argument has been given some empirical support.

Empowerment of Congregations

The flip side of an assumption that one ought not use *power over* congregations to get them to do what one thinks they should do is the enjoinder to seek to *empower* church members to define their own aspirations and to find their own ways of realizing them. This theme is clearly a major aspect of the cultural feminist argument (e.g., Ice 1987; Meyers 1988). Motivated perhaps by their own frustrating experience of powerlessness—of exclusion from religious vocations, of being second-class citizens in religious power structures, of not being taken seriously as church leaders, and of being repeatedly rebuffed in efforts to overcome those obstacles—many religious feminists appear to empathize deeply with lay church members, whom they perceive as being subjected to the same kinds of manipulation and subordination as they have experienced themselves. To them the church has too long tried to control people's lives, pretentiously telling them what is important, what is good, what they should be doing, and how to do it.

That image at best is of the church as "parent" and at worst of the church as "ruler."

They argue that clergy should seek ways of leading lay church members to take control of their own religious lives, to define their goals as individuals and as members of religious communities, and to develop ways of bringing those objectives into reality. The relationship of the church to the lay member should be that of "teacher" and "facilitator" rather than "parent" or "keeper."

This theme, of course, is but one of the battle cries of the Reformation, the priesthood of all believers. Prior to the Protestant Reformation, Roman Catholic ecclesiology assumed that the church was indeed the wise parent watching over spiritually immature and religiously inferior lay people. Some observers would argue that this orientation of Catholicism toward lay persons has not changed significantly. Rome's response to many pressures for internal structural and cultural change has been negative, as illustrated in recent church decrees on qualifications for ordination and control of reproductive fertility. Today in Latin America, of course, lay people find a new affirmation in "liberation theology" and in the "base communities" movements (Royle 1991).

Within the feminist argument, however, one finds the assertion that such Protestant criticisms of Roman Catholicism are tantamount to "the pot calling the kettle black." This criticism is leveled especially at Protestant clergy. The basic point some critics make is that many Protestant ministers are also so impressed with their theological erudition, their "holy" status as ordained ministers, and their occupying formal leadership positions in religious hierarchies that they, too, look down upon the lowly lay person as spiritually immature and religiously inferior. Assuming that they know what is best for the church, these Protestant clergy tend to manipulate lay church members and take just as much of a "parent" or "keeper" role as their Roman Catholic counterparts. The "official" position of the Protestant denominations may be the religious autonomy of the lay person, but the idea sometimes gets lost in the day-to-day implementation. The "reality" in many Protestant churches is also one of clergy authoritarianism.

So the cultural feminist cry is for a return to the Protestant principle. "Return to your historical roots, ye clergy! You are not as wise, virtuous, or ethereal as you think you are. You are the *servants* of the church, not its rulers. Your role is to help lay believers on their own spiritual journeys, not to tell them where and when to go!" Ministers should try to empower lay members to live their own religious lives— to listen to questions and aspirations, suggest possibilities perhaps not considered, present the Gospel in understandable terms, and to love and support members in their own choices.

As in the criticisms of the misuse of power, the discussions of churches failing to empower their lay members to take control of their religious lives couch the problem primarily in terms of the historical pattern of *male domination* of the ministry. Given their privileged access to positions of power, men are more likely than women to define their clergy role in terms of enhancing their own power rather than that of the congregation. Given their experience of powerlessness, women are more likely than men to strive to empower their members and to eschew any magnification of their own power over the laity. In short women should be more inclined than men to seek to augment the power lay church members have over their private and collective religious lives. Can we find evidence to support this statement?

The interview schedule contains four questions uniquely related to the issue of lay empowerment. Those four items are as follows:

91. I believe that lay people, not the clergy, should decide the direction in which the church will go.

106. One of my ministry goals is to enhance the power my members have in the mission and operation of their local church.

108. My ministry will be most successful if I can lead my congregation to get along without me.

110. A collaborative leadership style works best for me in working with the congregation.

All of these items are stated in feminine terms. Thus we combined them in the same manner as was done on the power index above, giving all respondents one point for each item they said characterized them clearly and one negative point for each item they clearly rejected. Each clergy respondent, therefore, received an "empowerment score" based on his/her replies to the four questions. The general tendency in the empowerment scores distribution (see table 3.5) is for clergy to manifest highly divergent tendencies to strive for the empowerment of their congregations. The median score is 1, which is also the modal score. Very few of the ministers have scores at either end of the continuum, although there is a slight tendency for the clergy as a group to endorse empowerment of congregations more than to reject it.

Again, the focal question is whether female clergy manifest more interest in lay empowerment than men. To ascertain whether that is the case, we cross-tabulated the empowerment scores with sex. The results of that comparison (table 3.6) once again collapse the lowest and highest score categories. The pattern in the table tends to support

Table 3.5. Distribution of Empowerment Scores

	Little Empowerment					Much Empowerment			
Score	-4	-3	-2	-1	0	1	2	3	4
Percent	1	3	6	16	16	21	19	13	5

Table 3.6. Cross-Tabulation (Percent) of Empowerment Scores with Sex of Clergy

Empowerment Score:		Males	Females
-2		13	6
-1		20	13
0		14	18
1		23	20
2		16	22
3		14	21
	totals	239	273

Note: Correlation (gamma) = .22.

the cultural feminist argument. *Interest in lay congregational empowerment is related to sex.* Proportionately more women than men obtain high empowerment scores, while more men than women have low scores. The strength of the correlation (gamma) in this relationship is .22, not terribly strong but statistically significant. This pattern tends to support the cultural feminist argument concerning differences in the orientation women and men have toward the appropriate location of power in the churches.

Use of Power versus Lay Empowerment

One question that may be posed at this juncture concerns the possible relationship between proclivity for using power and interest in congregational empowerment. Given the arguments about clergy using power oneself *or* seeking to empower the laity, one would expect the two concepts to be correlated. Clergy who are interested in protecting their own power would be expected to show little interest in enhancing the power of the congregation, and conversely those whose egalitarianism moves them to press for lay empowerment would not be expected to seek self-aggrandizement. There seems to be nothing in the cultural feminist position that would lead one to argue *against* such a prediction. Is there in fact a negative relationship between these variables?

We cross-tabulated power scores with empowerment scores to examine this possibility. If the speculation noted above is correct, then clergy with high power scores should also manifest *low* empowerment scores, and *vice versa*. The results of the comparison supported that prediction. The correlation emerging from the cross-tabulation was -.13. Power seeking is negatively related to seeking to empower the laity.

Since sex is related to both power and empowerment scores, it is possible that the two variables are correlated differently when controlling for sex. The simultaneous effects of sex on both variables could influence the relationship between them. Accordingly, we cross-tabulated power score with empowerment score, controlling for sex. The results indicate that *sex specifies the relationship between power score and empowerment score*. The relationship holds among the *male* clergy, where the correlation increases slightly to -.19, but the correlation tends to *disappear among the women*, for whom the coefficient is but -.06 and is statistically nonsignificant.

Curiously it is the *men* who seem to manifest the consistency one would predict on the basis of the feminist argument, not the women. This pattern implies that there is no significant tendency for women to either like or dislike the use of power if they also press (or do not press) for congregational empowerment. At this point, one can only speculate about possible explanations for this pattern. The conjecture that immediately comes to mind considers a possible ambivalence clergywomen may have toward their own use of power. To be accepted by most congregations, women clergy feel varying degrees of pressure to perform their role as pastor in ways that resemble precedents set by their (usually male) predecessors. This would include expectations of "taking charge" as the local pastor. Couple this reality with the struggle in which women clergy have sought to enhance and solidify their own identity as religious leaders, and it is quite possible that some clergywomen find themselves seeking *both* congregational empowerment and stabilization of their own status as leaders. Whether dynamics such as these (or something else) explain the sex differences noted above remains to be seen.

Desire for Formal Authority

Closely related to concepts of 'power' and 'empowerment" is the issue of formal authority—being in the right position to influence others legitimately. Having authority in social settings is a matter of "having the right" to influence others. In the Judaeo-Christian tradition, this right to influence others in religious matters has usually been reserved to males. Today most church members assume that their pastor or priest will be a man. It is one of their "of course" assumptions, which to many believers is on a par with the idea that "of course" the sun will rise in the East and not in the West. It is "natural." This form of authority has been termed "traditional authority" by Max Weber (Gerth and Mills 1946), and it remains a powerful basis for a claim to exclusive access to legitimate authority. It is hard to change.

However, Weber pointed out that there are other forms of authority as well. A second type he discussed is "legal-rational" authority. Whereas traditional authority is based on assumptions of legitimacy by long-standing practice—the appeal that "this is the way we've always done it!"—legal-rational authority is a matter of *enactment*. Groups and societies calculatingly decide that specific qualifications must be met for a person to be in a position of authority, and they "make a law" stating that it shall be so. Examples of persons with this form of authority include physicians, lawyers, military officers, and public school teachers. Some religious groups have elevated the grounding of the status of men as exclusive ordained leaders from traditional to legal-rational authority. They have established a formal norm specifying that only men will be accepted by the group as ordained clergy. Much of the women-in-ministry movement involves a systematic attack on the legitimacy of such rules, as well as on the immutability of the force of tradition, of course. And some of these efforts have met with success. All four denominations in this study, for example, have endorsed the ordination of women, and all of the ministers included in the sample, half of whom are women, have been placed as pastors. Yet it is also clear that women in other denominations do not have access to leadership positions as sanctioned in rational-legal terms, as seen in the Roman Catholic Church worldwide and among the Missouri Synod Lutherans and most Southern Baptists in the United States.

The third form of authority discussed by Weber is "charismatic" authority. The term *charismatic* derives from the Greek word *charisma*, meaning "gift." Charismatic persons are "gifted" persons, individuals who are able to attract attention to themselves on the basis of their unique qualities. Their ability to attract a following by others is not based on tradition or some formal rule; instead it derives from the force of their personality and talents. They are referred to as "charismatic leaders," and their right to influence others is a matter of "charismatic authority." Examples of this type of authority include

Ghandi, Hitler, and Martin Luther King, Jr. Other examples in the religious sphere are Jesus of Nazareth, the Prophet Mohammed, Amy Semple McPherson, and Billy Graham.

Ice (1987, 81) suggests that today women in ministry depend most heavily on charismatic authority. The women in her study were "*oriented* toward this type of influence; they believe in it as a way of life" (emphasis in the original). Ice also notes, however, that each of them in fact had been ordained and thus had legal-rational permission to be doing the work in which they were involved. Ice's point is well taken, because in spite of legal-rational legitimation, clergywomen constantly face the classical double standard. They have to prove themselves more clearly than men, and they have to demonstrate their abilities (their "charisma") again and again in each new social arena they enter.

This belief in charismatic authority has become another point of emphasis in the cultural feminist discussion of male/female differences in approach to ministry. Wanting and holding formal legitimation of one's position is held up for ridicule as a sign of (male) insecurity in ministry. Many men "need" the props of traditional and legal-rational authority to secure them in their positions of leadership, so the argument goes. Women, on the other hand, may not need those legitimations. They can identify with the powerlessness of the laity more readily than can the men, because women themselves have experienced exclusion from positions of authority. Thus they can relate to lay church members more empathetically than the men can, and the more informal and egalitarian style of leadership to result from that lay identification will be better for the church in the long run.

At the same time, however, the women-in-ministry movement is consciously, systematically, and tenaciously pressing for the formal legitimation of women's ministry—driving for legal-rational authority. It is pressing for the ordination of women, placement in positions of religious leadership as parish ministers and priests, appointment to faculty positions in theological seminaries, and installation in high-level positions of denominational leadership. Thus the movement does not speak with one voice on the issue of the desirability of possessing legal-rational authority. On the one hand, the movement criticizes the traditional ministry system for depending so heavily on legal-rational bases of clerical authority. On the other hand, it works feverishly to remove barriers women face when they seek such formal legitimation. Ice (1987, 81–82) also recognizes this paradox. She asks, for example:

> Will the immediacy of authentic faith and interpersonal influence idealized among women enter increasingly into the official interpretations of institu-

tional authority...? Charismatic appeal has special impact right now in role shaping and in ministerial effectiveness. When they can relax from the rigors of establishing a social role, will they continue to regard charismatic credibility as the primary professional religious authority?

It is important to point out that this internal paradox in the movement also constitutes an important division among religious feminists themselves. In fact it is one of the points that tend to separate the structural from the cultural feminists. It is primarily the structural feminists who are pressing hard for the legal-rational authority embodied in the ordination and placement of women. And it is mainly cultural feminists who cast aspersions and tend to reject the present masculine system as a whole. Thus the point is one of the defining factors in the distinctions with which we began the investigation.

Nevertheless, the question remains as an object of *empirical* examination—do women clergy who are actually serving as pastors of congregations tend to like (want, strive for) formal authority as much as do the men? The cultural feminist assertion suggests that they do not (e.g., Meyers 1988, 10–13; Ice 1987, 92ff.; Nason-Clark 1987, 332–333; Stevens 1989, 266). Is this the case?

An Index of Authority Orientation

Eight of the items on the data-collection instrument measured some aspect of clergy attitude toward possession of formal authority. Those items are:

33. I believe that only ordained clergy can properly administer the Lord's Supper (Holy Communion).

54. I cannot be the leader I want to be if I do not have authority to implement my own decisions.

55. My daily working theology has little to do with my professional ministry studies.

92. My authority as a minister rests primarily on my professional training and ordination.

97. I think that democratic decision making is a poor basis for local church policy.

99. I consider myself accountable primarily to the denominational administrators in my region.

100. I think ordination to the ministry places too much distance between ministers and lay people.

109. It is more important to me to maintain congregational solidarity than to follow denominational policy.

As with the other indices above, we combined these items to form an index of attitude toward formal authority. Clergy were considered to manifest positive attitudes toward possessing formal authority (and were given positive score points) if they indicated that five of those items were "like them"—items 33, 54, 92, 97, and 99. They were also given increases in positive score if they stated that the remaining three items—55, 100, 109—were *not* like them. The pattern in distribution of "authority scores" (see table 3.7) portrays a picture similar to that observed in previous distributions. The general tendency is for clergy scores to be fairly symmetrically distributed across the range of possibilities. The median score is quite central 0. That is also the modal score. It is clear that the clergy in the study were not monolithic in their attitude toward possessing authority. Some persons wanted it, while others did not.

Table 3.7. Distribution of Authority Scores

	Not Want Authority												*Want Authority*	
Score	-7	-6	-5	-4	-3	-2	-1	0	1	2	3	4	5	6
Percent	0.2	0.6	1	4	5	13	14	21	16	12	8	4	2	0.6

The next question, of course, is whether sex differences are predictive of variations in authority score. According to some cultural feminist argument, men should manifest higher authority scores than women. Wanting formal authority for oneself is contrary to cultural feminist argument. The results of cross-tabulating authority score with sex of clergy indicate that the variations in authority score are *not* due to sex differences. The correlation (gamma) that resulted from the comparison is only -.08, and it is not statistically significant. The distribution of clergywomen across the range of authority scores is virtually identical to that observed among the men. *These data do not support the idea that men tend to want formal authority more than do women.*

Desiring Both Authority and Power

Before moving to the next concept, it may be interesting to note the possible association between wishing to be in positions of formal

authority and being willing to use power in relating to the congregation. As noted above, more males than females among the ministers
questioned were willing to use power to get things done in their
church. However, clergy authoritarianism appears to be a different
matter, for there is no significant relationship between sex and desiring to be in positions of formal authority. Does this also mean that the
two concepts, therefore, are unrelated?

Not at all. We compared power and authority scores, and the
result indicates that clergy who wished to be in positions of formal
authority also manifested a greater willingness to use power over the
congregation, with the correlation from that comparison being .25. We
ran the same comparison controlling for sex, and the results are very
similar to the zero-order association. Power and authority scores are
positively related among the men with a correlation of .20, and the
coefficient among the women is slightly larger at .28. *Among both male
and female clergy, persons wishing to be in positions of formal authority were
also the more willing to use power over their congregations.* There are no
meaningful sex differences in this relationship.

Solving Problems in the Church

Another point made by some religious feminists concerns differences
in how clergy function when confronted with the need for congregational decision making or problem solving. The basic distinction
involves how ministers approach such tasks. The masculine strategy
for decision making and problem solving focuses on structure, rationality, sometimes called "science." The feminine design, by contrast,
centers on intuition and dialogue or "process" (see, e.g., Ice 1987,
60–71; and Miller-McLemore 1988). In caricature the masculine tactics
would resemble a highly structured, formally created committee of
men slavishly following *Roberts Rules of Order* in pursuit of the most
logical approach to the problem. The satirical parallel to the feminine
approach would have several women who share some interest engag-
ing in informal conversation during a coffee break and groping for
insights that feel right intuitively. The difference focuses on closed
structure and rationality in contrast to open process and intuition. As
noted in chapter 1, these propositions are not limited to religious feminism, of course, but are found in the broader movement as well (for a
contrary argument, see Robb 1985; and Epstein 1988).

Four items on the data-collection instrument were designed to
measure such differences in approach to decision making and problem solving. Those questions are as follows:

38. When dealing with difficult decisions in the church, it is usually my "gut feeling" that serves me best.

46. There is no substitute for rational, analytical thought for solving congregational problems.

96. I think it is more important to do the work of the church efficiently than to have a lot of people involved in it.

104. I feel uncomfortable in the absence of clear organizational guidelines for ongoing church programs.

These items were combined to form a composite index of preference for rational structure. The ministers were given positive and negative points toward a "rational structure" score in the same manner as in the construction of the previous indices. As was the case with previous composite indices, the distribution of clergy along the continuum of scores on the rational structure index (see table 3.8) indicates *little overall tendency to prefer or to reject rational and structured approaches to decision making and problem solving.* The modal score is 0, as is the median. Very few clergy have either high or low scores. So as a group the ministers tend to be "middle-of-the-road" concerning acceptance or rejection of rationality and structure in decision-making situations, manifesting at the same time wide differences in score.

Table 3.8. Distribution of Rational Structure Index Scores

	Dislike					*Prefer*			
	Rational Structure					*Rational Structure*			
Score	-4	-3	-2	-1	0	1	2	3	4
Percent	2	4	13	17	26	23	13	3	0.4

We may now ask whether any of those variations were due to the influence of sex. The pattern in table 3.9 indicates *a clear relationship between sex and preference for rational structure.* The differences between women and men in their rational structures scores are more pronounced than was found in any previous cross-tabulation. Proportionately nearly twice as many men as women manifest high scores of 1 and 2. And greater percentages of women than men are found in the lowest score categories. The correlation that emerges from the comparison is -.40, a figure larger than that found in any other relationship examined to this point. *Sex is a clear predictor of preference for rationality and structure in congregational decision making.*

Table 3.9. Cross-Tabulation (Percent) of Rational Structure Scores
by Sex of Clergy

Rational Structure Score:		Males	Females
-2		9	27
-1		14	19
0		26	26
1		26	21
2		25	8
	totals	237	275

Note: Correlation (gamma) = -.40.

Ethical Legalism

Closely related to preference for rational structure in problem solving
is the matter of ethics. Of all professions, perhaps only legislators and
persons working in the criminal justice system (broadly conceived)
work more closely than clergy in matters of ethics and morals—good
and bad, right and wrong. Religious systems typically present themselves as representing the highest values and moral standards in their
society. Religious functionaries are usually expected to be the normative pillars of their community, upholding and representing in their
speech and deportment the standards for which others are expected to
strive. It is that moral backdrop that made the scandals involving popular television evangelists in the United States such newsworthy
events in the 1980s. To many people, religious issues are synonymous
with ethical issues.

The study of ethics in general has long recognized that there are
many orientations and approaches to moral choices. Ethical schools of
thought have developed, each based on a particular guiding principle
such as: the correct *motive*, the best *outcome*, taking *responsibility* for
actions, and so forth. Not everyone views ethics in the same way.
What is considered "ethical" can be (and often is) determined by
widely differing criteria.

As noted above (see chap. 1), some feminist commentators on the
ministry have argued that a minister's sex will be predictive of the
approach he/she will take to ethical issues (e.g., Briggs 1987). These
differences, at least in theory, have crystalized into what is portrayed
as "masculine" and "feminine" approaches to morality. The guiding
principle that is said to characterize "masculine" ethics is duty or
legalism. The axiom undergirding "feminine" ethics is responsible car-

ing (see Ice 1987, chap. 7). Clergymen are viewed as seeking "the correct answer" when dealing with difficult moral choices—searching for precedent, moral maxims, rules of conduct—hence the label "legalism." Clergywomen, on the other hand, are portrayed as being less interested in dealing with moral issues in terms of the correct answers, instead preferring to focus on the *process* of arriving at the decision and on *responsibly caring about the consequences* any decision may have for persons involved in the situation. Ice says, for example (1987, 125), that for women ministers:

> moral leadership...is idealized not as perfect exemplary conformity to perfect rules of human goodness; not just as knowing a great deal about the official positions and defenses regarding right choices; not as prescribing appropriate religious compensations when the rules are disobeyed. It is rather idealized as authentic, exemplary struggle toward perfect caring community; loving life and people as best one can....Women respect social (including religious) rules of conduct as important moral resources. But the impact of action on persons remains the essential evaluating criterion for them.

A great deal of this discussion of divergent ethical orientations of male and female ministers reflects the broader debate within feminist circles and social and behavioral sciences in general (e.g., Epstein 1988). As noted in chapter 1, linking the distinction between legalism and responsible caring to sex differences is usually attributed to the works of Chodorow (1978) and Gilligan (1982), especially the latter. Gilligan viewed masculine morality as the "ethics of justice" and feminine morality as the "ethics of caring." This distinction seems to have attained the status of a "bandwagon" in many segments of the women-in-ministry movement, that in spite of some evidence to the contrary produced by other (feminist) observers (e.g., Greeno and Maccoby 1986).

Is there any evidence in these data to support the distinction between women's and men's ethical systems? Three items on the questionnaire measured some facets of the issue. They are:

51. I often will bend church rules if they don't meet the needs of the congregation.

52. I think today's church members need to hear the correct position on ethical issues delivered from the pulpit.

57. My primary concern in concrete moral choices is applying the best rules for conducting human life.

The first of these items is a "feminine" statement, and the other two are "masculine." We combined the three to form a composite measure of tendencies toward and away from "legalism" (see table 3.10). Once again the general tendency is for clergy to manifest widely divergent scores. Both the modal and median scores are 0. However, there is also a slight tendency for the group as a whole to manifest more *high* scores than low. About 45 percent of the cases fall in the "legalistic" end of the continuum, whereas only 29 percent are on the other end. More ministers think in terms of "rules" than not.

Table 3.10.   Distribution of Legalism Index Scores

	Little Legalism				*Much Legalism*		
Score	-3	-2	-1	0	1	2	3
Percent	3	9	17	26	25	13	7

To determine the extent to which these differences in legalism score are attributable to sex, we cross-tabulated those two variables. The resulting picture is contained in table 3.11, generally showing more men than women with relatively high legalism scores as in score categories 1 and 2, and more women than men with low scores of -2, -1, and 0. The correlation resulting from the comparison is -.28 and is statistically significant. Thus the cultural feminist argument that *men tend to manifest more ethical legalism than women* is supported.

Table 3.11.   Cross-Tabulation (Percent) of Ethical Legalism Scores by Clergy Sex

Rational Structure Score:	*Males*	*Females*
-2	8	17
-1	15	19
0	22	28
1	31	19
2	25	17
totals	224	243

Note: Correlation (gamma) = -.28.

General Interpersonal Style

Another point of possible difference between men and women is general interpersonal style. The idea that men and women relate to other people in ways unique to their sex has been a matter of protracted discussion (see, e.g., Maccoby and Jacklin 1974; Tavris and Offir 1977; and Epstein 1988, chap. 10). Some of the sex differences in mode of social interaction incorporated in the image with which much of that exchange deals are listed in table 3.12. As noted in chapter 1, many of the conclusions that the sexes differ in ways like these seem to be based on evidence which is at best weak and may even be highly selective and inconclusive. The debate goes on and on.

Table 3.12. Sex Differences in Social Interaction

Masculine	*Feminine*
aggressive	passive
extrinsic relationships	intrinsic relationships
instrumental behavior	expressive behavior
manipulative	compliant
dominance	subordination
authoritarian	egalitarian
defensive	vulnerable
impersonal	personal

These general assumptions have also found their way into the discussions of differences in how male and female clergy relate to other people. The overdrawn stereotype of the male minister, which congeals from various sources, depicts him as a terribly insecure individual, striving to prove himself a man in the eyes of others, emotionally incapable of exposing his own inadequacies and failures, fearful of dealing with deep and raw emotions, and (unsuccessfully) compensating for all of these problems by parading his accomplishments and seeking positions of increasing social dominance. The equally mythical clergywoman, by contrast, is quietly confident, happy to work successfully in the background, living comfortably with her own vulnerability, openly receptive to her own emotions and to those of others, humbly foregoing the status associated with public recognition, and content to work systematically in the lowly vineyard for which she is responsible (e.g., Ice 1987, 95, 127–28; Meyers 1988, 21–22; Stevens 1989, 268–69). Is there any truth to such images?

The interview schedule included several "like-me" questions

designed to measure differences in interpersonal style. They dealt in
various ways with clergy willingness to be open, available, and vulnerable. The nine items focusing on those concepts were:

34. I am uncomfortable when people open up and share their
    innermost feelings with me.

36. As a minister it is important for me to remain somewhat
    detached from members of my congregation.

37. It is hard for me to ignore requests from my congregation
    even when I feel overwhelmed with work.

53. I do not feel free to express my true feelings about things
    with anyone in my congregation.

56. I know I have my congregation's confidence when they
    openly discuss with me their critical assessments of my pro-
    gram proposals.

93. I prefer to use my professional title in relating to the local
    community.

98. I feel uneasy when members of my congregation touch me in
    any way physically.

103. As a church leader, it is important that I reveal no points of
     personal weakness to the congregation.

107. I prefer that church members address me only by my first
     name.

In combining these items to form a composite index of "open interpersonal style," the scoring used the *feminine* criterion. (The previous
indices were scored using the masculine criterion for defining the high
end of the continuum of scores.) Persons indicating that items 37, 56,
or 107 were "like them" were given positive increments to the scale
score. Clergy stating that the remaining items were *not* like them were
also given positive score points. Thus low scores indicate an interpersonal style that is closed, unavailable, and defensive. High scores indicate openness, availability, and willingness to be vulnerable.

The collapsed distribution of interpersonal style scores (see table
3.13) is spread across the entire range of possibilities. Yet the distribution is somewhat skewed, with the modal and median scores at 2.
Accordingly, as a group the ministers appear a bit more "feminine" in
orientation than appeared to be the case on the other variables. More
than one-half of the cases fall in the "positive" end of the spectrum,
while only 17 percent are in the negative portion.

Table 3.13. The Collapsed Distribution of Interpersonal Style Scores

	Closed, Defensive					*Open, Receptive*			
Score	-2	-1	0	1	2	3	4	5	6
Percent	11	6	12	13	13	11	11	9	14

The cross-tabulation of sex with style score reveals little or no relationship between the two variables. The distributions of style scores for males and females are almost identical. Proportional variations of men and women in different score categories are both small and curvilinear. The correlation representing the pattern in the table is only .11 and is statistically nonsignificant. The analysis of these data, therefore, *do not support the argument that male and female clergy differ significantly in interpersonal style.* Clergymen and clergywomen seem to resemble each other closely in an overall tendency for a feminine interpersonal style of openness, accessibility, and vulnerability.

Preaching Style

Preaching is a role activity of central importance in most Protestant traditions. In Sunday morning (and sometimes Sunday evening) worship services, the sermon is usually the central focus of the worship experience, with other worship events, such as hymns and scripture, selected on the basis of how well they fit with the sermon rather than vice versa. There are exceptions to that pattern, of course, but it has been virtually a defining attribute of the Protestant church service, particularly in the free church tradition.

How preaching is done varies widely. Some ministers are considered "good preachers" by other clergy and lay persons. Others are not so impressive. These judgments can be very important. You will almost never find a minister who does *not* excel in sermon preparation and delivery (especially the latter) who is also defined as "popular," "successful," or "influential." In the free church tradition, the "significant churches" typically call as their pastor only those ministers who do a good job in the pulpit, the so-called golden-voiced orators.

Some persons in the women-in-ministry movement argue that men and women engage in the art of preaching so differently that one may speak of feminine and masculine preaching styles (e.g., Ice 1987, 93; Stevens 1989, 267). The differences between these orientations begin with the relative importance the sexes place on the activity. Men supposedly rank preaching higher in importance than women. Men typically focus their sermons on theological and intellectual issues, while women reportedly emphasize concrete issues and the existential needs of church members. In line with what some perceive as men's desire to be in positions of power and authority, men purportedly use the pulpit as platforms from which to display their erudition more than women do. And men are viewed as "talking down" to lay church members in their sermons, whereas women are not. For many men the sermon is another way in which they find themselves competing with each other and dealing with the potentially emasculating spectre of failure. The success of their work week often stands or falls on the congregation's response to the Sunday morning message.

Five "like-me" items on the questionnaire deal with preaching in one way or another. Those questions are:

32. I make my major contribution to my congregation through my preaching.

35. My sermons typically focus on theological beliefs.

41. My sermons simply involve one believer speaking to another.

44. I usually focus my preaching on the concrete concerns of my people.

47. When I preach, I always try to remember that I speak as a representative of Almighty God.

These items hardly exhaust the total range of possible dimensions of "preaching style," but they were the ones that survived the elimination of questions in the requirement to be parsimonious. In combining these questions to form a composite index of "masculine preaching style," we awarded positive points for indicating that items 32, 35, and 47 were "like me,' and for the opposite response to questions 41 and 44.

The distribution of scores on preaching style is quite symmetrical (see table 3.14). It is also highly grouped toward the midpoint, with very few cases found at either extreme. This centralization of scores *may* be due to some inadequacy in the items composing the index. It is possible that the set does not differentiate well enough between persons inclined to masculine or feminine preaching styles. On the other hand, it is also possible that the items are quite adequate and that the respondents simply manifested few strong tendencies one way or the other. This latter possibility is certainly plausible, because the structure of preaching in these denominations tends to be somewhat standardized. In any case, there are at least five clearly useful score categories for use in comparing female and male ministers.

Table 3.14.   Distribution of Preaching Style Scores

Score	Not Masculine									Highly Masculine	
Score	-5	-4	-3	-2	-1	0	1	2	3	4	5
Percent	0.2	1	5	15	19	22	20	12	5	1	0.2

Are those sex differences actually predictive of variations in "preaching style" score? The results of cross-tabulating these scores with sex of minister indicated that the two variables tend to be independent of each other. There are few differences in the proportional distribution of females and males in the various score categories. The correlation resulting from the comparison is only -.07, and it is statistically nonsignificant. This section of *the analysis does not support the idea that clergymen have more masculine preaching styles than do clergywomen.*

Criteria of Status

Even though religious ideology associated with the ministry portrays the ideal clergy person as self-effacing and devoted strictly to the service of others, there is clear evidence of status striving among them (see, e.g., Lehman 1990). As a profession, the ministry involves differences in authority, power, privilege, and prestige. Some ministers are "more equal than others"—the old cliche applies. For most clergy, the major criteria of their position in those internal professional stratification systems closely resemble the determinants of social differentiation found in other occupations. Ministers' power and privilege typically vary with the size of the church they serve, their skill in the (preaching) ministry, the level of their formal education, the socioeconomic status of their congregation, their annual income, and so forth. Most ministers work within hierarchical organizations that designate incumbents of various positions as having more power and authority than others. The ministry is a very "human" profession—highly stratified—in these ways.

Since those realities of social stratification conflict with basic egalitarian values inherent in Christian ideology, the ideal must be reinforced regularly in order to keep clergy properly humble (at least outwardly). This social control is accomplished through a variety of mechanisms, such as routine ideological rhetoric extolling the compliant ideal, official ridicule of behaviors defined as inappropriate, or, if nothing else, simply denying the realities of professional stratification. Status striving, though rampant, is periodically criticized as unbecoming of a proper minister of the Gospel. These mechanisms pervade all denominations—from the complex hierarchies of the Roman Catholic Church to the diffused authority systems of the Baptists and other congregationally based organizations.

Religious feminists have focused some of their criticism of the "masculine" ministry system on the realities and excesses of stratification among male clergy. They are critical of the status striving that the masculine system has promoted historically—competing for ever larger churches, parading university and seminary degrees, pressing for increasing salaries—and the general haughtiness of "fat-cat" ministers defined as having succeeded in these terms.

In place of those traditional criteria of ministerial status, a competing set of determinants has been set forth. Within many circles of religious feminists, persons are admired (given status) if they have shown signs of persevering through suffering, of working hard in marginal vocational placements (i.e., small churches or positions usually defined as low in prestige), of being available to serve others twenty-four hours a day and seven days a week, serving as "mentors" to other (younger) clergywomen, building up their congregations and the surrounding community, and so on. These ideas constitute a "feminine" status system that stands alongside and competes with the traditional "masculine" one (e.g., Miller-McLemore 1988; Ice 1987, 49, 60). (Actually the basic points in that feminine status system appear to but recapitulate the "official" image of the ministry that the denominations have long sought to realize but cannot.)

Do men and women differ in their acceptance and implementation of the feminine status system? Do more men than women reflect the traditional "masculine" values of power and privilege? The data-collection instrument includes a few questions designed to address that matter. Those items are as follows:

45. I contribute the most to my congregation by sharing in their celebration or their suffering.

49. I would really feel successful as a minister if I were serving a large church.

94. I think there is too much talk among ministers about salaries and "promotions."

102. I would like to be remembered as a helpful mentor to other ministers.

105. The measure of success of my ministry is my positive influence on the community.

The scoring of these items was based on the feminine position. Clergy received positive points on a score of "feminine status criteria" if they stated that question 49 was *not* like them and if they indicated that the other items *were* like them. High scores indicate acceptance of feminine status criteria, while low scores suggest rejection of those values. As the distribution of the collapsed feminine status scores indicates, the clergy actually do differ widely in their acceptance of feminine status criteria (see table 3.15). The respondents are distributed across the entire range of possibilities. Nevertheless, there is also some skew in the pattern. More ministers had positive scores than negative ones, indicating a slight tendency for the sample to exhibit more acceptance of feminine status criteria than the masculine system.

Table 3.15. Distribution of Feminine Status Criteria Scores

	Reject Feminine Status Criteria			Accept Feminine Status Criteria		
Score	-2	-1	0	1	2	3
Percent	19	16	22	15	12	16

The major question is whether more women than men indicate acceptance of these feminine criteria of ministry status. The results of cross-tabulating feminine status score by sex of clergy indicate that there is no meaningful association between them. The correlation emerging from the comparison is only .03 and is statistically nonsignificant. *Thus we have no evidence here that sex is predictive of rejecting the masculine status system and endorsing feminine status criteria for the ministry.*

Involvement in Social Issues

The final composite measure deals with clergy involvement in social issues. One of the themes in religious feminist discourse is the argument that male clergy manifest too little interest in social concerns outside of the church. The traditional masculine system focuses their attention on the local church and what they are expected to do in order to succeed there. Instead of devoting time and energy to understanding community, national, and worldwide issues, male ministers reportedly have "tunnel vision" in their work, perceiving and attaching importance only to matters of direct concern for their ministry to the local congregation. Clergymen are said to be more interested in matters of personal morality than in those of social concerns, especially neglecting matters like conserving the environment, preventing international war, dealing with world hunger, addressing the dangers of nuclear energy, and correcting the plight of disadvantaged groups in society (e.g., Ice 1987, chap. 1; for the opposite argument, see also Stevens 1989).

Is it true that women clergy are more interested and involved in social issues than are the men? The questionnaire contains a few items dealing with social issues. They are:

42. I try hard to get my people involved in social issues that affect their lives.

43. I encourage my congregation to innovate when dealing with current issues instead of sticking with traditional patterns and programs.

111. One of my goals in ministry is the eradication of social inequalities in the church.

We combined these three items to create an index of concern about social issues (see table 3.16). The pattern indicates that the clergy differ widely in their orientation to social issues, distributing themselves broadly across the range of possible scores. One may ask whether the scores of women and men are distributed differently. The cross-tabulation of social issues scores with sex differences does not reveal any significant linear relationship between the two variables. The correlation is .10, which is in the direction some feminists would predict, but it is so weak that it is statistically nonsignificant ($p < .10$). *This pattern does not adequately support the assertion that more women than men are interested in social issues.*

Table 3.16. Distribution on the Social Issues Concern Index

	Low Concern				*High Concern*		
Score	-3	-2	-1	0	1	2	3
Percent	7	17	18	20	17	10	11

Summary

The analysis in this chapter focused on the argument that women clergy will tend to manifest a feminine style of ministry while men are inclined to a masculine approach. Simple cross-tabulations of the male/female dichotomy with each of the individual items measuring differences in approach to ministry revealed little evidence that many variations in approach were based on sex differences. Only 19 percent of the items were significantly associated with sex, and all but two of those items were the "like-me" questions. No differences in time allocation were associated with sex of clergy.

The analysis then combined subsets of the "like-me" items to create composite measures of specific dimensions of approach to ministry. The nine dimensions of ministry strategy were:

> using power over the congregation
> seeking congregational empowerment
> desiring positions of formal authority
> formal/rational decision making
> ethical legalism
> open interpersonal style
> preaching style
> criteria of clergy status
> involvement in social issues

Sex differences were predictive of variations in four of those aspects of ministry style.

1. More men than women tended to use social power in dealing with their congregation.

2. More women than men sought to empower their congregation to define their own objectives and find their own ways to pursue them.

3. More men than women used rational and formally structured modes of decision making.

4. More men than women dealt with ethical issues in a legalistic way.

These patterns were all consistent with the arguments of religious cultural feminists concerning specific ways in which women and men will differ in their approach to ministry. However, even in these instances the male/female differences were slight, with both women and men distributed across the entire ranges of ministry-style scores.

Nevertheless, on five dimensions of approach to the pastoral ministry, there were no significant differences between men and women.

Male and female clergy tended to be relatively similar in their approach to having formal authority, style of interacting with individuals and groups in the congregation, approach to preaching, ministerial status criteria, and involvement in social issues. On these facets of ministry style, the cultural feminists' arguments were *not* supported empirically. The associations involving those variables were extremely weak and statistically nonsignificant.

The next chapter continues the analysis by introducing other variables—other ways in which individual clergy and their communities differ from one another—in order to determine how those other factors influence ministry style and its relationship to sex differences.

4

What Kind of Minister Is Involved?

THE ANALYSIS PRESENTED in the previous chapters demonstrated that Protestant parish clergy differed widely in their approach to several dimensions of pastoral ministry. On each aspect of ministry style considered in the study, some clergy tended to be characterized by a "masculine" strategy, while others were more inclined toward a "feminine" manner. Some comparisons of these divergences with the male/female dichotomy also indicated that variations in approach were associated with sex differences. More men than women manifested a liking for social power over the congregation, a rational and structured approach to decision making, and a legalistic stance in dealing with ethical issues. More women than men sought to find ways in which their congregation could develop autonomy and power over its own collective life. On other dimensions of ministry style, however, the contrasting "masculine" and "feminine" tendencies appeared to have little or nothing to do with sex differences. Male and female clergy were equally disposed to occupying positions of formal authority, openness of interpersonal style, a traditional view of preaching, assumptions concerning what should give clergy social status, and involvement in social issues. The cultural feminist argument concerning sex differences in approach to pastoral ministry was sup-

81

ported, therefore, on four dimensions of clergy style, but it was not sustained on five other facets.

It would be a mistake to consider only sex differences when examining variations in ministry style. A wide range of other factors at least potentially associated with approach to pastoral ministry must be examined as well. It is important to remember that there is probably no aspect of human thought, emotion, and action that is explainable by reference to but a single other variable. *Homo sapiens* is too complex a creature for its permutations in functioning to be captured by such simplistic thought. The days when social and behavioral scientists were content to "explain" the intricacies of human activity in relation to a single class of other factors are long gone. Easy references to instinct (McDougall 1908), cognition (Festinger 1957), reinforcement (Skinner 1953; Thibaut and Kelley 1959), and even culture (White 1949) as the sole determinants of variations in human behavior are analytical temptations to which few experienced observers are likely to succumb today.

The same point applies to gender and sex differences. Even among the "maximalists," impressed by what they perceive as biological, cultural, and social-psychological factors creating important differences between men and women, few observers will pretend to explain the varieties of human functioning solely in relation to sex differences. A lot of other things help to make us what we are. And those other variables usually do not operate in isolation but instead interact with characteristics like sexual identity to create a complex web of interrelated forces underlying differences in human thought and action (cf. Epstein 1988).

In this chapter, the analysis focuses on several other factors plausibly related to variations in approach to ministry, factors that constitute different criteria for specifying *what kind of minister we are talking about*. The goal is to determine whether various ways of classifying clergy are predictors of differences in ministry style and whether they have any effect on the possible association between approach to ministry and sex of clergy. So what are some of these other factors we need to examine? In this chapter we examine the effects of denomination, racial and ethnic identity, and type of placement as pastor. Chapter 5 will deal with the effects of other personal characteristics, peculiarities of the congregation, and uniquenesses of the surrounding community.

Denominational Differences

The first factor to consider is the fact that the clergy in the study were participants in four different denominations—Baptists, Methodists,

Presbyterians, and United Church of Christ (UCC). Each body represents a specific historical tradition of theology, polity, ministry style, and worship. In polity, for example, the Baptist and UCC ministers officially have little formal authority and are subject to a congregational locus of power and decision making. At the opposite extreme are the Methodists, who have organized themselves in a hierarchical manner with power and decision making officially located nearer to the top. The Presbyterians are defined as coming between these types of structure, with power and authority delegated to deliberative bodies structurally located somewhere between the local congregation and central denominational offices.

The analytical question, of course, is whether these denominational differences are predictive of divergent approaches to pastoral ministry—the use of power, congregational empowerment, desire for positions of authority, interpersonal style, preaching, status criteria, involvement in social issues, mode of decision making, and ethical legalism. Do denominations differ in how clergy spend their time and how much importance they place on specific clergy roles?

In general *the results of cross-tabulating clergy style with affiliation indicate few if any significant differences between denominations in the approach their clergy take to ministry.* On the nine dimensions of ministry style defined in the "like-me" questions, only one comparison produces an association approaching statistical significance. That relationship involves denomination and clergy desire for positions of formal authority. About 50 percent of the Methodist and Presbyterian clergy manifested such ambitions, while only about one-third of the Baptist and UCC ministers were so disposed ($p < .06$). This pattern is consistent with what one would expect on the basis of the variations in church polity outlined above—more clergy in relatively authoritarian structures admit to seeking formal authority than those in decentralized organizations.

Does this pattern help explain the absence of a relationship between wanting formal authority and sex of clergy? The answer is no. *When controlling for denomination, there is still no significant association between desire for formal authority and the male/female dichotomy.* Denominational differences have no detectable effect on a relationship between authority score and sex.

The same general pattern emerges from comparisons of amount of time spent in clergy roles and denomination. In virtually all of the cases, *there are no significant differences between denomination and hours spent in specific ministerial activities.* The one exception to this generalization involves the amount of time clergy spent in local church administration. The Baptist clergy tended to spend slightly less time ($p < .01$)

running the local church than did the other ministers, but the difference was very slight. Given the number of comparisons involved, that relationship could be a statistical fluke, although it is consistent with informal perceptions some people have that Baptists tend to be less formally structured in their local church operations.

Finally, similar results emerge from cross-tabulations of denomination with differences in the relative importance clergy place on specific roles. Baptists tended to place lower degrees of importance on conducting funerals than did ministers in the other bodies. And the UCC ministers tended to place less importance on teaching formal classes than did the other clerics. In both of these cases, controlling for denomination in the association between role priority and sex differences has no effect on the initial relationship—which is *no* relationship. Similarly, Baptist and UCC clergy tended to place greater importance on being involved in social issues than did the other clerics, but that association appeared to have no effect on the relationship between sex and perceived importance of social issues. In all comparisons of these two variables, more women than men viewed involvement in social issues as something important.

To summarize, denominational differences appear to be slightly predictive of variations in a few measures of clerical role definition—desire for formal authority, time spent in local church administration, and the importance placed on conducting funerals, teaching formal classes, and involvement in social justice issues. Nevertheless, in no case did those denominational patterns have any effect on the relationship between ministry style and sex differences. In short, *denomination does not seem to be an important factor in ordering differences in clergy approach to the pastoral ministry.* These results would not support the argument that denominations differ in any important way on the question of differing approaches clergy take to their work.

Race and Ethnicity

The results of the analysis involving racial and ethnic differences among clergy, on the other hand, show racial/ethnic-group status to be quite an important predictor of clergy role definition. As shown in table 4.1, ethnicity is significantly related to scores on eight of the nine dimensions of differences in approach to pastoral ministry (involving the "like-me" items). (In order to present the results of the remainder of the analysis as parsimoniously as possible, the results of cross-tabulating variables from here on will be portrayed in terms of rank-order correlations (gamma). For a nontechnical explanation of correlations between variables, see Kerlinger 1979, chap. 5.) And most of those correlations are stronger than those observed in the associations between ministry style scores and sex of minister. *In most of those relationships, the white clergy tend to manifest more "feminine" scores, while members of racial/ethnic groups are characterized by more "masculine" patterns.* More racial/ethnic than white ministers expressed desire for power over their congregation, rejected ideas of congregational empowerment, wanted positions of formal authority, showed closed interpersonal style, preferred rational decision making, and manifested ethical legalism. On two other dimensions of approach involving the "like-me" items, however, the opposite tendency emerges from the analysis. That is, racial/ethnic ministers were *more* inclined than white ministers to accept the "feminine" status criteria; likewise, racial/ethnic clergy tended to be more involved in social issues than were white clergy. Finally, there was no significant difference between white and racial/ethnic ministers concerning their approach to preaching, just as this dimension was unrelated to sex differences in earlier segments of the analysis.

Table 4.1. Correlations (Gamma) between Approach to Ministry Scores, Clergy Ethnicity, and Sex

Dimension of Approach			Ethnicity Controlling for Sex	
	Sex	Ethnicity	Male	Female
Power over congregation	-.15	-.30	-.25	-.34
Empowerment of congregation	.22	.13	(.10)	(.11)
Formal authority	(-.06)	-.20	-.24	(-.14)
Interpersonal style	(-.11)	.31	.33	.27
Preaching style	(-.07)	(-.10)	(-.06)	(-.12)
Status criteria	(.03)	-.44	-.35	-.55
Social issue involvement	(.10)	-.42	-.48	-.34
Rational structure	-.40	-.38	-.33	-.40
Ethical legalism	-.28	-.35	-.26	-.39

Note: Coefficients in parentheses are statistically nonsignificant.

These comparisons of racial/ethnic and white clergy group all four racial/ethnic groups together in the analysis—Hispanics, African-Americans, Asian-Americans, and American Indians. In many ways what is labeled as simply "racial/ethnic" involves quite a mix of social experiences and cultural traditions. Can this be justified? The analysis proceeds with the four racial/ethnic subgroups aggregated for at least two reasons. First, the number of respondents in each group is small, especially the American Indians and the Asian-Americans:

Hispanics	21
African-Americans	53
Asian-Americans	11
American Indians	4

(The proportion of women and men in each group was about fifty-fifty.) To try to analyze them separately would involve considerable difficulty statistically and would make generalizations highly suspect. The numerical base is simply too small.

Reinforcing the reservation noted above, comparisons of the specific racial and ethnic groups with the indicators of ministry style produce almost no significant differences by subgroup. The exceptions to this pattern involve the scores on involvement in social issues, where the Hispanic and black clergy indicated higher levels of involvement than did the Asian-Americans and the American Indians. This pattern reflects the well-known campaigns for civil rights and ethnic power, especially among blacks but also among Hispanics, efforts at social change where the churches have played a major role (cf. Paris 1985). The Asian and Indian communities, on the other hand, have not displayed such activities to the same extent as the African Americans. Part of the reason for this difference among American Indians is that their significant social activists have tended to be anti-church (Gilkes 1992). Accordingly, in the following analyses, the racial/ethnic clergy were grouped together. Hopefully the future will provide a more adequate sample for distinguishing any patterns of difference between them. It is also worth noting that in the United States, anyway, even though specific racial/ethnic groups indeed have unique histories, they all tend to share a legacy of oppression and "otherness"—even a marginality to the larger society dominated by whites. This commonality of experience may have resulted in similar approaches to ministry (Royle 1991).

At this point one may only speculate about possible reasons for these patterns of relationship between ministry style and ethnicity. The first impulse is to account for them in terms of the social stratification positions characteristic of racial/ethnic and white congregations. Clergy from nonwhite groups typically serve as pastors of congregations that are also dominated by racial/ethnic group members. Black clergy usually serve predominantly black churches, Hispanic clergy care for Hispanic communities, and white Anglo-Saxon Protestant (WASP) clergy work with WASP churches. Since "racial/ethnic" social status is defined partly in terms of social and economic subordination, the congregations served by racial/ethnic pastors on average would tend to be lower in socioeconomic status than those for which white ministers care.

Status in society as a "racial/ethnic group member" historically has involved diminished access to paths of horizontal and vertical social mobility. The dominant "breadwinners"—typically the men—have experienced difficulty in attaining positions in society that resulted in economic or social resources that bring social status, power, and comfortable life-style. In agrarian societies this arrangement involves being relatively barred from land ownership, and in industrial societies the pattern involves exclusion from socially significant occupations. In these circumstances it has been difficult for men to "be somebody" in their own eyes, to their family, or in the community. This pattern characterizes the experience of many African-Americans, and it probably also corresponds to the biographies of men in the other racial/ethnic communities as well.

That kind of system tended to make the ministry an attractive option for African-American men with status aspirations and the social skills to carry them out. The ministry was an avenue within which they could become "somebody." In fact in many locales, racial/ethnic clergy became so set apart as "special people" that they took on general leadership roles that spilled beyond the walls of the church and covered the social and cultural life of the community as a whole. This emergent leadership probably was not a simple result of the black clergy seizing an opportunity. Instead it appears to have been a matter of resource mobilization by the community, a response by those clergy to the demand for direction by the African-American congregations (Gilkes 1992). With the racial/ethnic church as the major institution for gathering the community together and focusing its attention on important issues, the local racial/ethnic minister was strategically placed to be a significant force in the life of his people.

Accordingly, the "male ministry game" involved much higher stakes and carried larger historical demands for racial/ethnic men than for their WASP counterparts. And those who opted for that path to success and attained it tended to cherish and guard it fervently. The issue of women taking their place alongside men in the pastoral ministry is a very different ball game in racial/ethnic religious communities than in white congregations. The pulpit is defined as "men's space" and the pew is considered "women's place" more in traditional black churches than in predominantly white bodies (Lincoln and Mamiya 1990, 274).

These characteristics of "racial/ethnic" status based on race or ethnicity are likely to spill over into differences in the ways in which racial/ethnic and white ministers relate to their people. As persons to whom wisdom, virtue, and leadership are attributed, most ministers—both white and otherwise—internalize the role and come to believe that they in fact possess those attributes. If they also perceive that their church members are less gifted than they are themselves, it could easily propel them to assume a superordinate and highly active leadership role, something they assume their members expect them to do. They learn to act like the kind of persons that significant others tell them they are. To the extent that the role of "minister" involves more of these dynamics in racial/ethnic congregations than in WASP churches, one would expect to observe the patterns noted in the analysis above, that is, more racial/ethnic ministers than WASP clergy manifesting the attributes labeled as the "masculine system." More racial/ethnic clergy than white ministers assume power over their congregations, prefer formal authority, deal with ethical issues legalistically, and seek structure in decision making in order to maintain control and order in the congregation. The interpersonal style of racial/ethnic clergy is more aloof and guarded as a way of maintaining leadership status. Greater racial/ethnic (especially African-American) involvement in social issues, on the other hand, is probably a simple artifact of the historically heightened salience of many social issues to their communities.

It is important to note that *at this point in time these patterns do not appear to be exclusively "male" phenomena.* The relatively distinctive characteristics of the role of pastor in racial/ethnic religious bodies may have had its origins in patterns of *men* seeking to attain status in a society where many other high-status occupations were closed to them. However, the data in this study indicate that *the racial/ethnic distinctions do not apply exclusively to men today.* We also correlated racial/ethnic status with ministry style scores, while controlling for the sex of the minister (see table 4.1). The general pattern is for the same patterns of relationship between race/ethnicity and ministry style scores to appear among *both female and male ministers,* that is, both the male and female racial/ethnic clergy tend to be the more masculine in approach. The possible exceptions to this—the statistically nonsignificant correlations involving congregational empowerment and formal authority— are most likely artifacts of the reduction of the number of cases involved in the correlations after controlling for sex. Racial/ethnic men tend to have more masculine ministry styles than white men, and racial/ethnic women are inclined to manifest more masculine approaches to ministry than white women. The pattern appears to be a part of the ministerial subculture regardless of sex differences. So what apparently began historically as a pattern of racial/ethnic male status attainment may now be a part of the general pastoral ministry system for both men and women. Where a role is established firmly, women may have little choice but to adopt it (Royle 1991).

Racial/Ethnic Status and Specific Roles

Similar patterns to those just discussed above emerge from a comparison of racial/ethnic status with the amount of time clergy spend in specific ministerial roles and the degree of importance they place on them. As concerns the importance the roles have to the clergy, the racial/ethnic ministers tended to place greater importance on nearly every role activity than did the white ministers—preaching, teaching, visitation, counselling, church fellowship, church administration, denominational involvements, community activities, personal development, and social action. The one exception to the pattern involved conducting funerals; white clergy tended to place more importance on that role than did the racial/ethnic clergy, but that correlation is very weak and barely statistically significant ($p < .05$). There seems to be a generalized tendency among the racial/ethnic clergy to place relatively high degrees of importance on *all* of their role activities. Unfortunately, the interview schedule did not also ask the respondents to *rank* the various subroles in relation to each other. That step would have provided additional data for use in interpreting the racial/ethnic differences. So it is not possible to know whether the generally high importance placed on most roles by racial/ethnic clergy is due to their unwillingness to allocate differing priorities to various role activities or is a result of some other factor(s).

The data in table 4.2 do indicate, however, that not all of the relationships between race/ethnicity and role importance eventuate in differential amounts of *time spent* in various roles. Racial/ethnic ministers tended to spend more time than did white ministers in some roles but not others, that is, correlations emerge concerning teaching formal classes, counselling, church fellowship, community activities, personal development, and social justice issues. The last difference—time in social justice issues—is considerably stronger than the rest, most likely indicating the greater salience of social justice issues to racial/ethnic clergy. But the analysis indicates no meaningful differences between white and racial/ethnic clerics in time spent in preparing and delivering sermons, conducting funerals, visiting members, local church administration, and involvement in church structures beyond the congregation.

The one thing that possibly differentiates these latter activities from those apparently more associated with race and ethnicity is the amount of control one has over them. The pressure for sermon preparation is a virtual constant in the life of ministers; they have little control over whether or not to do it—it is a standard expectation every Sunday. They also have little or no control over time spent conducting

Table 4.2.   Correlations (Gamma) between Clergy Role Priorities, Time Spent in Roles, and Ethnicity

Specific Clergy Roles	Time Spent	Importance
Sermons	—*	-.47
Funerals	—	.09
Teaching classes	-.12	-.44
Visitation	—	-.27
Counselling	-.26	-.42
Church fellowship	-.25	-.25
Administration	—	-.31
Other church structures	—	-.29
Community activities	-.25	-.48
Personal development	-.15	-.36
Social issues	-.45	-.37

*Statistically nonsignificant correlation.

funerals. Deaths of members of the community simply must be dealt with as they occur. Visitation is also something of a constant. And if we can believe the chronic complaints of ministers concerning the way local church administration and denominational requests eat up their time, there probably isn't much control over the time clergy spend in those activities either. So those role activities found to be unrelated to racial/ethnic status probably have that independence largely because they are role activities demanding time and energy independently of the minister's volition. Time spent in those activities is more likely an artifact of the expectations of others, not just the minister's wishes. The ministers probably have more control over the amount of time they spend in the other role segments.

Controlling for White/Racial-Ethnic Status

Significant differences in most aspects of ministry style emerged from the comparisons of racial/ethnic clergy with WASP ministers. Where differences are found, most of the time the racial/ethnic clergy tended to exhibit more "masculine" approaches to ministry than did the white clerics. These patterns of relationship between racial/ethnic status and the various indices of approach to the pastoral ministry introduce an important cautionary note into the analysis—most significantly, don't overgeneralize.

One possible implication of these patterns could call into question the entire thrust of the study. The basic question of this particular undertaking focuses on differences in approach to work ascribed to sex differences. Cultural feminists impressed with possible uniquenesses of women's approach to ministry have conceptualized virtually all of those variations in terms of gender. The traditional style is "masculine," and the recent innovations attributed to women are described as "feminine." These maximalists often also subsume race prejudice and discrimination under "patriarchy." *However, to this point the analysis of the role of race and ethnicity in approach to ministry has produced stronger and more significant relationships than has the examination of sex differences in ministry style.* We could be barking up the wrong tree!

Perhaps. However, there is a better approach, and that is to recognize that these patterns simply tend to confirm some perceptions articulated by other observers of the racial-ethnic religious scene. The dynamics of religion in subordinate and superordinate communities are *not* always the same. Lincoln and Mamiya (1990) develop an elaborate and persuasive argument that African-American religion is unique on the contemporary stage. They reject the notion that "black religion...is but the replication of the white experience, [with]...an African patina" (xi). Many patterns in the black churches developed at least indirectly as a result of the oppression African-Americans have experienced in American society. To Lincoln and Mamiya (1990, 10ff.), the black church is characterized by at least six roles (perhaps eight) in dialectical tension, divergent sets of orientations that interact with each other to give the church its characteristics at a given time and locale:

> priestly vs. prophetic
> other-worldly vs. this-worldly
> universalism vs. particularism
> communal vs. privatistic
> charismatic vs. bureaucratic
> resistance vs. accommodation

Many of those tensions derive from the social experiences of black people in this society. (It is likely that the tensions also constitute basic parameters of many white churches as well, so it is probably a mistake to take Lincoln and Mamiya's descriptions as exclusively applicable to the black churches.) Nevertheless, the picture they paint resonates with some of the findings above; that is, the racial-ethnic churches differ systematically from those in the white community.

Another important point to remember is that the cultural feminist assertions that gave rise to this investigation derive from the perspectives of middle-class *white* women. They do not necessarily apply to racial-ethnic women at all. Grant (1989, 4–5) points out, for example, that even though one can discern at least three broad perspectives in feminist theology—Biblical, liberation, and rejectionist—they are all too exclusively "white" and are not generalizable to blacks. In fact, she also sees them as "racist" (Grant 1989, 195). Andolsen (1986) presents a similar argument. She states that white feminism doesn't understand black women and thus cannot speak for them. Furthermore, she indicates ways in which white feminists—sometimes knowingly—have supported racism by participating in racist political and economic structures and by refusing to deal with the specific concerns of racial minorities.

A more fruitful approach for our purposes is to reexamine the initial comparisons of dimensions of ministry style with sex of clergy (see chap. 3), while controlling for race/ethnicity. The question is whether sex is a predictor of approach to ministry among whites in one way but among racial and ethnic groups in another way. This approach remains focused on the central research question while acknowledging the effects of white/racial-ethnic status.

We ran correlations between sex differences and scores on the nine dimensions of approach to ministry (the "like-me" items), controlling for race/ethnicity (see table 4.3). The patterns of relationship among only the white ministers closely resemble those observed in the initial analysis; in fact the value of the coefficients that show statistically significant correlations are almost identical in the total and white groupings. Among white clergy, more men than women sought power over their congregation, preferred rational structures for decision making, and preferred a legalistic approach to ethics. More women than men sought to empower their congregations to control their own collective life and work. One association emerges as significant among the white clergy but is nonsignificant among the total sample, and that is the relationship between the male/female dichotomy and involvement in social issues. Among the white clerics, more women than men got involved in social issues, a pattern consistent with predictions based on cultural feminist argument.

The picture is more difficult to discern when considering the racial/ethnic clergy alone. Some of this difficulty arises from the much smaller numbers of racial/ethnic clergy in the sample—only ninety of them. With a sample of that size, it becomes difficult for an association between two variables to have statistical significance—the smaller the sample, the harder it is to attain statistical support. To compensate for this reality, we used a statistical criterion of 10 percent ($p < .10$) to define statistical significance among the racial/ethnic clergy.

Table 4.3. Correlations (Gamma) between Approach to Ministry
Scores and Sex of Ministries, Controlling for Racial-Ethnic Status

| | Compared to Sex of Ministers: | | |
Dimension of Ministry Style	All Cases	White	Racial/Ethnic*
Power over congregation	-.15	-.15	(-.08)
Empowerment of congregation	.22	.22	(.18)
Formal authority	(-.08)†	(-.05)	(-.16)
Interpersonal style	(.11)	(.08)	(.19)
Preaching style	(-.02)	(-.07)	(-.03)
Status criteria	(.03)	(.02)	.28
Social issue involvement	(.10)	.16	(-.11)
Rational structure	-.40	-.41	-.33
Ethical legalism	-.28	-.29	(-.11)

*Since the sample included only 90 racial/ethnic clergy, in comparison to 426 white ministers, the probability level for statistically significant associations among racial/ethnic clergy was set at .10. The criterion for other correlations was .05.

†Coefficients in parentheses are statistically nonsignificant.

In spite of this compensation, very few correlations between sex of minister and approach to ministry emerged from the analysis of racial/ethnic ministers. As in the larger sample, there is a clear association between sex and rational decision making. More men than women placed high value on rationality and structure when dealing with church decisions. And *unlike* the pattern in the larger sample, *more women than men tended to reject the masculine status system and to accept the feminine criteria of clergy status.*

If one were to be most liberal and virtually ignore the test of statistical significance where the *magnitude* of the correlation among racial/ethnic clergy is nearly the same (or greater) as in the white sample, then one would say that there may also be correlations between sex differences and three other dimensions of ministry style, that is, congregational empowerment, desire for formal authority, and interpersonal style. More women than men sought to empower their congregations to run their own life and interacted with others in an open and vulnerable interpersonal style. More men than women sought positions of formal authority. However, these patterns are *not* notable if one applies the test of statistical significance, liberalized though it was when applied to the racial/ethnic clergy. There are simply too few racial/ethnic clergy in the sample to get a clear picture of patterns of variation within their category.

Andolsen (1986, 93–98) identifies at least one peculiarity of black women's perspective that may help explain why racial-ethnic women differ from white women in the analysis above. She argues that "feminist separatism is not a viable political philosophy for most black women" (98). Black women have criticized black men for not sharing power in black associations, but not to the point of rejecting black men. Black men and women know that they still need each other in the struggle against racism. *White* women have defined their feminism as a matter of oppressed women against oppressing men. Not so black women. "Black women refused to see themselves as involved in a struggle for liberation *over against* (emphasis in the original) black men. Black women experienced themselves as joint members of an oppressed group: the black race in white America. Black women saw themselves as drawing strength from an alliance with black men in a historic struggle for black liberation" (93). So if black men are not "the bad guys," then why dump the problems of black churches at their feet? It would make no sense, so they don't do it.

Accordingly, the remainder of the analysis will proceed with the initial question of sex differences and will set the matter of race and ethnicity aside for examination in the future. This strategy does not imply that variations in ministry style between members of white and racial/ethnic groups are unimportant. They are intriguing. Instead the decision to leave them for future research is a simple attempt to retain focus and to acknowledge the complexities noted above.

1. The goal is to finish what we started—*to examine sex differences proposed by white cultural feminists*—and to avoid changing topics midway through a study.

2. One must accept the argument that the religious experiences of racial-ethnic communities does not always resemble those of whites.

3. Some of the patterns noted in the analysis above tend to support the argument that racial-ethnic women do not define their religious situation in the same terms as white feminists.

4. The racial-ethnic sample is both small and heterogeneous, so it would be a mistake to stretch the analysis so far as to make generalizations deriving from an inadequate empirical base.

There is a vast literature on racial/ethnic religious systems (e.g., Baer 1988; Lincoln and Mamiya 1990), indeed a substantive specialty with which many others must be much more familiar than I. The questions of the role of interactions between racial/ethnic status and sex differences in ministry style deserve far more systematic attention than can be given within this undertaking.

For this reason, we shall eliminate the racial/ethnic clergy from some segments of the remaining analysis, concentrating instead on the patterns amongst the white ministers. That approach may be the better part of wisdom for yet another reason, that is, most of the arguments concerning women's approach to ministry have developed mainly out of the thought and experience of white clergy. The patterns of racial and ethnic differences noted above, therefore, constitute a not-so-subtle warning about the dangers of overgeneralization.

Appointment as Copastor

Another factor that could influence the relationship between ministry style and the male/female dichotomy is the type of pastoral placement the ministers had, type of appointment in terms of whether or not it was as "copastor." All of the ministers in the sample were in positions as either solo minister, senior minister on a team, or copastor of one or more congregations. Being a copastor involves unique arrangements on the job.

The copastorate is a ministry structure that has become adopted by increasing numbers, especially of white clergy, over roughly the last few decades. Its development also coincides with the increasing acceptance of women in ministry by many mainline Protestant denominations in the United States. In a copastorate, two or more individuals are appointed or called to perform pastoral functions with a congregation. The copastorate is different from traditional ministry "teams" found in many large churches. In those conventional multi-staff structures, the arrangement involves one person being designated as the "senior minister" with some degree of authority over the other clergy on the team. Those others would typically have highly specific role definitions in that church—as "minister of Christian education," "minister of music," "minister for visitation," and in some cases even "minister for church administration." The persons performing these specific clerical functions are normally defined as subordinate to the senior minister.

By contrast the copastors (usually two individuals) are defined as equals in status and authority in their work with the church. Some copastorates also involve a form of division of labor, with one person being primarily responsible for certain functions—such as preaching—and the other(s) having different primary responsibilities. But in spite of that functional specificity, the clergy on the team are assumed to be equals in status and authority. No one is singled out as the "senior minister."

(Incidentally, this arrangement is the *normative* pattern in ministry teams within the Uniting Church in Australia, where they are seeking to obliterate invidious distinctions about and among clergy.) There is some anecdotal evidence that the egalitarian ideal is not uniformly implemented in practice. The copastorate is a departure from traditional assumptions about the structure of ministry in large churches, and some lay members have difficulty adjusting their thinking to the idea. In some churches served by copastors, for example, some members of the congregation informally define one member of the team—more often than not, the man—as the "senior minister" and the other as the "assistant." This deviation from the egalitarian pattern can create difficulties in the day-to-day operation of the church, and copastors have to develop ways of dealing with it to bring deviant lay perceptions of the situation into line with the intended authority structure.

The copastor structure has been an especially popular option for clergy couples. In this sample, for instance, about 77 percent of the copastors were serving as such with their spouse. At least in theory such an arrangement is ideal for couples committed to a marriage partnership, as it allows them to carry the "partnership" ideal into their work as well as other facets of their married life. The copastorate allows them to avoid having one partner defined as subordinate to the other.

It is this egalitarian motif in copastor arrangements that requires examination. To the extent that copastors, especially marriage partners, assume an egalitarian structure of ministry from the outset, there may no longer be any basis for expecting to find any relationship between ministry style and sex differences, particularly on the dimensions for which egalitarianism is salient. Since the copastorate is *defined* as an egalitarian approach to ministry, will clergy working in such an arrangement manifest the same sex differences in ministry style as those serving in more traditional arrangements? That is the question we address here.

The analysis compared ministry style scores with sex of clergy, controlling for whether or not the respondent was serving in a copastorate (see table 4.4). (This analysis involves white clergy only, because there were only five placements as copastor among the racial/ethnic ministers.) The patterns are potentially instructive. Among ministers serving in traditional leadership structures—that is, *not* as copastors—the relationships between approach to ministry and sex differences are almost identical to those observed in the sample as a whole (see chap. 3). More men than women sought power over members of the congregation, preferred structure and rationality in decision making, and were legalistic in ethical matters. More women than men sought to empower their congregation to chart its own course. There are no significant correlations between sex differences and the other dimensions of ministry style (the "like-me" items).

Table 4.4. Correlations (Gamma) between Ministry Style Scores and Sex of Clergy, Controlling for Position as Copastor* (White Clergy Only)

Dimension of Approach	Copastors	Non-Copastors
Use of coercive power	(-.18)†	-.12
Empowerment of congregation	(.16)	.24
Formal authority	(-.18)	(.01)
Interpersonal style	(1.20)	(.10)
Preaching style	.40	(-.09)
Status criteria	-.38	(.02)
Social issue involvement	(.22)	(.12)
Rational structure	(-.15)	-.40
Ethical legalism	(-.27)	-.30

*There were forty-seven ministers who were serving as copastors; only five of these were males.

†Coefficients in parentheses are statistically nonsignificant. For copastors the criterion level was $p < .10$. For others the ciriterion level was $p < .05$.

There were also a few significant relationships between sex of clergy and how male and female ministers relate to specific role responsibilities in traditional appointments. Male clergy tended to spend more hours than female clerics in teaching formal classes (gamma = -.11) and in visitation of members and prospects (gamma = -.10). Women tended to spend more time working in church structures beyond the congregation (gamma = .12). Nevertheless, note that these correlations are *very* small, indicating but minimal differences between males and females in this regard. Comparisons of sex differences to stated importance of clergy roles also result in a few significant correlations. That is, more women than men placed high importance on conducting funerals, participating in church structures beyond the congregation, and involvement in social justice issues. The high female emphasis on social justice parallels earlier findings using the "like-me" items that deal with social issues. Women's greater focus on involvement in extra-local church structures is also carried out in the amount of time they spend in such activities.

The patterns tend to deviate from those observed in the whole when considering only *ministers in copastoral appointments.* Among copastors the male/female dichotomy is predictive of ministry style on only two dimensions—preaching and status criteria. In those cases, proportionately more *men* than women manifested a *feminine* approach. There was a greater tendency among *men* than women to reject the traditional masculine emphasis on preaching and to prefer feminine criteria of clergy status. Even using a probability level of .10 as a criterion of statistical significance fails to result in significant correlations between sex and other dimensions of approach to ministry. There are too few male copastors in the sample.

The results in table 4.5 show the mean scores of men and women instead of correlations. The differences between male and female *solo* pastors emerge in the same patterns as discussed above—males more masculine and females more feminine, concerning using power, empowerment of others, mode of decision making, and ethical legalism. The differences between those mean scores are statistically significant.

Table 4.5. Mean Ministry Style Scores of Men and Women Serving as Solo Pastor and Copastor

Dimension of Ministry Style	Males* Solo Pastors	Females Solo	Copastors
Power over congregation	-.05§	-.41§	-.40
Empowerment of congregation	.50§	1.06§	1.03
Formal authority	.05	-.01	-.33†
Interpersonal style	2.03	2.50	2.13‡
Preaching style	-.21	-.31	-.15
Status criteria	.11	.23	-.11‡
Social issue involvement	-.44	-.15	.13†
Rational structure	.31§	-.45§	-.50
Ethical legalism	.40§	-.16§	.09‡

*Insufficient number of males serving as copastor.

†Copastors more feminine than solo pastors.

‡Copastors more masculine than solo pastors.

§Women more feminine than men.

There are also differences in mean ministry-style scores among the *women only* between solo ministers and copastors (see table 4.5). The female copastors tended to be the more feminine concerning desire for formal authority and involvement in social issues, but the solo pastors tended to be a bit more feminine in matters of interpersonal style, status criteria, and ethical legalism. However, given the small number of cases, *none of these differences are statistically significant.*

Accordingly, a note of caution is warranted at this juncture. *Of the people surveyed, only five males and forty-two females were serving as copastors of their congregation.* A total of forty-seven cases is simply not an adequate empirical basis for making anything approaching final judgements on these questions. The results must be regarded as suggestive only.

The same general caveat applies to comparisons of sex differences to relative emphasis on clergy roles. Only one item dealing with time spent in specific roles is significantly associated with sex of clergy among copastors. As was the case among persons in traditional appointments, more men than women copastors spent large amounts of time visiting members and prospects (gamma = -.52). Consistent with the egalitarian motif in the copastor arrangements, men and women tended to spend equal amounts of time across the spectrum of different role activities that their job involves. A similar pattern appears in the analysis of role priorities. Men and women copastors tended to place different degrees of importance on teaching formal classes (gamma = -.65)—men stressed this activity more than did the women. But no such significant differences between males and females show up concerning the other roles. Again, the egalitarian thrust of the copastorate seems to show through. These patterns are consistent with widely shared perceptions about the copastorate. Men who want to be copastors, especially those *not* serving with their wives, tend to be *very* egalitarian. Often their interest in serving on a copastor team seems to be the most effective way they have of expressing their opposition to sex-typed ministries.

Accordingly, the patterns *suggest* the general idea that clergy serving as copastors are not likely to manifest the same sex-specific approaches to ministry as will be found among ministers in more traditional placements. However, since we really have too few copastors (especially males) in the sample, any conclusions of this nature must await analysis of evidence no one has in hand at the moment.

Clergy Placed as Senior Minister

Another specific type of clergy placement worth examining is the position of "senior minister" in a multiple staff situation. Unlike the copastor situation discussed above, the senior minister role inherently involves social differentiation and ranking among members of a clergy team. The senior minister is by definition in a superordinate position over the other persons on the staff. He/she is "the boss." Even in specific churches where the senior pastor is defined with more political caution as but "first among equals," there is usually no doubt about who is supposed to be "in charge." Again, it is widely accepted that a minister has more status and potential influence if he/she is the senior pastor at a large church than if he/she is in a smaller solo charge, and there is a great deal of anecdotal evidence that such senior positions are the object of a great deal of competition among clergy. Everyone on the ministry team may be equal, but the senior pastor is regarded as "more equal than others" (see Lehman 1990).

There is evidence of tacit acceptance of this internal status system even among those who sometimes criticize it. In some religious feminist circles, when the gains clergywomen have made in the last few decades are tallied up, the conversation frequently comes around to the question "What's next? Now that we have this many placements as pastor, and that number of women working as seminary faculty, and this other count of women in denominational administrative positions, what door should we strive to open next?" Two types of goals frequently emerge in the conversation that then follows: *placement of women as senior pastors of "significant churches," and recruitment of women to "significant positions" of ministerial leadership within the denomination—for example, bishops, heads of major departments, directors of significant boards, and so on.* Even among women seeking to influence (if not modify) traditional religious structures, some religious jobs are defined as more important than others. Publicly they may deny it, but privately it remains a tenacious symbol of success to many of them.

To pursue this line of thought, the analysis separates out white men and women who were serving as senior minister in multiple-staff situations in order to compare them with their less prestigious brothers and sisters concerning their approach to ministry (see table 4.6). (There were no racial/ethnic women in the sample serving as senior ministers.) *Among clergy who are in multiple staff situations and are not copastors—the "senior ministers"—the male/female dichotomy is more predictive of approach to ministry than among those in solo pastorates.* Among senior ministers only, there are sex differences on more dimensions of ministry style, and the strength of those relationships is greater than those observed previously. More senior males than senior females sought power over their congregation, wanted to be in positions of formal authority, preferred rational and structured modes of decision making, and took legalistic approaches to ethical issues. More senior women than senior men sought ways of empowering their congregation and displayed openness and vulnerability in interpersonal relations with members of the congregation. With the addition of authority issues and interpersonal style, these are the same dimensions of approach to ministry that have demonstrated sex differences in previous phases of the analysis, only those relationships are even clearer in this subgroup.

Table 4.6. Correlations (Gamma) between Ministry Style Score, Type of Placement, and Sex of Clergy

		Senior vs. Solo Pastor†	
Dimension of Approach	*Sex of Clergy**	*Males*	*Females*
Power over congregation	-.54	.29	-.27
Empowerment of congregation	.53	(-.11)	.36
Formal authority	-.34	(.10)	-.30
Interpersonal style	.54	(.03)	.53
Preaching style	(-.20)‡	(.04)	(-.10)
Status criteria	(-.17)	(.03)	(-.20)
Social issue involvement	(.18)	.27	.29
Rational structure	-.32	(-.09)	(-.01)
Ethical legalism	-.52	(.09)	(-.18)

*Compares men to women among "senior pastors" only.
†Compares senior ministers to solo pastors, specified by sex.
‡Coefficients in parentheses are statistically nonsignificant.

These same patterns are supported in the analysis shown in table 4.7, where the mean ministry-style scores are listed for males and females serving as senior ministers and solo pastors. Sex differences in mean score are much greater among senior ministers than solo pastors. The one exception to this pattern involves rational decision making, in which case the *solo* clergy manifested greater sex differences than did the seniors, again in the sex-stereotypical direction.

However, these more apparent sex differences do *not* emerge when we examine specific role activities. *Among senior ministers, there are very few significant differences between men and women concerning hours spent in clerical role activities and the degree of importance placed on them.* More women than men spent large amounts of time in social justice issues (gamma = .36), and the same pattern holds for the relative emphasis clergy placed on working with social justice concerns (gamma = .35), so there is some consistency here. Female senior pastors also tend to place more importance than the men on conducting funerals (gamma = .50) and involvements in church structures beyond the congregation (gamma = .40), but those preferences do not also translate into differences in time spent in those activities.

The differences between male and female senior pastors concerning the dimensions of ministry style based on the "like-me" questions then led us to ask a slightly different type of question, that is, is holding a "significant placement" predictive of variations in approach to ministry when holding sex constant? Or to put it differently, *does sex of*

Table 4.7. Mean Ministry Style Scores of Men and Women Serving as Senior Minister vs. Other

Dimension of Ministry Style	Males* Other	Senior	Females† Other	Senior
Power over congregation	-.26	.49	-.34	-1.00‡
Empowerment of congregation	.54	.28	.97	1.68‡
Formal authority	-.05	.18	.04	-.77‡
Interpersonal style	1.99	2.10	2.17	4.17‡
Preaching style	1.19	-.13	-.26	-.43
Status criteria	.12	.15	.16	-.24
Social issue involvement	-.53	-.05	-.18	.30
Rational structure	.33	.16	-.46§	-.48
Ethical legalism	.39	.51	-.07	-.43‡

*Male senior ministers more masculine than solo ministers concerning power, empowerment, and authority.

†Women senior ministers more feminine than solo ministers on all dimensions but "rational structure."

‡Greater male/female differences among senior ministers than among solo ministers.

§Greater male/female differences among solo ministers than among senior ministers.

minister make any difference in relationships between ministry style and the prestige of one's present job? If it is true that clergywomen are less impressed than men with traditional criteria of clergy success, then one would expect the status of one's appointment to be associated with one's approach to the job more among men than among women.

The results of analysis portrayed in table 4.6 do not support such a prediction. *Being "senior minister" is more predictive of ministry style among women than among men.* For the clergymen, the solo/senior dichotomy was associated with but two dimensions of approach to ministry—seeking power over the congregation and involvement in social issues. More male senior pastors than solo ministers sought power over the congregation or were involved in social issues.

In contrast to the men, more women in *solo* pastorates than senior ministers sought power over their congregation. The same pattern applies to wanting formal authority; more female solo pastors than senior ministers wished to be in positions of formal authority in their church. These patterns *may* be an artifact of the differential expectations associated with the two types of leadership structures. In the solo situation, the minister is expected to provide direct leadership in a broad range of activities and issues, while the senior minister has the luxury of concentrating on a more focused set of involvements. In short, solo clergy seek more power and authority than do senior ministers because they are expected to. A more cynical interpretation, but one which is also plausible, would explain the greater desire for power and authority among solo pastors in terms of the lesser prestige of their position. The senior minister *already has* considerable power and authority over other clergy on the staff and a relatively large congregation. Thus she has a different type of "luxury," a diminished need to seek out those kinds of fulfillments.

It is important to remember that the solo pastor assumes responsibility for virtually *everything* in church life. For female clergy who, like clergymen, experience their first professional placements in solo circumstances, this situation is an opportunity as well as a burden. It gives the clergywoman structured occasions in which to demonstrate her competence, to maintain broad power and authority in church life, and to retain a central place in the minds of the lay members (Lawless 1988, 102). Kleinman suggests that it often proves strategic for clergywomen to take advantage of those circumstances. Writing about female seminary students, she says, "Since the female [ministers]... expect parishioners not only to challenge their nontraditional professional ideology but their claim to the ministerial role as well, they feel an even greater need than men to have a firm sense of professional authority in their...relations with clients. [They]...are placed in a situation where they cannot fully accept the [feminist] rhetoric and ideology lest they diminish the role-model strength needed to survive in a male-dominated field" (Kleinman 1984, 82). "In entering the professions as marginal members, male-like behavior is the resource available to women who seek recognition as professionals" (97). "Because the wider public 'lags behind' the [feminist] humanistic rhetoric, some of the female students use that rhetoric in ways circumscribed by old cultural understandings and adjust to that wider context by reverting back to old ["masculine"] ways" (99). Evidence of whether these patterns will withstand replication must await other research.

Another type of pattern emerges from the comparison of women as solo pastors and senior ministers, that is, more female senior pastors than solo ministers sought ways of empowering their congregation. This result is consistent with the findings above concerning power and authority. The women who felt a need for more power and authority— the solo pastors—also expressed relatively little interest in giving increased power to their congregation. By contrast, those who showed little need for power and authority—the senior ministers—also demonstrated greater willingness to empower the congregation. Could it be that there is more of a sense of vocational security in the position of senior minister than the solo pastorate? Does the complex leadership structure of multiple staff situations actually extend a greater degree of social psychological protection to incumbents than the simpler (and more "lonely") leadership position involved in solo ministries? And why does this pattern show up among the *women* but not among the men? Again, these issues need to be addressed in the future.

Note next that among the female clergy, more senior ministers than solo pastors exhibited an open and vulnerable style of interacting with the congregation and were clearly concerned about social issues. The differences in concern about social issues could simply be another artifact of salience to the situation. Senior ministry placements are typically in relatively large churches, which, in turn, tend to be located in the larger communitites where social issues are more commonly perceived and discussed. Note also that these differences emerge among the *women* but not the men. It could be that the security offered by the senior position in a multiple-staff situation allows the clergywomen to act on social concerns, whereas the greater structural vulnerability of the solo pastorate keeps the women there more on their guard. It is also possible that the congregation willing to call a woman as pastor tends to be more socially conscicous in general than those that are willing to call only a man. The greater cosmopolitanism typically associated with larger communities (and their churches) would also provide support for clergywomen's concern for social issues.

The matter of differences in interpersonal style between women serving as senior or solo pastor is also interesting. As with many of these patterns, we can only speculate about why these associations between style and type of position emerge from the analysis, let alone why they characterize the women but not the men. Could it be that the women placed as senior minister *feel* more secure in their position than the solo pastors, something we also discussed above? After all, they have "made it" to a prestigious position in some degree of direct or indirect competition with other clergywomen *and men*. They must have *something* on the ball—some realistic basis for self-confidence. From that perception of stability in the job, they would also sense few reasons for wariness and thus would be freer to be open and forthcoming in their dealings with members of the congregation. It is also intriguing to ask the causal question, that is, whether those women attained their status on the basis of their open interpersonal skills or whether they developed such interpersonal competence as a result of the realities of the senior position—the security, the altercasting by lay persons, the ingratiations, and so forth. The cultural feminist argument would most likely lead to the former stance. Something at least approximating longitudinal data would be required to address that question, input that we do not have in this undertaking.

Note, finally, that there is *no* significant association between the senior/solo appointment distinction and preference for rational structure in decision making or ethical legalism. This pattern applies to *both* the men and the women. Mode of decision making and moral legalism have been among the dimensions of approach to ministry consistently found related to other variables discussed above, but they drop out in this instance. Why is this so? Perhaps a clue resides in one characteristic shared by the dimensions of ministry style that *are* correlated with prestige of placement, that is, power, empowerment, authority, and interpersonal style. These aspects of approach to ministry all involve *relationships* between clergy and congregation, connections of power, authority, and social interaction. Differences in decision-making strategy and ethical dogmatism, on the other hand, are more "private" or internal dispositions of individual functioning. Perhaps habits of intrapersonal functioning are less likely to be associated with appointments of dissimilar power and prestige than are tendencies to interact overtly with people in a manner which also assumes divergence in status.

Returning to the *racial/ethnic* clergy, there are both solo and senior ministers among the men in that subgroup. We asked whether this status difference was associated with variations in ministry style for racial/ethnic groups as well. Some of the patterns noted in the white data also emerge in the analysis of racial/ethnic clergy responses (see table 4.8). More racial/ethnic senior ministers than solo pastors sought power over their congregation and wanted positions of formal authority for themselves. Senior ministers also tended to be more legalistic than solo pastors. The ethnic senior ministers stressed involvement in social issues more than the solo pastors. In all of these associations, the senior ministers manifested the more "masculine" approaches to ministry. However, more senior ministers than solo pastors also *rejected the traditional masculine bases of clergy status,* indicating acceptance of more feminine criteria instead.

Once again there are few differences between men and women concerning time spent in clergy roles and the extent to which they are considered important. Among the white men, being senior minister is related to time spent in but three activities. More senior ministers than solo pastors spent a lot of time in sermon preparation and delivery (gamma = .21) and in church administration (gamma = .33). Senior ministers also tended to place greater personal importance on these matters—more importance attached to preaching (gamma = .41) and to church administration (gamma = .28). Conversely more solo pastors than senior ministers spent large amounts of time in visiting church

Table 4.8. Correlations (Gamma) between Indices of Ministry Style and Type of Placement among Male Racial/Ethnic Clergy

Dimension of Self-description:	Solo/ Senior	Specific Role Activity	Solo/ Senior
Power over congregation	.45	Sermons	.51
Empowerment of congregation	—*	Funerals	.37
Formal authority	.45	Teaching classes	—
Personal style	—	Visitation	—
Preaching style	—	Counselling	—
Status criteria	.39	Church fellowship	.29
Social issue involvement	.70	Administration	.15
Rational structure	—	Other church structures	.41
Ethical legalism	.46	Community activities	.20
		Personal development	—
		Social Issues	—

*Statistically nonsignificant correlation.

members and prospects (gamma = -.24). These patterns most likely reflect divergent expectations of clergy working in the two types of situation. That is, senior ministers can spend considerable time on sermons, because preaching tends to be one of their major responsibilities and they have assistance to take care of other matters. Senior ministers, typically in large churches, also get caught up in demands of local church administration to a greater degree than solo pastors. The greater time spent in visitation by solo ministers may also reflect the fact that they alone are responsible for it.

Two other roles are evaluated differently by the male senior and solo pastors—conducting funerals and working in church structures beyond the congregation. More *solo* pastors than senior ministers placed much emphasis on funerals (gamma = -.29) and on involvement in denominational structures (gamma = -.27).

There were even *fewer* differences in role behavior and role preference between senior and solo ministers among the white *women,* and they tended to emerge in different areas from those noted among the men. Female senior ministers tended to spend more time in counselling (gamma = .36) and on social justice issues (gamma = .48) than did the female solo pastors. Senior women also tended to assign more importance to church administration (gamma = .38) than did women working alone. By contrast, more female solo pastors than senior ministers placed high degrees of importance on being involved in community activities. This last pattern may derive from the fact that solo charges are more often located in small communities where the local minister can be more easily integrated into community-wide activities than can be done in larger locales.

For the racial/ethnic men, only one specific role emerges as more important to senior ministers than solo pastors, and that is teaching formal classes. This pattern conforms to the observation that in traditional black congregations the preacher is also expected to be an "educator" (Gilkes 1992). However, several differences between senior and solo racial/ethnic pastors appear in the analysis of time spent in various roles. The correlations in table 4.8 indicate that more racial/ethnic senior ministers than solo pastors spent large amounts of time in sermon preparation, funerals, church fellowship activities, church administration, church structures beyond the congregation, and community-wide activities. The basic reasons for those variations probably parallel those that apply to clergy serving white congregations.

Summary

The role that sex and gender play in ministers' approach to their work varies widely, depending on what "kind" of minister one is considering. Several modes of classifying parish clergy are predictive of approach to ministry and of a relationship between the male/female dichotomy and ministry style. The picture can get quite complicated.

Nevertheless, the criteria for classifying clergy that is intuitively the most obvious—denominational affiliation—turned out to be the major exception to that generalization. Denominational labels tended to be *unrelated* to scores on the indices created from the "like-me" items, to variations in the number of hours ministers spent in specific ministerial roles, and to the degree of importance clergy placed on those role activities. The pastors in these four denominations tended to be far more alike in these ways than different. There are apparently few (if any) denominational norms producing denomination-specific patterns of approach to the dimensions of pastoral ministry included in the study. This outcome tends to support the perception that these "mainline" Protestant bodies have departed from any historical uniquenesses they may have had at one time. While the clergy in the study are not monolithic in ministry style, whatever differences do exist among them probably derive from factors other than denomination. One pragmatic consequence of those findings is that we have an empirical basis for continuing to analyze the data for all four sets of clergy together.

Classifying clergy by race and ethnicity, on the other hand, produced patterns of results that dictated keeping the analyses of racial/ethnic and white clergy separate. Racial/ethnic status was associated with differences in nearly all dimensions of ministry style measured by means of the clergy self-descriptions. The consistent pattern was for white ministers to describe themselves in more "feminine" terms, while the racial/ethnic clergy presented self-portraits characterized by relatively "masculine" traits.

These differences probably derive from historical circumstances barring racial/ethnic men from most rewarding occupations but not from the Christian ministry. Attaining ordained ministerial status was one of the few avenues of vertical social mobility open to them, giving them platforms for community leadership and influence, and leading them to assume that their opinions and actions were needed by their lay members. Today that pattern no longer appears sex-specific. Racial and ethnic differences in ministry style appeared among *both* male and female clergy, with racial/ethnic clergy of both sexes appearing more masculine than their white counterparts. These racial/ethnic variations were very stable and appeared to be more important than sex differences within the white and racial/ethnic ranks. Sex-linked differences in approach to ministry were far more prevalent among whites than racial and ethnic groups. These patterns are consistent with the fact that cultural feminist thought has derived almost exclusively from the experiences of *white* women, and they support the observation that the perspective of women in racial-ethnic churches differs significantly from that of the white majority.

Type of pastoral placement was also predictive of variations in approach to ministry. The three types considered were solo pastorates, copastorates, and senior minister appointments. The status of copastor involves placement in a pastorate shared with usually one other person, often one's spouse, a position in which both (all) members of the ministry team are defined as equals in status and authority. As one would expect, given the egalitarian theme in the definition of the post, among copastors there were few significant relationships between sex differences and ministry style.

However, conceptualizing type of placement in terms of being "senior" pastor in a ranked ministerial team was considerably more predictive of approach to ministry. Among the senior ministers alone, sex was highly predictive of variations in clergy self-descriptions, where the sex differences were both strong and clear. The tendency for women and men to have feminine and masculine scores, respectively, was quite pronounced. However, those differences did not emerge when considering the specific role activities. Finally, simply occupying a high-profile position as senior pastor (in contrast to solo minister) was associated with differences in self-descriptions as minister among the women but very little among the men. Women in placements as "senior minister" tended to manifest more "feminine" ministry styles, whereas female solo pastors appeared disposed to choose the more "masculine" approaches. These patterns applied mainly to the clergy self-descriptions items; they were not apparent in the measures dealing with specific clergy roles.

So here we have evidence to support the notion that clergy ministry style takes shape as a result of complex interactions between sex differences, race and ethnicity, and type of pastoral position. The next chapter will indicate how other variables also fit into the picture.

5

Situational and Background Factors in Ministry Style

THE ANALYSIS IN the previous chapter demonstrated that differences in approach to ministry by Protestant pastors were patterned by norms deriving from several social identities—sex, race and ethnicity, and type of pastoral position. Sex differences among clergy were predictive of several dimensions of ministry style, especially using power over the congregation, seeking to empower the laity, preferring rational structures for decision making, and dealing with ethical issues in a legalistic manner. However, the analysis also showed that predicting ministry strategy was much more certain in terms of racial/ethnic identity than sex differences. Ministers of racial and ethnic groups consistently manifested more "masculine" approaches to ministry than did the white clergy. And the extent to which sex-based norms influenced ministry style appeared to depend heavily on whether the pastor had been placed as solo minister, copastor, or senior minister of a ministry team. These patterns suggest a complex web of interrelated forces shaping a minister's approach to pastoral work.

Yet the picture is even more complicated than that. The analysis introduced in this chapter shows the effects of other factors—differences in various background characteristics of clergy and variations in the social context of ministry. A few of these other variables appear to

111

make no difference in ministry style. Nevertheless, some of those factors seem to constitute significant conditions affecting the style a person's ministry will take. Those examined here include variations in community size and region; additional personal attributes of age, formal education, and social status characteristics; family relations involving spouse's education and occupation; seminary cohort; and tenure on the job. Unless otherwise indicated, the analysis will focus on the white clergy. Given the differences in approach to ministry associated with racial/ethnic versus white status revealed in the previous chapter, it is important to keep those subgroups separate. Unfortunately, the sample does not include a sufficient number of racial and ethnic clergy to permit analysis of their ministry characteristics in much detail.

Community Characteristics: Region

A person familiar with geographic patterns of religion in the United States might expect to find specific ministry styles varying according to geographic location. There is a long history of geographic differences in American religious life. As Stump points out:

> Regional cultural differences in the United States are strong and persistent…and encompass many dissimilarities in the nature of religious belief and practice. Most denominations in America, for example, have strongly regionalized distributions.…Regional differences in religious belief and practice also manifest themselves in the relative importance of religious liberalism and conservatism…, the diversity of denominational affiliation…, and even the size of religious broadcasting audiences. (1986, 209)

The Northeast, for example, has been characterized as socially and culturally "liberal" in relation to a variety of issues such as feminism, civil rights, world peace, the environment—and religion. Similarly, the Southeast and Midwest are often caricatured as being very conservative in both religious and secular terms. The "Bible Belt" still refers to an identifiable area of the country. It is possible to plot on a map the places where Roman Catholicism or Judaism have significant numbers of adherents.

In view of patterns like this, it is reasonable to ask whether ministers living in different regions also manifested systematically divergent approaches to the pastoral ministry. If religious belief, affiliation, participation, and ethics vary geographically, are the ways in which Protestant pastors approach their work also patterned by regional norms?

To pursue this question, we classified each pastor as living in the Northeast, Southeast, Midwest, Southwest, Mountain, or Far West regions of the United States. We then cross-tabulated each indicator and composite measure of ministry style with regional location. The results are consistently negative. *There are no statistically significant differences between regions concerning clergy self-descriptions, time spent in clergy roles, and relative importance of those roles.* In spite of other findings of regional variations in religious life, region is not a useful predictor of differences in approach to the pastoral ministry in these four mainline Protestant bodies.

Community Characteristics: Size of Place

Another potentially important determinant of pastoral role definition is the size of the community in which the church resides. As Hargrove (1971, 197-215) points out, the urbanization of American life has had profound effects on the churches, influences with which local congregations are still trying to cope today. The decline of rural communities and the burgeoning of metropolitan areas has created relatively unique problems for churches in each type of environment (see also Winter 1961; and Schaller 1967).

Effects of urbanization and industrialization were probably first noticed in the rural churches. As a result of population loss, declining financial resources, and emigration of talent, today very few churches in rural communities resemble the stereotypical "little brown church in the dale," i.e. the solid, stable *Gemeinschaft* of neighbors expressing their community solidarity through participation in their local church. Instead rural congregations are dwindling in number and in size, and those that remain are typically struggling just to keep their doors open. In efforts to deal with that situation, some denominations and ecumenical organizations have established special programs to support rural congregations. Some of that special attention has involved training clergy to take leadership roles not only in their local congregations but also in relation to the surrounding community in general, to encourage and organize people to deal with the changing realities of their collective life more effectively.

This is not to imply that the metropolitan churches are free of such problems. Continued urbanization and industrialization have shaped urban and suburban congregations as well. The high rates of geographic mobility of urban dwellers tends to make them an atomistic and culturally heterogeneous lot. Instead of sharing long local histories, which provide a basis for community, mobile urban dwellers have to depend on family, work groups, and special interest organizations for a sense of belonging.

Hargrove (1971) argues that some residents of metropolitan areas *seek out* churches in the hope that they will find a sense of community within them, instead of merely "expressing" a preexisting sense of locality-group solidarity as was characteristic of the traditional rural church members. However, the churches in this situation sometimes find it difficult to meet those needs successfully. This is because they are "organizational churches" (instead of "community churches"). In "organizational churches" the maintenance of the organization itself is a matter of paramount concern. They must constantly recruit new members, solicit operating funds, draft lay leaders to implement social programs, and so forth. Those located in the inner city also tend to depart from the model of the church as primarily the "worshipping community" and devote church resources to programs addressing social problems of substance abuse, poverty, homelessness, and the community policies that breed such difficulties. As a result they can lack the "warmth" urban dwellers are seeking, so that in the end they cannot provide the "community" for which they were sought out in the first place.

These perceptions of churches in locales of differing size have promoted the idea that the job of the pastor will differ widely from one milieu to the next. The tasks to be performed in rural churches should be quite different from those required in the downtown city church, and neither of these environments should call for the kinds of congregational objectives one would expect to find in suburban churches. The extent to which one must pay attention to organizational survival will vary in each situation, as will the need for operating funds, recruiting competent ministerial leadership, boosting member morale, dealing with heterogeneous congregational membership, and other issues.

The question we address here is whether or not ministers serving churches located in different types of communities also approach their work differently in terms of the concepts with which we have been dealing in this analysis of ministry style—their self-descriptions, use of time, and priorities placed on specific clergy roles. Comparisons of scores on the "like-me" indices and community size indicate only two significant relationships. Community size was associated with criteria of clergy status. The smaller the community, the more likely the ministers were to reject the traditional masculine status criteria in favor of the feminine bases of status. The relationship is quite weak (gamma = .15), so it may not be important substantively, but it is statistically significant.

The second correlation that emerges from this analysis is between community size and involvement in social issues. Clergy in larger places tended to be more involved in social issues than those serving in smaller locales (gamma = -.11). Again the coefficient is very small, and one could easily attach too much importance to it. Nevertheless, it does square with typical assumptions that urban dwellers tend to be more involved in social issues than their rural cousins.

That interpretation is supported in the comparison of community size and time spent in specific clergy roles. Ministers serving in large communities tended to spend more hours actually dealing with social issues than did those in smaller places (gamma = -.21). Persons working in large communities also tended to spend more time than those in small locations counselling parishioners (gamma = -.11), a pattern that reinforces perceptions that life in large communities is more stressful than what one will endure in small towns. Finally, more clergy in large places than small sites spent a great deal of time in local church administration (gamma = -.16). Running the metropolitan church may be a more demanding job than administering the affairs of the rural congregation.

Church administration also looms larger in ministers' priorities in urban settings than in small charges. Ministers in churches located in large communities tended to place more importance on local church administration than did those in small places (gamma = -.22). This is the only clergy role on which size of place is predictive of both ways of dealing with specific roles, (1) the stated importance of the role to the minister and (2) the amount of time actually spent doing it. More city clergy than small-town clergy *both* placed great importance on local church administration *and* spent more hours actually doing it.

Finally, ministers working in small communities placed more importance on involvement in church fellowship activities (gamma = .11) and local community affairs (gamma = .10) than did city dwellers. Again, the correlations are *very* small, though statistically significant, so one must be cautious in generalizing from them.

In summary, then, *differences in community size appear to be but minimally associated with variations in ministry style.* The few correlations that emerge from the analysis lend some support to the perception that life in large places can be more complex, stressful and demanding than in the small town or village. The same point applies to "running the church" in those different types of locale. Nevertheless, one must not lose sight of the fact that significant associations appeared in relation to but a *small minority* of the measures of clergy self-perceptions, time spent in specific role activities, and the importance the ministers place on those roles. And the correlations that do emerge as statistically significant are quite small. Accordingly, size of community is probably not an important predictor of differences in approach to the pastoral ministry.

Personal Attributes: Age

Another set of factors that may influence ministry style is the variety of ways in which the clergy differ from one another as individuals. The analyses in chapters three and four have already dealt with two such variables, sex and race/ethnicity. Sex was predictive of some differences in approach to the ministry, while racial and ethnic identity was associated with just about *all* of them. Here we want to consider two more ways in which ministers differ from one another, age and formal education.

Church folklore has long considered age as an important predictor of differences in how clergy approach their work. But the variety of pictures of clergy to be gleaned from those folk assumptions is as contradictory as the traditions are longstanding. On the one hand, the older minister or priest is portrayed as the stable fount of wisdom, persistently nurturing his (sic) flock and guiding them through their tribulations with profound insight and gentle persuasiveness. The actor Barry Fitzgerald immortalized this model in his rendition of the wise old priest in the film *Going My Way*. In this mode the young minister appears at best as one with a lot to learn and at worst as the upstart novice who will ruin the whole show if not corralled. On the other hand, older priests and pastors sometimes share the same negative images as are imposed on older workers in other occupations, that is, as the out-of-touch, inflexible, self-centered, and domineering autocrats who have outlasted their usefulness and who should be made to step aside to allow the next generation of leaders to take over and bring the church into line with the real world.

So we asked whether age was associated with differences in the ministers' approach to their work. Do the older clergy differ significantly from younger ones in their replies to the "like-me" items, the hours spent in clergy role activities, and the importance they place on ministerial roles? The answer generated by comparisons of age with each of the measures of ministry style is quite negative.

Age predicts very few differences in approach to pastoral ministry. The only self-description item significantly related to age is acceptance of feminine criteria of clergy status. More older respondents than younger ones tended to reject traditional masculine status symbols in favor of those valued by cultural feminists. As concerns the relative

importance placed on clergy roles, older ministers placed more importance than younger ones on conducting funerals (gamma = .08), personal counselling (gamma = .08), and visiting church members and
prospects (gamma = .13). This pattern implies that older clergy tend to
be a bit more "pastoral" in orientation than younger persons, placing
importance on these nurturant aspects of their work. However, the
pattern does not carry over into parallel differences in time actually
spent in those role activities. *None* of the measures of time spent in
specific roles are related to differences in age.

Note once again that overall the correlations associated with age
are *very weak* and that they constitute only 9 percent of the total of possible relationships. At the 5 percent level of significance, one would
expect to see almost as many correlations emerge as statistically significant based on sampling error alone. Furthermore, none of these statements of importance are translated into differences in time actually
spent in those roles. So it is probably safest to conclude that *age is not a
useful predictor of these variations in ministry style.*

Personal Attributes: Formal Education

The other personal attribute to consider here is the level of formal education the ministers obtained. While some people assume that all ministers receive the same level of formal training, in fact there are wide
differences in clergy's educational attainments. Some of those dispari-
ties are based on the requirements of the particular denomination in
which the minister is working. Religious bodies differ widely in the
kinds of educational backgrounds they want (and permit) their ministers to obtain. At one extreme are groups in which candidates for ministry must complete specific courses of study in colleges or universities
and then attend particular theological institutions sponsored by the
group. Upon completion of those studies, they must complete what
amounts to an apprenticeship under the tutelage of an experienced
ordained religious leader. At that point they are considered qualified
to *apply* for acceptance into the ministry in that denomination. While
the application is seldom denied, their entrance into ordained pastoral
ministry at that point is by no means guaranteed. The point is that
*there are rigid formal requirements and procedures for acceptance as a legiti-
mate religious leader* in those groups.

At the opposite extreme are the smaller and less highly structured
denominations within which formal ordination requirements are few.
In these groups persons aspiring to the ministry must merely convince
a subgroup of religious leaders of the reality of their being called by

God to serve, coupled with some discernible demonstration that one has sufficient charisma to make lay members sit up and take notice. There are no requirements of formal degrees from colleges, universities, or theological seminaries. In fact members of these informal bodies often distrust and ridicule those who enter the ministry through completion of high levels of formal education.

The majority of religious functionaries work within denominations having educational requirements falling somewhere between these two extremes. The ministers included in this study were in "mainline" Protestant bodies, where educational requirements for ordination tend to be relatively high. *Most* of them would have completed a bachelor's degree prior to entering a theological seminary or divinity school. Upon completion of the theological training, they would have become formal candidates for ordination as functioning clergy within their denomination, and they would then pursue placement in a pastoral position. Some of them would have gone on to complete additional formal education, increasingly the doctor of ministry degree, which is regarded by many as the "union card" for getting placement in a large church. (These variables are actually strongly related in these data. The correlation between education and holding a "senior minister" appointment is .50, with highly educated clergy overrepresented as incumbents of senior staff positions.) In the actual percentage distributions of educational attainment among clergy in the sample (see table 5.1), the distribution of all the cases ("total") indicates that about three-fourths of the ministers in the sample took the typical educational route—undergraduate degree followed by theological seminary (the old B.D., or bachelor of divinity, or the more recent M.Div., or master of divinity; equivalent degrees constituting the basic "union card" for ordained ministers). The white clergy (about four-fifths of the cases) followed that same pattern. The racial/ethnic ministers, however, departed from the middle. Among racial/ethnic ministers, greater proportions attained both *less* than the typical requirements *and more* than the basic requisites. Many racial/ethnic ministers had gone on to higher degrees, especially the doctorate.

This pattern also indicates, then, that denominational "requirements" are not totally determinative of the amount of formal education clergy receive. Some underachieve, while others go beyond the stated minima. The question we asked, then, concerns whether or not those variations in individual educational attainment were significantly related to differences in ministry style. Does the "amount" of formal education ministers receive determine anything about the way in which they define their role as pastor?

To pursue that question, we cross-tabulated the measures of level of formal education with the various measures of clergy self-descrip-

Table 5.1. Educational Attainment of Clergy

Educational Level	Total (%)	White (%)	Racial/Ethnic (%)
Less than B.A./B.S.	2	1	6
B.A./B.S.	5	5	8
B.D./M.Div.	74	78	56
Th.M.	3	3	3
D.Min.	10	10	13
Th.D.	1	1	1
Ph.D.	5	3	13

tion, time in role activities, and importance placed on specific roles. *There proved to be no significant correlations between level of education and scores on the "like-me" questions.* Use of power, authority, interpersonal style, and so on, are *un*related to educational attainment.

However, four of the eleven measures of time spent in specific role activities are significantly related to level of education. The higher the level of formal education, the more time the clergy spent in personal counselling of parishioners (gamma = .18), church administration (gamma = .20), community-wide activities (gamma = .25), and working with social issues (gamma = .26). Most of these role activities are also associated with size of both community and congregation, so what emerges is a clustering of role activities associated with the more educated clergy serving as senior ministers in large metropolitan churches, in contrast with smaller charges in smaller places served by solo pastors with more standard qualifications. All of these variables are significantly intercorrelated. The determinants of these differences appear to be more a matter of the requirements of the external situation than the internal proclivities of the minister.

Level of education is also associated with the degree of importance the respondents placed on two roles, conducting funerals and participation in church fellowship activities. Ministers with high levels of formal education tended to place less importance on funerals (gamma = -.11) and church fellowship (gamma = -.19) than did those with lower educational attainments.

Status Characteristics: Size of Congregation

Although clergy and other denominational spokespersons typically deny it, like anyone else ministers are concerned about their social status. In fact ministers may have larger-than-average egos, because like

actors, trial lawyers, and elected government officials, they are habitu-
ally "on stage" and others constantly seek their opinions. Eventually
some of them come to believe that all of the attention they get is simply
as it should be, viewing themselves as "special people." Moreover, the
ministry as an occupation is also ranked internally. Some clergy are
"more equal than others," all clergy know it, and some of them are
quite concerned about it (e.g., Lehman 1990).

The traditional criteria of social status in the ministry closely parallel those that apply to other occupational groups—education, income,
power and authority in the work organization (e.g., whether "senior
minister" or not), and size of congregation. We have already examined
some of these status characteristics, that is, type of placement (senior
minister) and formal education. Here we look at the remaining two—
size of church and income.

We measured differences in size of church by obtaining the number of people attending a typical Sunday morning worship service (see
table 5.2). Overall the distribution is quite skewed. Most of these ministers were serving fairly small congregations, although nearly 20 percent of them had typical attendances on Sunday morning of more than
200 people. (The differences in the distributions of racial/ethnic and
white clergy are statistically nonsignificant.)

Table 5.2.   Rate of Church Attendance

Size Category	Racial/Ethnic*(%)	White*(%)
fewer than 50	23	16
50–100	38	34
101–150	18	19
151–200	5	12
201–250	3	7
251–300	4	4
301–350	1	2
more than 350	8	6
Total	100	100

*The race/ethnic and white categories describe Clergy, not church attendees.

In any case, we then cross-tabulated size of congregation with
each measure of ministry style; the results closely parallel the outcomes discussed immediately above. That is, only one dimension of
clergy self-description is associated with differences in church size,
and that is "interpersonal style." Ministers serving large congregations
tended to manifest more open interpersonal styles than those working

in small churches (gamma = .11). Once again the coefficient is very small, so one must be cautious about generalizing from it.

We then compared the male/female dichotomy with each dimension of clergy self-description, controlling for size of congregation (see table 5.3). The general pattern in the table indicates that *sex predicts differences in ministry style more in large churches (more than 150 attending) than in small ones (150 or fewer)*. In large churches, more men than women seek to use power over the congregation and want to be in positions of authority, but those correlations do not appear among ministers in smaller churches. Sex of clergy also makes more of a difference in large churches than small ones concerning congregational empowerment, involvement in social issues, and ethical legalism. The opposite is the case for wanting rational structure for decision making. Sex is unrelated to interpersonal style, preaching, and status criteria in either small or large situations. These patterns are not unlike those obtained when comparing the interactions of ministry style, sex differences, and type of placement—especially as senior minister. Sex is more predictive of divergent ministry styles among those in high-status positions than those in more ordinary charges. Each of the significant correlations is in support of the cultural feminist argument.

Table 5.3. Correlations (Gamma) between Sex of Clergy and Dimensions of Ministry Style, Controlling for Size of Congregation

Dimension of Ministry Style	Sex of Clergy	
	Small Church	Large Church
Power over congregation	—*	-.29
Empowerment of congregation	.16	.39
Formal authority	—	-.20
Interpersonal style	—	—
Preaching style	—	—
Status criteria	—	—
Social issue involvement	.14	.30
Rational structure	-.47	-.31
Ethical legalism	-.28	-.35

*Statistically nonsignificant correlation.

We also compared church size to the relative importance ministers place on clergy roles and the time they actually spend in them. The most consistent pattern to emerge from that analysis involves local church administration and preparation and delivery of sermons. The larger the congregation, the more ministers placed *importance* on church administration (gamma = .23) and involvement with sermons (gamma = .17). Similarly, size of congregation is directly related to the amount of *time spent* in church administration (gamma = .25) and preaching (gamma = .09).

Stated importance of four other clergy roles is *negatively* related to church size. That is, the larger the congregation, the *less* ministers tended to emphasize church fellowship activities, involvement in church structures beyond the congregation, participation in community-wide activities, and commitment to social issues. One suspects that the increased demands of large churches in terms of liturgy, general program administration, working with committees, and so forth tend to squeeze these kinds of activities out of one's agenda in favor of more pressing matters.

Finally, church size is also related to the hours spent in two other role activities, working with funerals and doing personal counselling. More pastors of large churches than small ones spent large amounts of time in funerals (gamma = .28) and counselling (gamma = .20). Larger congregations would likely have a greater likelihood of ad hoc demands for these kinds of things than would small churches. Accordingly, it is most likely this differential external demand for funerals and counselling that accounts for the slight differences in time spent in those activities by clergy serving different-sized congregations.

Status Characteristics: Family Income

The final status characteristic to consider is family income, a common determinant of socioeconomic status and lifestyle. We obtained information on income by asking, "Which of the following categories includes your annual family income, including allowances (such as housing, car, etc.)?" The median family income of the ministers was between $30,000 and $35,000, with the white clergy earning significantly more than the racial/ethnic ministers. This figure may seem high to some readers, but one must remember that it represents *total family income* earned by both spouses and includes any allowances the ministers receive for their housing, automobile expenses, retirement, and so on. With slightly more than 80 percent of ministers' spouses contributing to family income by earning a salary, the figure isn't excessively high at all, especially considering the extra expenses many ministers have for clothes, entertaining, and so forth.

In any case, we cross-tabulated family income with each of the measures of approach to ministry; the results are somewhat similar to

Table 5.4.   Ministers' Family Income

Income Category	Racial/Ethnic (%)	White (%)
less than $20,000	15	6
$20,000–24,999	16	14
$25,000–29,999	12	15
$30,000–34,999	15	13
$35,000–39,999	11	10
$40,000–44,999	3	7
$45,000–49,999	8	9
$50,000 or more	20	26
Totals	100	100

those obtained in relation to other facets of social status. As concern the scores based on the "like-me" items, only two are significantly associated with income differentials. Income is positively related to interpersonal style and involvement in social issues. The higher the minister's family income, the more likely he/she is to have an open and nondefensive interpersonal style (gamma = .13) and to be involved in social issues (gamma = .12). Once again the relationships are *very weak*, so one must be careful about generalizing about them and their implications. Income is *not* predictive of use of power, desire for authority or for rational structure, or the other scales.

However, differences in family income are associated with differential emphasis on three of the specific role activities—teaching formal classes, local church administration, and community-wide activities. Ministers with high incomes tended *not* to place high importance on teaching (gamma = -.09) or community involvements (gamma = -.14). By contrast there is a direct relationship between family income and importance placed on local church administration (gamma = .19).

The emphasis on church administration is followed up with actual behavior, that is, the higher the family income, the higher also was the time spent in local church administration (gamma = .22). Income is also directly related to time spent in counselling (gamma = .19) and funerals (gamma = .16). These patterns are consistent with those noted in connection with differences in size of congregation (above).

So what is the general picture thus far? Comparisons of size of church and family income with ministry style produce results that show some consistency with those obtained when examining other status characteristics, such as formal education and, to a lesser extent, placement as senior minister. First, church size, family income, and education tend to be *un*related to most dimensions of clergy self-description (the "like-me" items). It is primarily interpersonal style that is influenced by status, with high status persons being more open and willing to be vulnerable and low-status ministers more likely to be closed and defensive, and those correlations are quite small. Differences in other dimensions of ministry style are not associated with variations in status. That is, use of power, congregational empowerment, wanting formal authority, and so forth appear to exist independently of having more or less prestige and other resources. Differences in ministers' statements about how they approach their work do not seem to derive from these status differences within the ministry.

If anything status differences among clergy influence what they concentrated on in their work. Higher-status persons tended to emphasize church administration, personal counselling, and funerals, while persons with less status preferred to focus on community involvements and church fellowship activities. These patterns probably derive from the different types of demands made on clergy working in different sized churches and communities.

As is the case involving placement as senior minister (chap. 4), sex of minister has more of an impact on self-description scores among those serving in *large* churches. Men and women differed in their approach to ministry more if they were serving a large church than if they were placed in a smaller charge. Perhaps in large churches, men and women feel more confident to be themselves than do those with smaller charges. Some of this difference is associated with placement as senior minister, since such positions exist almost exclusively in relation to the larger congregations.

Family Relations: Spouse Education and Occupation

As noted above, most of the clergy participating in the study were married to a spouse who was also gainfully employed. Most of the respondents' spouses also had significant attainments in formal education. So they shared a working life-style and some degree of parallel perspective on life's other concerns.

Until the last decade or so, there was widespread acceptance of the idea that the family was a "separate sphere" from work and that what went on in each domain had little or no relevance to the other (Piotrkowski 1979; Finch 1983). Family affairs were assumed to be "private" matters, while work took place in the "public sphere," and these separate systems functioned independently of each other. Finch

(1983, 4) points out that this idea is "empirically insupportable..., theoretically naive..., and it serves actually to obscure certain important features of social life" (see also Piotrkowski 1979, 276). There are numerous ways in which work and family influence each other in both long- and short-term perspectives.

The most commonly perceived contact between work and family involves several ways in which the job affects the home. "Work" as we usually conceive of it typically takes the employed person out of the home, eliminating the amount of time and energy that person can devote to household work. The nature of the job often dictates where the family will live. It also largely determines the level of economic resources the family has at its disposal, thus establishing a level of living or life-style for all family members. In this way the job influences the nature of the family's domicile, the circle of friends likely to be available to them, the kinds of leisure activities members can participate in, the quality of health care members receive, and on and on.

Traditionally wives have been the ones dependent on their husbands in this situation. The man's job has been what patterned family living for most people. However, it is a mistake to assume that wives are merely passive objects in the operation of that work/family system. When a woman marries, she usually knows full well that she is not marrying only the man; she is also marrying his job. Women "opt in" to a work/family system, expecting real benefits from it and experiencing their husband's career vicariously. To do so simply makes economic sense, avoids difficulties of noncompliance, and provides a framework for defining her role as "wife" (Finch 1983, 150ff.).

What has been less obvious are the ways in which family matters influence work. How one performs one's work doesn't depend exclusively on conditions in the workplace. Events outside of the office or factory also affect how one relates to work. Whether one simply *stays on the job*, for example—job turnover—can be influenced by numerous events external to the job per se, including family variables. Family needs and responsibilities, a working spouse, number of children, children's schooling, role conflicts between work and family roles, and so forth can impact job tenure (Mobley 1982, 108). Worker stress, another fact of life in the world of work, can come from *nonjob* sources including the family—problems with spouse or children, marital problems, change in residence, illness and death in the family (Werther 1985, 422–25).

Family situations and events typically have influenced the patterns of remunerative work of women more than of men. If a woman is married, with or without children, her occupation suffers. She can experience discrimination from an employer concerning her being hired, trained, retained, or promoted. Her husband's attitudes will influence the nature of her work patterns. His career moves can disrupt her own otherwise orderly career progression. Her children's requirements for care can make her *appear* unreliable as an employee, and conflicts over such things at home can distract her from concentration on the job (Montagna 1977, 397).

Even less often recognized are the actual contributions women routinely make to their husband's work and careers. Finch (1983) points out that wives often contribute to their husbands' careers in numerous ways. Wives do this by providing domestic labor to free the man for other things, giving her husband moral support to do his own work effectively, providing peripheral activities for him (like entertaining), doing "back-up" work like conveying messages, and actually doing some of the man's work at home. Simply by "deciding" to be devoted to the success of a man's career creates conditions at home to facilitate his achievements. *So what a spouse does can directly contribute to or detract from a worker's performance on the job.*

Given this evidence of "give and take" between work and family, the analysis seeks to determine whether there is any detectible relationship between the ministers' approach to work and their spouse's work involvements. Does the education and occupation of *spouse* have any impact on the clergy's ministry style? Are there different relationships between approach to ministry and spouse's work for men and women?

We approached these questions first by obtaining the spouse's level of formal education and his/her occupation. For education we asked: "What is the highest level of formal education your spouse attained?" A number of patterns are immediately apparent in the data (see table 5.5). First, the spouse of most clergy manifested educational levels below their own achievements. With most clergy possessing at least the standard seminary degree (B.D./M.Div.), the spouses of most racial/ethnic clergy, both males and females, showed lower levels of education. The same was true for the wives of white clergymen. However, the husbands of white clergywomen departed from that pattern, exhibiting educational attainments more in line with those of their spouses. Note, finally, that the wives and husbands of racial/ethnic clergy also showed the *highest* levels of formal education, the Ph.D. degree, while none of the white spouses achieved that level.

The spouses' occupational classifications were obtained by asking: "Which of the following categories best describes your spouse's occupation?" The general tendencies in those figures indicate, again, that most of the clergy spouses were gainfully employed (see table 5.6). Among those not employed, wives of white and racial/ethnic men held the greatest proportions, while unemployed husbands of white women were the least common. Proportionately more of those white

Table 5.5. Educational Attainment of Clergy Spouse (Percent) by Sex and Race/Ethnicity

Educational Level	Racial/Ethnic Pastors Wives (%)	Husbands (%)	White Pastors Wives (%)	Husbands (%)
Less than B.A./B.S.	35	44	36	13
B.A./B.S.	25	39	39	17
B.D./M.Div.	3	6	3	38
Th.M.	0	0	1	2
M.A./M.S.	32	6	18	15
D.Min.	0	0	0	5
Th.D.	0	0	0	0
Ph.D.	5	6	0	0

clergywomen were also married to other clergy than appeared in the other categories, often reflecting placement as "copastors." White men and women had more spouses in religious and secular professional pursuits than did racial/ethnic ministers, whose spouses tended to be concentrated in other white-collar and skilled blue-collar jobs.

Table 5.6. Occupational Classifications of Clergy Spouse (Percent) by Sex and Race/Ethnicity

Occupational Classification	Racial/Ethnic Clergy Wives (%)	Husbands (%)	White Clergy Wives (%)	Husbands (%)
Clergy	3	11	4	44
Other professional	38	21	44	34
Admin/proprietor	15	26	7	9
Technical	0	16	2	3
Sales/clerical	18	0	11	2
Skilled manual	0	11	1	4
Unskilled manual	0	0	1	1
Not employed	26	16	31	3

Do any of these educational and occupational differences among clergy spouses have anything to do with the respondents' approaches to the pastoral ministry? As usual, the answer is "it depends." *The answer depends on whether you are talking about the man or the woman, which spouse characteristic is under consideration, and the aspect of ministry style on which one is focusing.* As shown in table 5.7, dealing with the self-description ("like-me") items, if spouse characteristics are related to the ministry style of one sex, they tend not to be so for the other sex.

Differences in spouse's education, first of all, are related to more dimensions of *men's* approach to ministry than to women's. Men with more *highly* educated wives tended to use power over their congregation more than did those whose wives had fewer educational credentials. And men whose wives had *lower* levels of education tended to (1) seek to empower their congregations, (2) endorse feminine criteria of clergy status, (3) prefer rational structure in decision making, and (4) view ethics in legalistic terms.

Differences in educational levels of *husbands of clergywomen,* on the other hand, are associated with only two facets of ministry style. Female clergy with highly educated husbands tended to promote congregational empowerment and relate to church members in an open manner more than women whose mates had accomplished less educationally.

Shifting to occupation of spouse, a similar but even more interesting pattern emerges. *Type of occupation* of spouse makes more of a difference for the ministry style of *male* clergy than female (see table 5.7). Women whose husbands had relatively *low* status occupations tended to accept feminine criteria of clergy status more than those with spouses in high-prestige vocations—only one dimension is affected.

Table 5.7. Correlations (Gamma) between Dimensions of Ministry Style and Education and Occupation of Spouse, Controlling for Sex of Clergy

Dimension of Ministry Style	Spouse Education		Spouse Occupation*		Spouse Employed?	
	Men	Women	Men	Women	Men	Women
Power over congregation	.16	—†	—	—	—	.43
Empowerment of congregation	-.16	.13	-.17	—	.18	-.40
Formal authority	—	—	—	—	—	.45
Interpersonal style	—	.14	.15	—	—	—
Preaching style	—	—	.27	—	—	—
Status criteria	-.25	—	—	.19	.17	—
Social issue involvement	—	—	-.14	—	—	-.46
Rational structure	-.30	—	-.16	—	—	.63
Ethical legalism	-.29	—	—	—	.24	-.52

*Level of occupational status, excluding person unemployed.
†Statistically nonsignificant correlation at $p < .01$.

But type of spouse's occupation is related to *five* differences in ministry style for the male clergy. Clergymen whose wives worked in *high-status* occupations tended to (1) seek to empower their congregations, (2) relate to church members in an open and nondefensive manner, (3) be highly involved in social issues, (4) place little emphasis on preaching in their ministry, and (5) prefer an intuitive and integrative approach to decision making—all *"feminine" ministry strategies*. The presence of the high-status wife is associated with men using more feminine ministry styles, but the occupational status of the female clergy's husband seems much less related to her approach to her work.

An equally unique set of relationships emerged from comparisons of variations in approach to ministry with *whether the spouse is employed at all*, as represented by the final set of figures in table 5.7. In these comparisons the differences between male and female spouses are reversed. That is, *whether or not the minister's spouse was gainfully employed at all makes more of a difference in the ministry styles of women than of men.* Clergymen with unemployed wives tended to be *high* on congregational empowerment, acceptance of feminine status criteria, and ethical legalism.

But having an unemployed husband is associated with twice as many differences in approach to ministry on the part of the female clergy. A note of caution—there were only five white clergywomen with husbands not gainfully employed. This small number of cases makes comparisons very difficult in view of requirements of ruling out chance differences based on sampling variation alone. But in spite of that fact, using a 10 percent criterion of statistical significance, some intriguing associations emerge from the analysis. Having an unemployed husband is associated with female ministers who also (1) use power over their congregations, (2) do not seek to empower their congregations, (3) wish to be in positions of authority, (4) have little involvement in social issues, (5) prefer rational structures for decision making, and (6) shun ethical legalism. In all but the last of these correlations, *the woman's approach to ministry tend toward the "masculine" end of the continuum if her husband was not gainfully employed.* Even though these correlations are significant at only the 10-percent level, the pattern is relatively consistent from one relationship to the next.

When the focus of the analysis shifts from the self-description items to the *number of hours* the respondents spend in specific role activities, no discernible pattern emerges. A few very weak associations between ministry style and spouse education and occupation appear, but none of them are noteworthy. These spouse characteristics basically tend to be unrelated to variations in time male and female clergy spent in specific roles.

However, meaningful patterns do emerge from the analysis of spouse occupation and the *importance* ministers place on specific clergy roles. (Spouse education is *un*related to stated importance of any clergy roles.) *Spouse's occupation is associated with differences in importance placed on ministerial roles more for the female clergy than for the males* (see table 5.8). First looking at the men, if the minister's wife was in a relatively high-status vocation, he tended to place more importance on personal counselling, church administration, and involvement in social issues than if she were in a low-status field. However, the *opposite* is the case for the women ministers. For the clergywomen, having a husband working in a high-status occupation was associated with placing *low* importance on preparing and delivering sermons, conducting funerals, teaching formal classes, visiting members and prospects, doing personal counselling, and being involved in community-wide activities.

The difference between men and women is even greater when considering whether spouse is gainfully employed at all. For male ministers, placing high importance on only one role activity—preparation and delivery of sermons—is negatively related to having a wife who was earning a salary. Among the women, on the other hand, relative emphasis on five role activities is related to whether or not hus-

Table 5.8.   Correlations (Gamma) between Importance Placed on Clergy Roles and Occupation of Spouse, Controlling for Sex of Clergy

Clergy Roles:	Spouse Occupation* Males	Females	Spouse Employed? Males	Females†
Sermons	—‡	.22	.33	—
Funerals	—	.38	—	-.68
Teaching classes	—	.12	—	—
Visitation	—	.19	—	-.55
Counselling	-.16	.19	—	—
Church Fellowship	—	—	—	-.74
Administration	-.19	—	—	-.60
Other church structures	—	—	—	—
Community activities	—	.17	—	—
Personal development	—	—	—	.55
Social issues	-.24	—	—	—

*Level of occupational status, excluding persons unemployed.
†Statisical criterion: $p < .10$.
‡Statistically nonsignificant correlation.

band was working. Having a husband gainfully employed is related to placing high importance on conducting funerals, visiting church members and prospects, being involved in church fellowship activities, and working on local church administration. Having an employed husband is negatively related to assigning high importance to personal development.

WHY THESE PATTERNS? While the correlations between spouse's education and clergy self-descriptions are mixed (and thus inconclusive), the relationships between those ministry-style scores and spouse's occupation are more consistent and thus intriguing.

1. If something about spouse's occupation influences ministry style for *men*, then it tends not to have such effects for *women*, and vice versa. WHY?

2. The occupational prestige level of *clergymen's wives* influences the men's approach to ministry, but the occupational prestige level of the husbands of female clergy has little or no such effects on women's approaches. WHY?

3. Whether or not *women ministers' husbands* are gainfully employed at all appears to affect the women's definition of their ministry, but the presence or absence of a working spouse is not as systematically related to the men's ministry style. WHY?

4. In each of the situations outlined in points two and three above, the presence of the (high status) working spouse tends to be associated with a more *feminine* ministry style. WHY?

5. Clergy*women* with husbands working in high-status fields tend to *play down* the importance of several ministerial roles, while those with husbands in less prestigious work tend to stress some of those roles more. WHY?

6. Clergy*women* with husbands who are simply *employed at something* tend to place higher importance on several roles than those whose husbands are unemployed. WHY?

Obtaining these patterns was a totally serendipitous outcome of the analysis. Thus, we have no measures of other variables that may account for them. We are simply left with an opportunity to speculate about them and to point them out as a possible focus in future research.

One possibility that must not be ruled out prematurely is the idea that the patterns are not meaningful at all but instead are statistical accidents. That explanation should always be considered a possibility, but it is not likely to be satisfactory in efforts to account for the patterns that emerge in this instance. It is probably safest to view the relationships involving spouse's *education* in this way. Education of spouse is *un*related to most variations in ministry style, and the directions of the few significant correlations are inconsistent. However, there is too much consistency in the correlations involving *spouse's occupation* for them to be merely artifacts of sampling variation of some sort.

One direction that could be fruitful for exploring the differences in ministry style associated with spouse characteristics involves the concept of "power." Family social exchange, decision making, the direction of social influence, and so forth will often be at least partly determined by the relative distribution of power between the husband and wife. "Power" in this case means the amount of discretion and leverage each partner has available as social capital with which to influence the relationship.

In the patterns noted above, this concept would enter the equation in the sense of relative power at home establishing habits which then carry over into work as well. Male clergy whose wives have little economic leverage at home (i.e., low-prestige jobs) tend to carry that pattern over into work and adopt a "masculine" ministry style, while those with wives in high-prestige occupations can't exercise as much power at home and hence adopt a more feminine approach to ministry. Similarly, female ministers whose husbands have no economic basis for power at home exercise dominance over those men and take a similarly masculine stance toward serving as "pastor." Conversely, women clergy with working husbands have some competition for power at home, where they then develop habits of consultation and cooperation that are also applied on the job, that is, a more feminine approach to the work of the ministry. This rationale would account for the patterns of men in response to the status of their wife's occupation and of women in reaction to whether or not their husband is employed. But it does *not* explain why the emergence of such effects for one sex does not also carry over to the other. Similarly, the appeal to power doesn't explain why the presence of spouses in high-status occupations leads male clergy to *em*phasize certain clergy roles, while the same situation has female clergy *de*emphasizing clergy roles, or why women with working husbands emphasize particular ministerial roles more than those whose husbands are not gainfully employed.

Another approach to the possible effects of spouse's occupation focuses on the concept of *'deviance from traditional patterns'*. Where one partner experiences what some would define as "deviant" patterns in spouse's occupation, that departure from accepted norms sets in motion social psychological responses in which the person seeks to adjust to the "abnormalities" in that experience. Where a male minister experiences a wife in a relatively high-status occupation—a situation that deviates from family arrangements that have predominated in the United States—he takes a role that merges well with his wife's status, foregoing masculine postures and adopting more feminine ones. In parallel fashion, where the female minister is married to an unemployed husband—deviation from the American norm—she takes a role that is more "masculine" both at home and at work. This explanatory strategy deals with the patterns involving the composite measures (the "like-me" items), but it does not necessarily resolve the difficulty in accounting for the divergent effects of spouse's occupation on the stated importance of various clergy roles.

Another dimension of the situation involves the differential consequences that variations in spouse characteristics can have for women and men. Given the traditional family economic structure in this society—males as major provider and females as either secondary provider or consumer—the nature of the wife's occupation, while important, is typically considered to have fewer economic consequences for the family than that of the husband. People tend to be less nervous if the wife is unemployed, for example, than if the husband has no remunerative work. These assumptions, therefore, are likely to involve different influences spouse's occupation will have on the way males and females feel about their work. Perceptions of the implications of spouse's work status, therefore, could also lead men and women to *approach* their own work quite differently.

Each of the approaches above assumes that the marriage situation is causally antecedent to the minister's approach to work. But that need not be the case at all. One could easily develop an argument that the situation at work had causal effects on family roles and hence on the employment status of the spouse. Which is the dependent variable (the "effect"), and which is the independent variable (the "cause")? The answer is not given in the data.

Finally, some social psychologists could easily argue that neither the home situation nor the approach to work is the causal factor. Instead, it is possible that individual ministers with either masculine or feminine personality configurations simultaneously self-select into marital arrangements and work situations that are mutually compatible. In that case both spouse's occupation and ministry style would simply be manifestations of what some balance theorists view as the inevitable flow of social and psychological forces. Although this "nature" is always in some state of *im*balance, it is also constantly striving to move toward greater equilibrium (e.g., Heider 1958; and Brehm and Cohen 1962).

No doubt many other theoretical orientations can provide leads for explaining the apparent associations between ministry style and spouse's occupation. Nevertheless, we must move on, hoping that the matter can be addressed systematically by additional research in the near future.

Cohort Effects: Years since Seminary

Another factor that must be taken into account is the period during which the ministers went through seminary and completed their theological education. The seminary cohort to which each minister belongs can be an important factor in her/his approach to ministry. Most people have simplistic perceptions of theological seminaries, because they have not been directly involved in theological education in any way. This point applies to the vast majority of church members, let alone those who have little contact with organized religion. To the laity what happens during seminary years is primarily a matter of training candidates to be caring and effective ministers, a harmonious program of study that also involves systematic study of the Bible and its languages, church history, systematic theology, and perhaps a dash of pastoral psychology thrown in for good measure. And they assume that the seminary experience is pretty much the same for everyone who attends.

Persons who have experienced theological education, on the other hand, know that this detached perspective on the seminary experience is quite inadequate. In the course of a theological education, students encounter scholarly conflict fueled by widely divergent ideological commitments. They are invited to grapple with perspectives on religious issues that won't reach most lay people for another fifty years—if then. If they are lucky, they discard the comfortable, closed Sunday-school image of religion that they brought with them and embrace a less cozy and open-ended orientation.

More to the point, the intellectual, ideological, and experiential content of theological education is constantly changing. Scholarship involving religious literature, history, philosophy, and so forth moves in irregular fits and starts. It is like a gigantic snowfield in the mountains, much of the time flowing imperceptibly like a glacier but occasionally dashing forward like an avalanche. Over a short period of time, it looks very stable and unchanging. From a longer perspective, it never appears the same at all.

Accordingly, what a contemporary seminary cohort encounters will be different in many ways from what its colleagues experienced as recently as ten years earlier. The place of women in ministry is actually one of the best examples of this principle. *The extent to which the seminary experience involves an encounter with religious feminist ideas varies greatly with the dates of attendance.* Up to about the 1960s, the place of women in the churches tended not to be an object of inquiry. While virtually everyone acknowledged that most local churches would wither away if the women withdrew their support and labor, it was also considered common knowledge that ordained pastoral and denominational leadership was really the province of men. Few people—men or women—challenged those assumptions. By the late 1960s and early 1970s, those postulates came under pressure that has continued up to the present.

The "atmosphere" in theological seminaries became much more highly charged with feminist thought during the 1970s. Enrollments of women rose sharply (e.g., Lehman 1985, 11–15). Female students developed local women's caucuses and other types of groups in order to present an organized challenge to traditional assumptions about their place in the church. They attacked the prevalence of exclusive male language in religious literature, liturgy, and structure. They pressed seminary administrators for major alterations of the seminary curriculum in the direction of women's interests. They lobbied for seminaries to recruit women as regular faculty. They pressed their denominational administrators to redress similar grievances and to appoint women to posts of significant leadership at the denominational level. And in setting this movement into motion, they showed early on that they had learned from the social unrest of the 1960s. Their strategies sometimes took the form of strident demands; they did not always offer polite requests. And they succeeded in opening many organizational doors that previously had been closed to them.

There is usually a division of labor in social movements just as there is in social organizations. Not everyone is capable of contributing to the overall success of the operation in the same way. By the late 1970s and early 1980s, the feminist thrust in the seminaries took on a different complexion. One group of women had challenged the seminaries and the churches in a variety of ways during the decade preceding. Using both rational discourse and emotional shock tactics, they had succeeded in shaking loose numerous sexist assumptions and had begun to raise the level of consciousness of people in religious institutions. However, in the process their pressures for immediate change had also alienated some church leaders and lay members. It was time to consolidate those gains, and it was up to the next set of seminary cohorts to accomplish that goal.

By the 1980s many seminary curricula had been restructured to incorporate women's issues, the purge of noninclusive language was progressing well, seminary faculties included at least a few female scholars, and mainline Protestant ministry placement systems incorporated at least equal opportunity norms if not some form of affirmative action. At least on paper, many of the objectives feminist seminarians had pursued in the previous decade had been attained at least in part. The seminary faculties still had a few reactionary individuals on board, but their voices had been silenced somewhat by the shift in prevailing norms. Individual courses had been scrutinized to ferret out vestiges of sexism. The curriculum contained courses that explicitly concentrated on feminist concerns.

Finally, the type of students had changed. Instead of small numbers of female students who entered immediately following an undergraduate education, the seminaries had increasing numbers of older women and men, many of whom had already raised their family and were embarking on new interests—even a second career. The proportions of women increased dramatically, frequently exceeding 50 percent of the student body. Not only did the age distribution of female seminarians change, but also the tone of feminist discourse settled down. The need for strident voices had passed. The 1980s saw a decline in feminist militancy and an increase in consolidation of gains and a form of collective bargaining. The marchers and demonstrators of the 1970s had succeeded in getting the attention of seminary administrators and denominational leaders. A new system was emerging and moving toward institutionalization. Feminism in seminary was still far from the promised land. But the gains of the past had created a new situation and were calling for different strategies. *And the extent to which feminist thought was a part of routine seminary discussion had increased markedly.*

Because of these shifts in the place of feminist values in mainline Protestant seminaries, it is useful to compare the respondents' seminary cohort with the place cultural feminism had in their ministry styles. We placed the ministers into "cohorts" based on their stated dates of graduation from seminary, using the cutting points discussed above—before 1970, 1971 to 1980, and since 1980 (see table 5.9). These dates correspond roughly to the period prior to the initial concerted feminist pressure, the decade of the initial gains, and the period of institutionalization and redefining goals. At least ninety percent of both racial/ethnic and white groups completed seminary. More racial and ethnic clergy did not complete a formal theological education. And more racial/ethnic ministers than white clergy completed their seminary work in more recent periods.

Table 5.9. Minister Groupings by Cohort
(Graduation Date from Seminary)

	Racial/Ethnic (%)	White (%)
Since 1980	42	36
1971–80	26	35
Before 1971	23	25
Did not graduate	10	4

Cross-tabulation of seminary cohort with ministry style scores indicates that some of the dimensions of approach to ministry previously found related to sex are also associated with seminary cohort. Ministers who completed seminary prior to the 1970s tended to use more power over the congregation (gamma = -.11), to be more involved in social issues (gamma = -.11), to prefer more rational structure for making decisions (gamma = -.19), and to be more legalistic ethically (gamma = -.10) than those in more recent seminary classes. None of these correlations are very strong, but they are statistically significant and are consistent with some of the relationships noted in chapter three. The increasing prevalence of feminist thought at theological seminaries is associated with graduates who are less inclined to use power, less rationalistic, less legalistic, and less socially involved.

Cross-tabulating ministry style with sex, while controlling for seminary cohort (see table 5.10), specifies the effects of seminary cohort even further. The most general pattern in the table is that *the more recently a minister finished theological seminary, the more likely sex is to predict approach to ministry.* Among ministers who completed seminary prior to 1971, only one dimension of ministry style was associated with sex; more women than men were involved in social issues. In the next two cohorts, sex differences predict four and five dimensions of ministry style respectively—ethical legalism, rational structure, and congregational empowerment in both of them, and using power over congregations and involvement in social issues in one each.

Calculations of the mean ministry-style scores tends to reinforce this picture as shown in table 5.11, which lists the scores by cohort and by sex. The general patterns in the table are as follows:

1. The overall tendency is for the ministry-style scores of males and females to *diverge* in the more recent seminary cohorts. The men become relatively more masculine, and the women become the more feminine in approach to ministry.

Table 5.10.   Correlations (Gamma) between Ministry Style and Sex of Clergy, Controlling for Seminary Cohort

Dimension of Ministry Style:	Before 1970	1971–80	Since 1980
Power over congregation	—*	-.17	—
Empowerment of congregation	—	.27	.24
Formal authority	—	—	—
Interpersonal style	—	—	.29
Preaching style	—	—	—
Status criteria	—	—	—
Social issue involvement	.32	—	.35
Rational structure	—	-.31	-.58
Ethical legalism	—	-.26	-.35

*Statistically nonsignificant correlation.

Table 5.11.   Mean Ministry Style Scores of Male and Female Clergy by Seminary Cohort

Dimension of Ministry Style	Males			Females		
	Before 1970	1971–80	Since 1981	Before 1970	1971–80	Since 1981
Power over congregation	.06	.08	-.40	-.29	-.41	-.44
Empowerment of congregation	.58	.61	.37	.83	1.06	1.10
Formal authority	.15	-.08	.27	.00	.16	-.25
Interpersonal style	2.33	2.18	1.61	2.44	2.43	2.46
Preaching style	-.26	-.19	-.07	.00	-.33	-.31
Status criteria	.33	-.08	-.02	.12	.08	.23
Social issue involvement	-.18	-.21	-.1.24	.06	.01	-.18
Rational structure	.21	.34	.51	-.47	-.15	-.68
Ethical legalism	.38	.36	.55	.06	-.12	-.14

2. However, there is a *con*vergence of style between men and women on their willingness to use power over their congregations.

3. *Both* men and women tend to diverge in recent cohorts concerning their approaches to congregational empowerment, desire for formal authority, preaching style, rationality in decision making, and ethical legalism.

4. But it was mainly the *men* who differ from one cohort to the next in matters of the use of power, interpersonal style, criteria of clergy status, and involvement in social issues. The women differ less than the men from one cohort to the next on these dimensions of ministry style.

5. As noted above, sex differences in ministry style are found primarily in the recent two cohorts of seminary graduates.

Similar patterns emerged from a comparison of seminary cohort with the number of hours clergy spend in specific role activities (see table 5.12). As is the case with the self-description items, there are no significant differences between men and women concerning time spent in specific roles among those who completed their theological education prior to 1971. For those in the 1971–80 group, men tended to spend more time than women in teaching formal classes, visiting church members, and involvement in community-wide activities. Among ministers who graduated since 1980, more men than women spent large amounts of time in sermon preparation and delivery and teaching classes, while those men tended to spend *less* time than women in church fellowship activities and in church structures beyond the congregation. (There were no such consistent differences between men and women in various cohorts concerning the relative importance they placed on those roles.)

Table 5.12. Correlations (Gamma) between Time Spent in Clergy Roles and Sex of Clergy, Controlling for Seminary Cohort

Hours spent in roles	Before 1971	1971–80	Since 1980
Sermons	—*	—	-.15
Funerals	—	—	—
Teaching classes	—	-.21	-.19
Visitation	—	-.16	—
Counselling	—	—	—
Church Fellowship	—	—	.26
Administration	—	—	—
Other church structures	—	—	.28
Community activities	—	-.13	—
Personal development	—	—	—
Social issues	—	—	—

*Statistically nonsignificant correlation.

Note the central pattern in these variations, that is, *it is the differ-ence between male and female clergy that increases as seminary cohort became more recent*. This shift might indicate that the presence of feminist ideas on campus was quite selective in its influence. Probably not all stu-dents present at the seminaries during a given period of time internal-ized feminist values to the same extent. The women appear to have internalized the cultural feminist perspective more than did the men. This interpretation would imply that having changes in the seminary curriculum, course content, and so forth is not sufficient to bring about universal adoption of feminist values. It isn't just a matter of head learning. If the increased prevalence of feminist thought on campus simply led to students soaking it up when they encountered it, then the men in the sample would have reflected it in their ministry as much as the women. But that doesn't seem to be what happened.

Instead, as feminist ideas and values became a part of seminary curricula, they also became integrated into a campus feminist subcul-ture, an integrated set of patterns for thought, feeling, and action focused on feminist values. Participation in that subculture most likely appealed far more to women students than to men. In fact, in many cases the women's caucuses and other feminist interest groups that arose on seminary campuses tended explicitly to exclude male stu-dents. Some members came to view these structures as training grounds for raising the consciousness of female students concerning sexist elements in the seminary, in denominational policies and prac-tices, and even in Christian tradition in general. It wasn't helpful to have men around. Accordingly, it is hardly surprising to find that sub-sequent to graduation from seminary during the 1970s and 1980s, some women manifested more feminist thought in their approach to ministry than did the men.

This interpretation also accounts for the relative absence of male-female differences in ministry style among clergy who completed sem-inary prior to the 1970s. Up to the 1970s, feminist ideas and values were relatively absent from seminary culture. The late 1960s was the time when a few women began the assault on religious sexism there. The feminist subculture, which now composes a part of the scene on most mainline seminary campuses, had not crystalized and was not a force to bifurcate the seminary years into masculine and feminine learning experiences. During that early period, if a woman embarked on a theological education, she did so on traditional men's terms—sex-ist language and theology, the stigma of occupational deviance, occu-pational marginality, and the danger of tokenism. In order to navigate theological education successfully, these earliest pioneer women had to think and act like men in a man's world. They developed their conception of ministry in the terms that predated their arrival—as men had defined and practiced ministry before them. As they then in fact succeeded as pastors in those terms following graduation—they were all pastoring churches at the time of this undertaking —once again it is not surprising to find few ways in which their ministry style differed from that of their male colleagues.

The question of how much *individual* students change their orientation to ministry during seminary education, that is, have it become more "masculine" or more "feminine," remains an open one. Since we do not have data on how students changed during their seminary years, this question will have to be addressed in future research.

Some observers might argue that these relationships are merely an artifact of age more than of seminary cohort, but the analysis does not support that interpretation. Age is significantly associated with but one dimension of ministry style, criteria of status (gamma = .13). Furthermore, age is not related to any dimension of approach to ministry when seminary cohort is held constant. We appear to be dealing with cohort effects more directly than with age per se.

Number of Years in Current Position

The final situational factor to be examined is "tenure"—the number of years the ministers had been serving their present church. To measure that variable, we simply asked them to tell us how long they had been in their present position (see table 5.13). For both racial/ethnic and white clergy, the median cases fall in the category of three to four years. Nevertheless, there was a significant difference in time in position between the racial/ethnic and white ministers. Ministers in racial/ethnic groups tended to display longer periods of service in their present position than did the WASP clergy.

Cross-tabulating job tenure with ministry style scores reveals a pattern similar to that obtained when examining seminary cohort (see table 5.14). That is, male and female ministers differed in approach to ministry more if they had been in their present position for a relatively short period of time. Among those who had been serving their present church for seven years or more, sex is predictive of only one dimension of ministry style, wanting rational structure for decision making. More men than women approached decisions in that way.

However, clergy who had been serving their present church for no more than six years differed by sex on six dimensions of ministry style. This was especially the case concerning using power over the congre-

Table 5.13.   Distribution (Percent) of Years Serving Present Church, by Race/Ethnicity

Years in Position	Racial/Ethnic	White
Less than 1	7	12
1–2	19	22
3–4	24	24
5–6	15	16
7–8	8	10
9–10	7	2
11 or more	21	13

Table 5.14.   Correlations (Gamma) between Dimensions of Ministry Style and Sex of Clergy, Controlling for Job Tenure

Dimension of Ministry Style	Up to 2 years	3–6 Years	7 years or More
Power over congregation	-.26	-.21	—
Empowerment of congregation	.34	.24	—
Formal authority	—*	-.23	—
Interpersonal style	—	—	—
Preaching style	-.24	—	—
Status criteria	—	.25	—
Social issue involvement	.32	—	—
Rational structure	-.45	-.49	-.26
Ethical legalism	-.30	-.33	—

*Statistically nonsignificant correlation.

gation, seeking to empower the laity, preferring rational structures for decision making, and being legalistic. It was also the case when considering wanting formal authority, preaching style, status criteria, and involvement in social issues. In each instance, the men manifested a more "masculine" stance than did the women.

We also compared the male/female dichotomy to time spent in role activities and importance placed on them (see table 5.15). As you see, there is no clear pattern of relationships based on tenure. Instead the significant associations appear relatively randomly in one tenure category or another. This outcome suggests that time in present position was not an important factor in men's and women's involvements in (or importance of) various clergy roles.

Table 5.15. Correlations (Gamma) between Hours Spent in Clergy Roles, Importance Placed on Clergy Roles, and Sex of Clergy, Controlling for Years in Position

Hours in Roles	Up to 2 years	3–6 years	7 years or more
Sermons	—*	—	-.23
Funerals	—	—	—
Teaching classes	—	—	-.18
Visitation	-.23	—	-.28
Counselling	.23	—	—
Church Fellowship	—	.11	-.33
Administration	—	-.17	—
Other church structures	—	—	—
Community activities	—	—	—
Personal development	—	—	—
Social issues	.32	—	—
Importance Placed on			
Sermons	—*	-.32	—
Funerals	—	—	.50
Teaching classes	—	—	—
Visitation	—	—	—
Counselling	—	—	—
Church Fellowship	—	—	—
Administration	—	—	—
Other church structures	.22	.36	.31
Community activities	—	.24	—
Personal development	—	.22	—
Social issues	.32	.30	.28

*Statistically nonsignificant correlation.

Patterns among Racial/Ethnic Clergy

The results of examining the effects of situational and background characteristics on approaches to ministry discussed above pertain to the white ministers. The effects of race and ethnicity noted in chapter 4 dictated separating white and racial/ethnic groups for analytical purposes. Even with more than four times as many WASP clergy as racial/ethnic clerics, some of the desired breakdowns described among the WASPs are difficult to implement, because the numbers of cases in certain analytical categories become quite small. With fewer than one hundred racial/ethnic ministers in the sample, it is even more difficult to explore the effects of situational and background factors on their ministry styles. In fact, in some cases the numbers become so small as to be totally inadequate as an analytical basis for generalization. Nevertheless, a few patterns are discernible in the analysis of racial/ethnic clergy, and we discuss them briefly here.

Table 5.16 contains the results of correlating ministry style scores with respondents' education, family income, church size, and community size. Racial/ethnic clergy with high levels of formal education tended to manifest the more "masculine" approaches to ministry. Formal education is negatively related to congregational empowerment, to having an open interpersonal style, and to accepting feminine basis of clergy status. It is positively related to manifesting ethical legalism. Racial/ethnic ministers with high levels of formal education tended to be more masculine in ministry style than those with fewer educational accomplishments.

A similar pattern emerges from comparisons of family income and approach to ministry scores. More high-income respondents than persons with low incomes exhibited closed and defensive interpersonal style, high emphasis on preaching, desire for rational structure, and ethical legalism—all "masculine" approaches to ministry.

Church size and community size are predictive of fewer aspects of ministry style, but where relationships appeared they tend to be in the same direction—working with large congregations and location in

Table 5.16. Correlations (Gamma)* between Ministry Style and Selected Situational and Background Characteristics of Minority Clergy

Dimension	Education	Family Income	Church Size	Community Size
Power over congregation	—†	—	.19	-.19
Empowerment of congregation	-.19	—	—	-.17
Formal authority	—	—	—	—
Interpersonal style	-.27	-.17	—	—
Preaching style	—	.20	—	-.12
Status criteria	-.30	—	—	—
Social issue involvement	—	—	.14	—
Rational structure	—	.19	—	—
Ethical legalism	.19	.24	—	—

*Statistical criterion: $p < .10$.
†Statistically nonsignificant correlation.

large communities were more associated with masculine style than feminine.

The major grounds for claiming a pattern in these relationships among the racial/ethnic ministers is *consistency*; in every significant correlation but one (community size and congregational empowerment), being a well-heeled and highly educated pastor of a large church in a large community is associated with exhibiting a "masculine" approach to ministry. Nevertheless, the reader should note that the correlations are neither strong nor all encompassing, so they should be interpreted with caution.

We also compared these four background variables with the relative importance racial/ethnic ministers placed on role activities and the amount of time actually spent in them (see table 5.17). The overall pattern in the results tends to reinforce the one obtained in table 5.16, that is, there tends to be a consistency in the direction of the relationships involved in the four factors. Highly educated clergy tended to emphasize teaching formal classes and actually spent more time doing it. Education is also associated with an emphasis on church fellowship, but either the more educated pastors tended to downplay visitation, or the less-educated ones tended to do more of it.

Table 5.17. Correlations (Gamma)* between Ministry Style and Selected Situational and Background Characteristics of Minority Clergy

Hours Spent on	Education	Family Income	Church Size	Community Size
Sermons	—†	—	.22	—
Teaching classes	.10	—	.16	—
Church Fellowship	—	—	—	-.23
Administration	—	.11	.24	-.29
Other church structures	—	—	—	-.28
Personal development	—	—	—	.23
Importance Placed on				
Teaching Classes	.32	—	.25	—
Visitation	-.43	-.20	-.16	—
Counselling	—	—	-.15	—
Church fellowship	.20	—	—	-.31
Administration	—	.20	—	-.11
Personal development	—	-.31	—	—

*Statistical criterion: $p < .10$.
†Statistically nonsignificant correlation.

High income racial/ethnic ministers tended to place high importance on church administration, and they indicated that they spend
more time at it. They also indicated that they placed relatively low
importance on visitation and on personal development.

Church size affected racial/ethnic ministers' use of time in some
ways, as we saw when examining the WASP clergy. The larger the
congregation, the more time the clergy spent in church administration,
preaching, and teaching formal classes. This pattern also appears in
relation to the level of importance they placed on teaching. However,
the opposite situation appears concerning visitation and counselling.
Pastors of large racial/ethnic churches tends to place *little* importance
on visiting members and prospects and on personal counselling.

Finally, racial/ethnic ministers working in large communities
tended to differ from their small-town counterparts concerning their
involvements in several specific clergy roles. The more urban ministers
tended to place high degrees of importance on church administration
and church fellowship, and they similarly tended to spend more time
in those activities. Those in large communities also tended to spend
more time working in church structures beyond the local congregation, and they appeared to devote *less* time to personal development.

Summary

The role situational and background factors played in the relationships between sex differences and approach to ministry varied widely
among the white ministers. Some such variables that have proven
important in other research on the religious scene, factors such as
region of the country, age of clergy, and family income, did not appear
to be useful in this undertaking.

Other factors were but marginally useful in predicting ministry
style. Differences in community size were of limited utility in predicting approach to ministry, with the possible exception of anticipating
that ministers in large communities would have to spend a bit more
time and energy on social issues, personal counselling, and church
administration. Differences in levels of formal education were also
associated with some specific role activities—counselling, church
administration, community involvement, and social issues. It seems as
though the external realities of large, urban churches with highly educated multiple staff called upon those ministers to concentrate on matters with which clergy in other situations (solo pastors with standard
credentials in smaller churches located in smaller communities) did
not have to deal as often.

Differences in size of congregation appeared to set limits on the relationship between sex differences and approach to ministry. The minister's sex was considerably more predictive of divergent ministry styles in large churches than in small ones. The dimensions that have reappeared at each stage of the analysis—use of power, congregational empowerment, formal authority, involvement in social issues, ethical legalism—were associated with sex differences mainly in the larger churches. This pattern also resembles that obtained when examining the effects of placement as "senior pastor," implying that the two outcomes reflect similar sets of realities and/or that the two sets of people are really but one.

The level of education obtained by the ministers' spouse was not very useful in explaining differences in ministry style. However, the nature of the spouse's occupation was related to the clergymembers' approach to ministry in some intriguing ways. Status of occupation of clergymen's wives was related to the men's ministry style, but the same did not apply to female clergy and their husbands' occupations. Conversely, whether or not the female minister's husband was working at all was predictive of her approach to ministry, but there was no such pattern for the men in relation to their wives working. Those patterns of family situations apparently influencing approach to work beg for further explanation, but they must be addressed in some future undertaking.

The year in which ministers completed their formal theological education was also an important factor in the association between sex differences and approach to ministry. Men and women differed in ministry style primarily if they finished seminary relatively recently. There were very few sex differences in approach to work among clergy who graduated from seminary prior to the 1970s. These patterns could have been artifacts of the introduction of feminist thought into seminary life during the 1970s and 1980s, ideas that obtained a hearing from more women than men. Or the cohort effects could have reflected a simple selectivity of persons with preexisting orientations that they brought to the seminary years. Prior to the 1970s and 1980s, both men and women "made it" on men's terms. After feminist values became a part of seminary culture, men and women could develop their approaches to work in more sex-specific terms.

Job tenure—length of time serving one's present church—was also related to ministry style and sex. Sex of minister was predictive of approach to ministry mainly among persons who had *not* been in their present position for a long time and primarily in relation to the clergy self-description scores (the "like-me" items).

Given the small number of racial/ethnic ministers in the sample, it was not possible to carry out as elaborate an analysis as was done with the WASP clergy. Nevertheless, four factors did appear to influence the racial/ethnic pastors' approach to ministry—formal education, family income, church size, and community size. These background characteristics were predictive of both some ministry style scores and levels of involvement in several specific clergy roles. Other background variables were either unrelated to differences in approach to ministry among the racial/ethnic subsample or involved too fine a breakdown in relation to the limited sample size.

These results further reinforced the point that the relationship between sex of clergy and approach to ministry is very complex. It is anything but a matter of women and men having divergent ministry styles simply because they are women or men. The approach ministers take to their work results from an elaborate interplay of forces, only one of which is the biological fact of sex and its psychological corollaries. Do men and women manifest different ministry styles? *It depends.* It depends on their ethnic community, the type of position they have, the size of church in which they work, the ministry cohort in which they find themselves, their relationships with their spouse, and the length of their tenure in their present position. And, of course, it depends on what you mean by "approach" to ministry or "ministry style." What applies to one aspect of the work of the ministry does not necessarily pertain to another dimension. Simplistic and facile assertions to the contrary simply do not square with the evidence.

6

The View from the Pew

THERE IS AN INTERESTING "parlor game" that is sometimes also played in therapy groups. The activity involves members of the group taking turns writing down some terms that they think describe themselves, while the other members of the group write down terms they would use to describe the individual under consideration. Quite predictably some glaring discrepancies emerge when the self-description is compared with the perceptions of others. In therapy sessions those divergences become devices for use in enhancing the individual's personal growth. Among friends in parlor games the same discrepancies can be deadly to relationships!

The act of comparing our self-images with the perceptions of others is something we all do at some level of consciousness during much of our waking life. And it isn't merely a "game" at all. It is a fundamental part of being human. We learn very early in life that other people develop ideas of what we are like and that it can be important to know what their perceptions are. They can constitute a healthy "reality check" on our various egocentricities.

Cross-checking Clergy with Lay Perceptions

Comparing self/other perceptions can also be a useful research strategy. We sought to employ a variant of this kind of "reality check" in this study of male and female approaches to the ministry. We supplemented the clergy's self-descriptions with the perceptions their members had of them. That is, we asked lay members of the churches in the sample *the same set of descriptive questions about their pastor as we had asked of the ministers themselves.* This step produced data for use in making direct comparisons between clergy self-descriptions and lay perceptions of those same ministers. Those comparisons allowed us to check for lay corroboration of clergy statements about their approaches to ministry. The central question was simply whether or not laypersons saw their pastor in the same ways as the pastor saw him/herself. The analysis also sought to identify other factors that explained variations in the way lay church members viewed their minister.

The Process of Person Perception

Asking church members to indicate the extent to which various concepts accurately describe their pastor is to ask them to engage in a specific act of "person perception": What is your minister like? Is he/she like this or that? What does she/he value highly? and so on.

Person perception has been defined as "the forming of judgements about other people...as social animals" (Cook 1979, 2). Most of us take for granted our ability to "size up" other people. We do it all the time. It seems so simple. But the concepts involved in Cook's definition of the process open up a wide range of subtle distinctions that should disabuse us of any simplistic ideas about it. In truth the process of perception appears to be an extremely complicated matter, one that social and behavioral science is just beginning to understand, a process that can produce results that say as much about the perceiver as the person perceived.

One of the most common *mis*conceptions of the process is that it is a *passive* matter, that is, that people perceive objects "as they really are" in much the same way as a tape recorder picks up sound and a camera records pictures, as though the sound or the image "out there" is simply recorded in our ears or eyes and thus is perceived. The problem with that assumption is that it clearly does not square with our actual experience. We in fact do not hear every sound reaching our ears. We pay attention to some of the sounds and ignore others—we select out the ones in which we are interested and disregard the others as noise. Similarly, we rarely see every image that in fact is before our eyes. We focus on particular light sources—again, those in which we are interested at the moment—and we treat as background other things that are equally "out there." If asked later on about other things that were in fact there to be seen, but objects on which we did not focus at the time, we rarely can remember them.

So perception is very active, not passive. We *select* things to hear, see, feel, and so forth. People are not passive recorders of anything; they are active agents selectively relating to experiences of various objects. This selectivity applies to the process of perceiving other people just as much as to the act of perceiving other objects. As Cook (1979) argues, person perception involves the "forming of judgments" about people, not merely the recording of images.

Another aspect of the "activity" involved in human perception is classification. Perception is not synonymous with mere "sensation." As we encounter objects, we do not relate to them as "raw input data" received from the object. We respond to a *series of categories* or classifications of objects that fit the object we are experiencing. For example, when meeting another human being walking down the sidewalk, our emotional and behavioral responses to that encounter depend very heavily on which of a series of categories we place the person in. First, the fact that we note that it is a "person" we meet, not an inanimate object such as a fence post or a mannequin, sets boundaries on our reaction. Then whether we classify the person as male or female, young or old, attractive or ugly, married or single, and on and on—all help determine how we deal with the person we perceive. Our reaction is based largely on what we have learned is "appropriate" for dealing with individuals who fall within the categories that apply. Again—Cook's definition—person perception involves "the forming of judgments" about people.

Finally, perceiving "persons" involves more than sizing up what is immediately available to the senses. It is done by the use of "trait words," which are terms that summarize past behavior of people and predict their future behavior. These trait concepts also involve evaluations of the characteristics in question and thus also of the person perceived (Cook 1979, 5). Our ideas of other people are rarely restricted to readily observable traits like height, weight, skin color, and mode of dress. We think of people more centrally in terms of things *we cannot observe directly*—for example, degrees of intelligence, patriotism, honesty, trustworthiness, humility, diligence, and so on. These traits tend to be the attributes that make human beings "persons" and result in our liking or disliking them, hiring or rejecting them, wanting to be with them or to avoid them. The definition specified that person perception of people dealt with them "as social animals" (Cook 1979, 2). The characteristics of people as social animals are not immediately available to the senses. These "invisible" characteristics, as we "perceive" them, come to us as a result of complex *judgements* we make based on many bits of discreet information we receive and then compare with our mental "file cabinet" of things we have experienced in the past.

So the process of "forming judgments about other people...as social animals," a matter of making judgments about traits we cannot observe directly but must infer from other things that we select out to notice, can be fraught with difficulty. The end result can say as much (or more) about the perceiver as the one being perceived. It can be correct or incorrect. Accuracy is by no means guaranteed, but instead seems to be related to identifiable characteristics of the perceiver, factors such as age, intelligence, personality, length of relationship with the person perceived, and so forth (Cook 1979, 127–32).

Social psychologists have identified at least four general factors that influence the process of person perception. Those determinants are (McDavid and Harari 1974, 203–4)

1. characteristics of the person perceived
2. characteristics of the perceiver
3. the relationship between perceiver and perceived
4. the situational context

In this study we have already presented data indicating that the persons perceived, that is, the pastors, differ widely according to a number of statements they have made about themselves. While it is true that we have no guarantee that those clergy statements are accurate (the ministers are, after all, but perceivers of themselves), the self-descriptions do provide a base line of data against which to compare the perceptions of the lay members.

Up to this point, the characteristics of the lay perceivers of the clergy are not known. We know only that they are all church members who have been identified by their pastor as "lay leaders" in their congregation. We know that they are divided about equally by sex. And we know that they have interacted rather extensively with the clergyperson serving as their pastor, an aspect of the relationship between perceiver and perceived. Finally, we know little about the broader situational contexts within which the lay members report their perceptions. Perhaps the one contextual factor that is known will be an important one—that is, they are responding to a stranger who has written to them asking a wide range of questions about their preacher, and the denominational leaders have encouraged them to cooperate with the research and tell what they think their pastor is like. Will they "be a snitch" if they have some negative images of their minister, or will they seek to protect him/her instead? There is no way to know for sure.

The Lay Survey

The survey of lay church members asked them to indicate their perceptions of their pastor. The structure of the survey was quite straightforward. The names of the lay members, first of all, were provided by the clergy in the study. At the end of the telephone conversation with each minister, the interview contained the following request: "One last item of business—the names of two laymembers. As outlined in the letter we sent you, we need the name and address of two laypersons you regard as leaders in the congregation—one man and one woman. Can you give me that information now please?" The information was recorded on a form containing the same identification number as the minister being interviewed so that the three persons could be linked directly in subsequent analysis. The request was for persons the ministers considered "leaders in the congregation," because the goal was to obtain perceptions of pastors from members who knew them well. We assumed that lay members identified by their pastor as "leaders" would have worked relatively closely with the minister and thus would know him/her better than lay members who were more marginal to the congregation.

In May 1990, the lay leaders whom the clergy had identified received a questionnaire, a letter explaining its use, a letter from a denominational leader encouraging participation in the survey, and a postage-paid return envelope. The initial mailing was followed up with two post cards two to three weeks apart as reminders for nonrespondents. The response data indicate that the level of lay cooperation in each denomination was quite satisfactory (see table 6.1). The overall response rate of 86 percent would imply that nonresponse bias is not likely to be a problem. Furthermore, using "time of response" as an indirect indicator of nonresponse bias (nonrespondents tend to resemble late returns more than early ones), the only variable indicating problematic degrees of representativeness was race/ethnicity. Members of racial/ethnic congregations did not respond as fully as did persons in white churches (gamma = -.29). While this outcome is not desirable, it does resemble the results often obtained when collecting data from members of racial/ethnic groups in the United States, so it is

Table 6.1.   Patterns of Response to a Survey Questionnaire by Lay
Church Members in Four Protestant Denominations

Denomination	Initial Sample	Number of Replies	Percent Replies
Baptist	252	215	85
Methodist	262	217	83
Presbyterian	230	207	90
United Church of Christ	260	225	87

Total response rate = 86%

not atypical. We assumed that in other ways the returns were representative of the target sample.

The questionnaire contained measures of laypersons' perceptions of their pastor, those questions being direct parallels to the items contained in the clergy interviews. For example, the ministers had been asked the extent to which the following statement was "like them":

I make my major contribution to my congregation through my preaching.

The questionnaire for the lay members asked the respondent to indicate how much the following statement was like their pastor:

He makes his major contribution to my congregation through his preaching.

Similarly, the lay members were asked to indicate how many hours they thought their minister spent in each clergy role activity considered in the clergy survey. The same applied to their perceptions of how much importance their pastor placed on each role.

Finally, the forms sent to the lay members were sex-specific in terms of the sex of their pastor. That is, for example, lay members of congregations served by female clergy were asked how much the following statement resembled that clergywoman:

She (emphasis added) will often bend church rules if they don't meet the needs of the congregation.

Members of churches served by men, on the other hand, were asked to respond to the parallel statement about their pastor:

He (italics supplied) will often bend church rules if they don't meet the needs of the congregation.

Both of these versions parallel the statement on the interview form previously administered to the clergy:

> I often will bend church rules if they don't meet the needs of the congregation.

Index Construction

Since the objective in analyzing the lay data was to make direct comparisons to the clergy data, the study incorporated composite measures of the various dimensions of ministry style. Those indexes were constructed in exactly the same manner as the measures utilized in the analysis of the ministers' responses. The same subsets of items from the laity as from the clergy were combined to create the composite measure of each dimension of approach to pastoral ministry:

willingness to use power over the congregation
desire to empower the congregation
seeking positions of formal authority
openness of interpersonal style
preaching emphasis and style
criteria of clergy status
involvement in social issues
preference for rational structure in decision making
ethical legalism

The extreme low and high scores on each index are collapsed to ranges that matched those observed in the clergy data (to facilitate direct comparisons discussed below).

The frequency distributions of lay members' scores on those composite measures (table 6.2) indicate, first of all, that the lay members' perceptions of each dimension differed widely. As was the case with the clergy, some lay members perceived their pastor in very "masculine" terms, while others perceived the minister in a more "feminine" mode. (This does *not* mean that the gender distinctions were involved in their own consciousness, for most of them probably would not have conceptualized the differences in those terms.) Accordingly, as was the case among the clergy, we have succeeded in demonstrating that each dimension indeed involves a "variable." The lay members did differ in how they perceived their pastor, and some of those variations paralleled the conceptual distinctions found in the cultural feminist arguments.

Table 6.2. Frequency Distributions (Percent) of Index Scores Describing Lay Church Members' Perceptions of Their Pastor's Approach to Ministry

Dimension of Approach:	Collapsed Scores*									
	-3	-2	-1	0	1	2	3	4	5	6
Power over congregation	29	17	17	15	11	6	6			
Empowerment of congregation		21	19	15	18	14	12			
Formal authority	12	13	15	18	15	12	16			
Interpersonal style		14	7	11	10	12	10	10		
Preaching style		19	20	24	37				10	
Status criteria		25	17	21	15	10	13			17
Social issue involvement		32	18	16	14	19				
Rational structure		9	9	21	26	35				
Ethical legalism		5	9	16	24	46				

*Score categories at either extreme were collapsed to match the range of scores obtained from the clergy.

The distributions also indicate that some scores are more evenly distributed than others. Lay perceptions of their pastor's interpersonal style and desires to be in positions of formal authority, for example, appear to have been spread fairly evenly across the range of scores. There was little tendency for a majority to lean one way or the other. Their views of other clergy characteristics, on the other hand, tended to be skewed in one direction. Most members tended to see little clerical use of power over the congregation. Conversely, they perceived a lot of "rationalism" and "legalism" in their minister.

In table 6.3 we have a summary of the results of asking the lay members about their perceptions of how much time their pastor spends in each clergy role activity and how much importance they thought their minister placed on each. Recognizing that such judgments would be difficult for some lay members to make, the issue of time spent in each role was introduced on the questionnaire as follows:

> The role of "parish minister" can be broken down into specific types of activity, such as preaching, counselling, visiting, etc. Listed below are several of those activities. As you come to each one, please indicate *how many hours you think your minister spends in that activity during a typical week.*
>
> YOU WILL PROBABLY NOT *KNOW* ANY OF THESE ACTIVITIES *FOR SURE.* WE ARE INTERESTED IN *WHAT YOU THINK*—YOUR BEST GUESS.

As was the case with the clergy (see chap. 2), there is wide variation in the numbers of hours indicated for each role activity. On every role except sermon preparation and delivery, several members thought their pastor didn't spend *any* time in that activity. And the maximum hours listed for each role ranges from a low of twenty for involvement in social justice issues to a high of sixty-three hours per week spent in local community affairs.

The average numbers of hours spent in each role also roughly parallel the patterns observed among the clergy themselves. Lay church members tended to perceive their pastor spending a great deal of time in sermon preparation and delivery, church administration, and visitation. They perceived rather little time spent by ministers in dealing with funerals, social issues, and teaching. Again, note that we are dealing with "variables." Not all lay church members perceived their pastor's use of working time in the same way.

The matter of asking the lay members how much *importance* they thought their minister placed on each of these roles was introduced on the questionnaire as follows immediately after the listing of roles in relation to the number of hours members thought the minister spent in them:

Table 6.3. Patterns of Lay Church Members' Perceptions of Pastor's Role Performance and Priorities

Role Activity:	Low Hours	High Hours	Mean	S.D.*
Sermons	1	48	9	5.9
Funerals	0	21	2	2.1
Teaching classes	0	51	3	2.7
Visitation	0	58	8	5.9
Counselling	0	56	6	5.6
Fellowship	0	57	4	3.7
Administration	0	59	9	7.7
Other church structures	0	61	4	4.0
Community activities	0	63	4	4.0
Personal growth	0	50	5	4.2
Social issues	0	20	2	2.5

Role Activity	Degree of Importance					
	0	1	2	3	4	5
Sermons	0.2	0.5	1	8	26	64
Funerals	1	6	12	28	26	27
Teaching	2	8	15	32	28	16
Visitation	1	6	12	24	25	32
Counselling	0.5	3	7	21	32	37
Fellowship	0.5	3	10	32	33	21
Administration	0.2	4	13	28	33	22
Other structures	2	6	16	32	31	13
Community	2	10	20	36	22	10
Personal growth	0	2	8	28	35	27
Social issues	2	9	20	29	22	18

*Standard Deviation

Now let's go over the same list in a different way. This time when you come to each activity on the list, please tell me *how important* that activity is to your minister.

Use a scale of "0" thru "5."
let "0" = not important to him/her at all,

1 = only the slightest bit important
2 = a bit more important
3 = more important to him/her than not
4 = quite important, but not the highest
5 = extremely important to him/her.

AGAIN, YOU PROBABLY WILL NOT *KNOW* THE ANSWER TO EACH
ONE *FOR SURE.* WE WANT TO KNOW *WHAT YOU THINK*—YOUR
BEST GUESS.

In considering the results of obtaining those lay estimates, two patterns emerge as noteworthy (see table 6.3). First, it is clear that the lay members thought their minister placed considerable importance on *all* of the roles. The distributions of responses are all highly skewed in that direction. Within that pattern, nevertheless, it is also apparent that the roles were differentiated in terms of importance. The role perceived as having the greatest level of importance placed on it is preparation and delivery of sermons, an activity that tends to be central to the work of ministers in these denominations. Roles perceived as relatively subordinate include involvement in local community activities, participation in church structures beyond the congregation, teaching formal classes, and involvement in social justice issues. Again, concerning each role, we have demonstrated that the lay members' perceptions vary widely. Now we turn to the central question involved in collecting these data in the first place. Are any of these differences perceived by laypersons related in any way to the descriptions the ministers gave of themselves?

Comparing Scores of Clergy and Lay Members

We compared the scores manifested by clergy and lay respondents on the composite measures of dimensions of ministry style (see table 6.4). In the comparisons the clergy scores are based on the ministers' *self-*descriptions, while the lay scores indicate their members' *perceptions* of the ministers. The correlations simply comparing the clergy and the laity *as groups,* the left-hand column in the table, indicate that they sometimes differed widely concerning the pastor's approach to ministry. More clergy than lay members portrayed the pastors as using power over the congregation, as seeking to empower the congregation, as attuned to masculine criteria of clergy status, and as highly involved in social issues. Conversely, the lay members were more inclined than the clergy to depict the pastors as highly rational and structured in decision making and as legalistic in ethical and moral choices.

We can only speculate about why these (sometimes strong) differences emerged from these comparisons of ministers and lay members. The explanation that seems most immediately applicable is that the ministers and lay members were playing by slightly different rules—that is, were applying somewhat divergent criteria for responding to

Table 6.4. Correlations (Gamma) between Composite Measures of Lay Perceptions of Pastor's Ministry Style, Clergy Self-Descriptions, and Sex of Ministers and Members, by Race/Ethnicity

Dimension of Ministry Style	Clergy vs. Lay as Groups	Sex of Clergy		Sex of Lay Member			Regression*	
		Racial/ethnic	White	Racial/ethnic	White	Race	Clergy Sex	Lay Sex
Power over congregation	.52	-.52	-.07	-.22	-.11	—	-.07	-.07
Empowerment of congregation	.37	—	—	—	.13	—	.06	.08
Formal authority	—†	-.20	—	—	—	-.09	—	—
Interpersonal style	—	.30	—	—	.17	.06	—	.11
Preaching style	—	—	—	—	—	-.09	—	—
Status criteria	.18	.19	—	—	—	—	—	—
Social issue involvement	.17	—	.16	—	.15	-.09	.09	.08
Rational structure	-.57	—	-.11	—	-.16	-.08	—	-.09
Ethical legalism	-.65	—	-.18	—	-.22	—	-.08	-.10

*The regression coefficients are standardized betas.

†Statistically nonsignificant correlation.

the "like-me" ("like-him/her") items. The clergy were probably trying to be straightforward in their efforts to describe their own ministry styles. The lay members, however, confronted with a set of subtle questions about their pastor and having been asked by that person to participate in the survey, most likely also tried to make their minister "look good." No doubt, both groups tried to describe the pastor as they themselves saw him/her. But when confronted with ambiguity, the lay members probably skewed their portrayals of their minister in what *they perceived* to be a more socially desirable direction—indicating very little "meddling" with the congregation, not excessively ambitious occupationally, not a "do-gooder," highly rational and structured in work, and using the "correct" criteria for making moral decisions. *There is probably more social-desirability bias in the lay data than in the clergy responses.*

Perceptions and Ethnicity

Before proceeding to the analysis of sex differences, it is important to examine the effects of race/ethnicity on lay perceptions of clergy. Race was sufficiently important in the breakdown of the clergy data to control for its effects in all analyses of the pastors' self-descriptions (chap. 4). It proved necessary to take the same step in examining the members' data. Comparisons of race/ethnicity of lay members with the measures of their perceptions of the pastors' approach to ministry indicate that on most dimensions *racial/ethnic group members tended to describe their minister in more masculine terms than did the WASP members.* This pattern emerges in the analysis of all composite measures except congregational empowerment, clergy status criteria, and ethical legalism. The size of those correlations range from .13 to .24, with a median of about .17. Very similar results were obtained from the analysis of race/ethnicity and lay perceptions of the ministers' time spent in clergy roles and the importance they place on those activities. Racial/ethnic members tended to view their pastor as spending more time in most of the roles and as placing greater importance on them than did the WASP members. Those coefficients range in size from .07 to .33, with a median of about .21. The greater tendency for members of racial/ethnic groups than whites to describe the pastor's approach to ministry in relatively "masculine" terms appeares in *both* data sets, that is, the laity saw the same differences as did the clergy themselves. Accordingly, it was necessary to hold race/ethnicity constant in subsequent analyses of the lay perceptions of clergy ministry styles.

Sex and Perceptions of Clergy: Composite Measures

The remainder of table 6.4 concerns the role that sex of clergy and of lay members played in the portrayals of differences in ministry style as measured by the composite indices of the "like him/her" items. The most central question, of course, is whether lay church members perceived their pastor's approach to ministry differently depending on whether their minister was male or female. One of the factors supposedly affecting person perception is the characteristics of the person being perceived—in this case the sex of the pastor. Is that so in this case?

White Members

Among the white members, sex of clergy is significantly predictive of pastor's ministry style on four dimensions—willingness to use power over the congregation, involvement in social issues, desire for rational structure, and ethical legalism. In each case the members tended to perceive "masculine" approaches to ministry in male ministers and "feminine" approaches in female ministers. This result is identical to that observed in the data from the clergy themselves, except that minister's sex also predicted the ministers' self-descriptions concerning congregational empowerment. Thus, *the lay perceptions tend to corroborate the self-reports of the pastors, and the sets of relationships among both lay and clergy tend to be in the direction predicted by the cultural feminist argument.*

The sex of the lay member is also associated with their perceptions of the pastor's ministry style, in this instance on all dimensions but three—desire for formal authority, preaching style, and criteria of clergy status. More *men* than women saw their pastor as using power over the congregation, desiring rational structure in decision making, and ethical legalism. More *women* than men viewed their minister as seeking to empower the congregation, having an open interpersonal style, and being involved in social issues. *Thus the women tended to perceive feminine qualities more than the men, and the men saw more masculine traits than the women, regardless of whether the pastor was male or female.* (Maybe the women also perceived these traits as the more desirable ones.)

Racial/Ethnic Members

The results of correlating ministers' sex with the *racial/ethnic* members' perceptions of their pastor differ from the outcome among WASP members. As shown in table 6.4, there is a strong association between sex differences of pastors and perceptions of the use of power over congregations, much stronger than that observed among white members. Male clergy were perceived as using power more often than female clergy. The same applies to wishing to be in positions of formal authority, which was perceived in male pastors more often than females. Racial/ethnic members also tended to perceive women ministers as having a more open and vulnerable interpersonal style than men ministers. And the racial/ethnic members perceived the traditional masculine criteria of clergy status more often in men than in women. All of these correlations are stronger than those observed in the analysis of the data from white members.

However, the sex of the racial/ethnic lay *member* is *not* very predictive of perceptual differences. Racial/ethnic men tended to perceive willingness to use power over the congregation more in clergymen than in clergywomen. But sex of member is not significantly associated with any other composite measure of members' awareness of the pastor's ministry style. Thus it appears as though white church members tended to project their own gender onto the object of perception *more* often than members who were a part of a racial or ethnic group.

Multivariate Analysis

So which of these factors—race/ethnicity, sex of minister, sex of lay member—is actually useful in predicting lay church members' perceptions of the pastor's ministry style? Any of them? All of them? To address this issue, the analysis turned to a set of multiple regression equations. (For the reader who is relatively unfamiliar with multivariate statistics, multiple regression produces a coefficient that represents the effect of a variable on a dependent variable when the effects of all other factors in the equation are held constant. In this case, the dependent variable is a score on a dimension of perceived ministry style, and the predictor variables are race/ethnicity, sex of clergy, and lay member sex. The larger the coefficient, the greater the effect of that factor on the dependent variable. (For a non-technical explanation of the technique, see Kerlinger 1979, chap. 11.)

The last set of columns in table 6.4 shows the results of the regression analysis. Race/ethnicity is predictive of five dimensions—formal authority, interpersonal style, preaching style, involvement in social issues, and ethical legalism. In each case the racial/ethnic group was the more identified with perceptions of "masculine" approaches to ministry, reinforcing patterns observed in earlier stages of the analysis. The beta coefficients representing the effects of minister's sex also tend to be consistent with previous findings, that is, male clergy are associated with "masculine" approaches and female clergy with "feminine" approaches involving scores on the dimensions of power over the laity, congregational empowerment, involvement in social issues, and ethical legalism. Finally, sex of lay member is predictive of perceptions of pastor's ministry style on all dimensions except formal authority, preaching style, and status criteria, reinforcing the correlations reported above. Each variable—race/ethnicity, sex of clergy, lay sex—predicts variations in some lay perceptions of clergy approach to ministry independently of the effects of the other two variables.

Sex and Perceptions of Clergy: Role Activities

The analysis also compared the sex of clergy and lay members to differences in lay persons' perceptions of the number of hours the pastor spent in clerical roles and how much importance he/she placed on them. The results of those cross-tabulations indicate that *the sex of both the perceiver and the perceived played a part in what the members reported* (see table 6.5)

White Members

The sex of the pastor is predictive of lay perceptions of time spent in several clergy role activities. Male ministers were seen as spending more time than females in sermon preparation and delivery, visitation, personal counselling, and local church administration. However, the opposite was the case involving social justice issues, where women were viewed as spending more time than men.

Lay perceptions of the *importance* the pastor placed on various clergy roles also differed according to the sex of the minister. Male pastors were observed as placing greater importance than females on dealing with sermons, teaching formal classes, and church administration. As above, the perceived sex differences reversed when considering other roles—more women than men were described as placing great importance on involvement in church structures beyond the congregation, personal development and growth, and social justice issues.

When the focus shifted to the *sex of the observers* —the lay members—a slightly different picture emerged. Male and female members differed in their impressions of the amount of time the pastor spent in

only three role activities: church administration, personal development and growth, and social justice issues. In each case females tended
to see the pastor as more active than did males. There are no significant differences between men and women concerning perception of
time spent in the other roles. The reported perceptions change dramatically, however, when the question deals with the degree of *importance*
the pastor placed on each role. On all roles but three (sermons, visitation, and church fellowship), women described their pastor as setting
greater importance on each pastoral role than men. So as was the case
when examining the scores on the various dimensions of ministry
style (table 6.4), *more lay women than lay men reported "positive" qualities
in their pastor regardless of the sex of the pastor.*

Racial/Ethnic Members

The picture that racial/ethnic lay persons gave of their perceptions of
their minister's involvements in clergy roles is quite different from
that obtained from the WASP members (above). On the one hand,
racial/ethnic members perceived their pastor as spending more hours
in most clergy roles if the minister involved was a *man.* Female pastors
were seen as less active than males. On the other hand, however,
almost no sex differences emerge in the analysis of the rest of the
racial/ethnic data. Sex of minister fails to predict the importance
racial/ethnic members think their pastor places on all clergy roles but
one, involvement in community affairs. The sex of the racial/ethnic
lay *members* is associated with perceptions of time the pastor spent in
only one clerical role, church fellowship. And sex of member is unrelated to perceptions of the degree of importance racial/ethnic ministers place on each role.

Multivariate Analysis

Finally, the possible effects of race/ethnicity, sex of clergy, and sex of
member on perceptions of clergy role involvements were subjected to
a multiple regression analysis (see table 6.5). A few fairly consistent
patterns emerge from that examination. First, as was the case when
analyzing the "like-him/her" data (above), each predictor variable—
racial/ethnic identity, minister's sex, member's sex—is related to differences in perceptions of involvements in some roles more than others. None of those relationships are very strong, and the amount of
variance explained in each equation averages only about 2 percent.

Table 6.5. Correlations (Gamma) between Lay Perceptions of Pastor's Involvement in Clergy Roles and Sex of Ministers and Members, by Race/Ethnicity

	Sex of Clergy		Sex of Lay Member		Regression*		
	Racial/ethnic	White	Racial/ethnic	White	Race	Clergy Sex	Lay Sex
Hours Spent in Roles							
Sermons	-.09	-.06	—	—	—	-.10	—
Funerals	-.23	—	—	—	—	—	—
Teaching classes	—†	—	—	—	-.11	—	—
Visitation	—	-.09	—	—	—	-.08	—
Counselling	—	-.08	—	—	-.09	-.09	—
Church Fellowship	—	—	-.08	—	—	—	-.08
Administration	-.17	-.19	—	.09	—	-.13	—
Other church structures	-.19	—	—	—	-.08	—	—
Community activities	-.15	—	—	—	—	—	—
Personal development	-.21	—	—	.14	—	—	.09
Social issues	-.28	—	—	.08	-.15	—	.07
Importance of Roles							
Sermons	—†	-.10	—	.19	—	—	—
Funerals	—	—	—	.10	—	—	.12
Teaching classes	—	-.11	—	—	-.13	-.08	—
Visitation	—	—	—	—	—	—	—

Table 6.5. (Continued)

Hours Spent in Roles	Sex of Clergy		Sex of Lay Member		Regression*		
	Racial/ethnic	White	Racial/ethnic	White	Race	Clergy Sex	Lay Sex
Importance of Roles							
Counselling	—	—	—	.11	—	—	—
Church Fellowship	—	—	—	—	-.09	—	—
Administration	—	-.13	—	.12	-.12	.07	.07
Other church structures	—	.12	—	.12	-.08	—	.07
Community activities	.21	—	—	.11	-.10	—	—
Personal development	—	.13	—	.15	-.08	.08	.11
Social issues	—	.19	—	.16	-.12	.12	.10

*Coefficients are standardized betas.
†Statistically nonsignificant correlation.

Second, race is associated with a few differences in perceptions of time pastors spend in clergy roles. Race is even more predictive of differences in lay descriptions of the importance their pastor placed on those roles. And in every instance where the relationship is significant, members of racial and ethnic groups attributed to their minister greater involvements in the role than did the white members.

Next, sex of pastor is predictive of but a few lay perceptions. *Male* clergy were seen as spending more time than females in dealing with sermons, counselling, visiting, and church administration. The opposite was the case concerning the degree of importance the members thought their pastor placed on other roles, that is, female clergy were seen as placing greater importance than males on involvement in church structures beyond the congregation, personal development and growth, and social justice issues.

Finally, the sex of the lay member is related to lay perceptions of clergy involvement in some professional roles. Where this was the case, female members tended to see their pastor as more involved in the role than did the male members.

Linking Members with Specific Pastors

The analysis up to this point in this chapter has concentrated mainly on the characteristics of lay church members' perceptions of ministers' approaches to ministry and whether the differences in those descriptions are explained by race/ethnicity, sex of minister, and lay sex. There has been a general tendency in the results of that examination to corroborate the self-descriptions of the ministers. That is, laypersons in congregations served by men showed a slight tendency to describe their pastor's ministry style in masculine terms, while members of churches led by women depicted their pastor in a more feminine mode. These outcomes lend some empirical support to the cultural feminists' arguments.

The remainder of this chapter will involve a different approach to the relationship between clergy self-descriptions and lay perceptions. The analysis involves a series of direct *comparisons between the self-portraits of the ministers and the perceptions of the lay members specifically from the churches they serve.* Using the identification numbers associated with the congregations involved in the study, it was possible to make direct linkages between the data obtained from the ministers and lay members of each particular congregation. This coupling enabled us to compare the lay perceptions with the self-descriptions of the specific individual they were trying to describe. The question that analysis sought to address, of course, was whether there was any correspondence between the pastor's self-description and the perceptions specifically of his/her members.

Comparisons Using the Composite Measures

The initial results of making those comparisons are interesting. The left-hand columns of table 6.6 indicate the extent of disparity between clergy and lay scores, controlling for ethnicity. The figures show the average results of subtracting the members' perception scores from the "like-me" scores obtained from their pastor, that is, the median differences across each set of comparisons. The results indicate that *there is relatively little deviation of the lay perceptions from the clergy self-images.* Among the white clergy and members, most of the medians are zero—on average the members tended to perceive their pastor very much as he/she had perceived self concerning formal authority, interpersonal style, preaching style, status criteria, and social issues. The pastors' scores average one point higher than the lay member scores on using power over the congregation and seeking to empower the congregation. Thus the ministers portrayed themselves as seeking to control the congregation and seeking to empower it slightly more than their members perceived. At the opposite extreme, the members perceived their pastor as wanting rational structure for decision making and being legalistic slightly more than did the minister. The basic patterns among the members of racial/ethnic groups are very similar, with the exception of additional deviations concerning criteria of clergy status and involvement in social issues.

The next set of columns in table 6.6 portray the results of correlating the ministry-style scores of pastors and their specific members, controlling for ethnicity. Among the WASP members and clergy, the correlations indicate a positive association between clergy self-portraits and lay perceptions on all dimensions of ministry style but three—congregational empowerment, preaching style, and ethical legalism. The same patterns emerge from the correlations using the racial/ethnic-group data; the associations are positive, but the significant relationships involve fewer dimensions of ministry style. In no cases are there negative relationships in either group.

The results are equally clear when the analysis involves controls for ministers' sex. For both male and female pastorates, most of the medians are zero—on average the members tended to perceive their pastor very much as he/she had perceived self concerning formal

Table 6.6 Comparisons of Lay Church Members' Perceptions of Pastors' Ministry Style with Self-Descriptions of Their Specific Minister, by Race/Ethnicity and Sex

Dimension	Median Difference between Member and Pastor Scores*		Correlation of Member and Pastor Scores		Median Difference between Member and Pastor Scores*		Correlation of Member and Pastor Scores	
	Racial/ethnic	White	Racial/ethnic	White	Clergymen†	Clergywomen†	Clergymen†	Clergywomen†
Power over congregation	1	1	.22	.09	1	1	—	.11
Empowerment of congregation	1	1	.13	—	1	1	—	—
Formal authority	0	0	—‡	.20	0	0	.18	.21
Interpersonal style	0	0	—	.15	0	0	.16	.13
Preaching style	0	0	—	—	0	0	—	—
Status criteria	1	0	.39	.12	0	0	.11	.14
Social issue involvement	1	0	.27	.24	0	0	.22	.25
Rational structure	-1	-1	—	.08	-1	-1	—	.12
Ethical legalism	-1	-1	—	—	-1	-1	—	—

*A positive number indicates that the minister's score was higher than that of the members; a negative number indictes the opposite.

†Majority group members only.

‡Statistically nonsignificant correlation (gamma).

authority, interpersonal style, preaching style, status criteria, and social issues.

The final set of columns in table 6.6 portrays the results of correlating the ministry-style scores of pastors and their specific members, controlling for the sex of the minister. Where members were served by female clergy, the correlations indicate a positive association between clergy self-portraits and lay perceptions on all dimensions of ministry style but three—congregational empowerment, preaching style, and ethical legalism, the same ones that emerges among whites in general. The same patterns emerge from the correlations using the data from situations involving male pastors. The associations are positive, but the significant relationships involve fewer dimensions of ministry style—formal authority, interpersonal style, criteria of clergy status, and involvement in social issues. There are no negative correlations in either group.

In summary, then, it is safe to say that *especially in white churches and those served by women, the members tended to perceive their pastor's approach to ministry concerning the "like-me/him/her" items in terms very similar to those in the pastor's self-portrait.*

Comparisons on Clergy Role Activities

The analysis performed the same types of comparisons between lay perceptions and clergy statements involving the number of hours the ministers spent in clerical roles and the degree of importance they placed on them. The general patterns in the results are quite similar to the comparisons of the responses to the "like-me" items (see table 6.7). The columns on the left-hand side of the table show the median differences between clergy statements and lay perceptions of clergy role involvements while controlling for race/ethnicity. The first thing to note in those figures is that there are very few differences between the racial/ethnic and white responses. Second, it is clear that there are fewer discrepancies between pastors' statements and lay descriptions when the question is on the relative importance the minister placed on the roles than when it was on the matter of hours spent in each one. The median hours divergence is typically zero in relation to the stated importance of the roles, while it is minus one pertaining to time spent performing them. The negative difference between the time clergy said they spent on the roles and the perceptions of the lay members indicates that the lay members tended to attribute more time devoted to the role activities than the pastor stated him/herself. This is especially the case in relation to hours spent in visitation by racial/ethnic clergy and hours devoted to personal counselling on the part of white ministers. The one exception to this pattern involved preparation and delivery of sermons among racial/ethnic ministers. In that instance the ministers indicated that they spent more time dealing with sermons than their members gave them credit for.

The next set of columns in table 6.7 indicates the correlations (gamma) between the descriptions of role involvements by particular clergy and their specific members, holding race/ethnicity constant. Most noteworthy in the figures is the fact that even though the correlations between clergy statements and lay perceptions are not very strong, they are positive and do cover almost every role. *The lay members tended to perceive their pastor's role involvements in ways that resembled the statements of the pastor him/herself more often than not.* That pattern appears to hold more consistently among white members than persons in racial/ethnic congregations. However, the possibility that white-racial/ethnic difference in the number of statistically significant correlations could be an artifact of the fact that the number of cases in the racial/ethnic sample is much smaller than in the WASP group. Finally, the distribution of the *non*significant coefficients suggests that clergy involvement in certain roles is somewhat difficult for lay members to perceive accurately. That seems to be the case particularly in relation to the pastor's involvement in personal development and growth and, to a less extent, concerning working with funerals and involvement in church fellowship activities. Perhaps the lay members have a greater chance to perceive the pastor's activities correctly in those role activities that are the more "public" or readily observable ones (Royle 1991).

The analysis next performed the same kinds of comparisons of clergy role involvements as above, only this time controlling for sex of pastor and including only the white cases. The results of those comparisons are contained in the right half of table 6.7. The median differences between clergy statements and lay perceptions, once again, are relatively small. That is especially the case concerning the degree of importance ministers placed on each role. Only in the cases of funerals and teaching classes did the pastors indicate that they placed greater importance on the role than did the lay members. And there were virtually no differences in the results obtained from members served by male and female ministers. On the matter of the number of hours pastors spend in each role activity, the general tendency was for the lay members as a group to perceive very similar amounts of time as that indicated by their pastor or to attribute more time in the role than the minister had reported. That kind of overestimate of time by lay persons was especially the case in relation to clergy involvement in per-

Table 6.7. Comparisons of Lay Church Members' Perceptions of Pastors' Involvements in Clergy Roles with Ministers' Self-Reports, by Race/Ethnicity and Sex

Clergy Roles	Median Difference between Member and Pastor Scores*		Correlation of Member and Pastor Scores		Median Difference between Member and Pastor Scores*		Correlation of Member and Pastor Scores	
	Racial/ethnic	White	Racial/ethnic	White	Clergymen	Clergywomen	Clergymen	Clergywomen
Hours in Activities								
Sermons	1	0	.21	.16	1	0	.20	.13
Funerals	-1	-1	—†	.24	-1	-1	.16	.28
Teaching classes	0	0	.23	.27	0	0	.29	.26
Visitation	-2	-1	—	.21	-1	-1	.19	.22
Counselling	-1	-2	—	.27	-2	-2	.29	.25
Church Fellowship	-1	-1	—	—	-1	-1	—	—
Administration	-1	-1	.29	.19	-1	0	.19	.18
Other church structures	-1	0	—	.13	0	0	—	.10
Community activities	-1	-1	.29	.27	-1	-1	.29	.27
Personal development	-1	-1	—	—	0	-1	—	.17
Social issues	-1	-1	.15	.19	-1	-1	.14	.23
Importance of Activities								
Sermons	0	0	—	.29	0	0	.20	.13
Funerals	1	1	—	—	1	1	.16	.28
Teaching classes	0	1	.23	.20	1	1	.29	.26
Visitation	0	0	.30	.22	0	0	.19	.22

Table 6.7. (Continued)

Hours in Activities	Median Difference between Member and Pastor Scores*		Correlation of Member and Pastor Scores		Median Difference between Member and Pastor Scores*		Correlation of Member and Pastor Scores	
Clergy Roles	Racial/ethnic	White	Racial/ethnic	White	Clergymen†	Clergywomen†	Clergymen†	Clergywomen†
Importance of Activities								
Counselling	0	0	.29	.14	0	0	.13	.15
Church Fellowship	0	0	—	.14	0	0	.11	.17
Administration	0	0	—	.08	0	0	.12	—
Other church structures	0	0	.23	.20	0	0	.12	.22
Community activities	0	0	.42	.26	0	0	.27	.25
Personal development	0	0	—	—	0	0	—	—
Social issues	0	0	.65	.27	0	0	.27	.25

*Positive numbers indicate clergy involvement greater than lay perceptions; negative numbers signify the opposite.

†White majority members only.

‡Statistically nonsignificant correlation.

sonal counselling. The one exception to that pattern involved sermon preparation and delivery, where clergymen stated that they spent more time than the lay members perceived.

Finally, the correlations between lay perceptions and clergy statements of role involvements indicate that the church members tended to perceive the same degrees of activity and prioritization as had been indicated by their pastor. All of the correlations were positive, they involved almost every possible relationship, and there were few if any differences in the responses of persons in churches served by male and female pastors.

As was the case involving the comparisons of lay and clergy descriptions of the composite measures of ministry style, *the members tended to perceive their pastor's approach to ministry concerning specific clergy roles in terms very similar to those used by the pastor him/herself.*

Summary

Using data collected from lay leaders in the churches served by ministers in the sample, the analysis sought to determine whether those church members would describe their pastor in roughly the same terms as those seen in the minister's self-portrait. Each lay member completed a questionnaire that asked the same questions about the pastor's approach to ministry as had been asked of the clergy themselves. This procedure then permitted direct comparisons between clergy and lay descriptions, item for item and person for person. The "like-me" items were combined into composite measures of the same nine dimensions of ministry style as utilized with the clergy data, and the indices were scored in exactly the same way in each case.

The completion of the questionnaire asking members to describe their pastor's approach to ministry was an exercise in "person perception," a complex process of making judgments about the minister's values, goals, attitudes, use of time, priorities, and so forth. Even though people make such assessments of other people all of the time, the process is difficult at best and can result in wide discrepancies between the perceptions of the viewer and the actual characteristics of the person perceived. So how accurate are the results?

A comparison of the distributions of responses from lay members and pastors *as groups* indicate that there are some different tendencies. On some dimensions the ministers scores are higher than those of the lay members, on others the case is reversed, and on a few there are no significant differences. Those divergences are probably an artifact of the difficulty lay members had in making the judgements and the resulting tendency to give more socially desirable replies than the clergy gave.

Church members from racial/ethnic groups tended to give more "masculine" responses than the white members on all three types of question—the "like-me" items, hours spent in clergy roles, and importance placed on roles. Thus it was important once again to analyze the data from these two groups separately.

The results of cross-tabulating members' perceptions of the pastor's ministry style with the sex of the minister tends to corroborate the reports of the clergy. Thus the analysis provides additional but indirect support for the cultural feminist argument. On some of the same dimensions as appeared in the analysis of the clergy data, "masculine" approaches are more attributed to male pastors, and "feminine" ministry styles are perceived more in female pastors. The sex of the *perceiver* is also predictive of the attribution of gender to the pastor, especially among the white laypersons. Women tended to see more feminine qualities, and men were inclined to see masculine traits, *regardless of the sex of the minister.* A regression analysis of the composite scores with race/ethnicity, sex of minister, and sex of lay member indicated that all three variables independently predict differences in perceptions of the pastor, generally reinforcing the previous correlations.

Both sex of minister and sex of lay member also predict differences in members' perceptions of the pastor's time spent in clergy roles and the importance placed on them. Especially among WASP members, sex of clergy predict perceptions in ways that tend to reinforce the patterns observed in the clergy data. Sex of the lay member also predicts differences in perceptions of pastor's involvements in clergy roles, with female members perceiving more time in several activities and greater importance attached to them than the males observed, again regardless of the sex of the pastor. There are fewer significant patterns among the racial/ethnic-group members. As above, a regression analysis of these variables tends to support the patterns observed in the correlations—race/ethnicity, sex of clergy, and sex of lay member predict variations in perceptions of pastor's role involvements.

The final step in analyzing the lay data involved matching the perceptions of pastor by lay members of specific congregations directly with the self-descriptions of the particular minister involved. Comparisons of the goodness of fit between the two data sets indicates that the lay members were relatively successful in their efforts to describe the pastor's approach to ministry, using the minister's own statements as the norm. More often than not the lay perceptions were sufficiently close to the self-descriptions of their pastor to basically corroborate the patterns in the clergy data. The correlations between the pastor's statements and the members' perceptions are all positive and involve nearly all of the dimensions of ministry style and role activities. Rightly or wrongly, pastors and their members tended to describe the pastor in similar terms.

7

The Big Picture

WE BEGAN THIS UNDERTAKING with what appeared to be a fairly straightforward question. Do female and male clergy approach their work in
gender-specific terms? The issue arose from recent discussions among
religious feminists, some of whom argue that men have developed a
uniquely "masculine" approach to implementing the call to Christian
ministry, while women have a dramatically different ministry style.
Other religious feminists disagree, asserting instead that while the
ministry system developed primarily by men manifests sexist characteristics that must be changed, the most strategic divergences to be
considered reside within the system rather than in sex differences
endemic to the participants.

This debate is an institutionally specific manifestation of similar
discussions taking place within current feminism in general. Among
the highly varied feminist schools of thought are two opposing camps
with seemingly polar sets of assumptions about the nature of women
and men—the "maximalists" and the "minimalists." The maximalists
argue that the sexes are fundamentally different cognitively, emotionally, and behaviorally as a result of the interaction of biological, psychological, and experiential realities that being male or female
involves. These uniquenesses purportedly lead men and women to
take different approaches to a wide variety of issues and problems,
including how they engage in occupational pursuits.

The minimalists, on the other hand, argue that any perceived sex differences in thought, feeling, or action are basically spurious. They assert that seemingly sex-specific characteristics are not endemic to males or females but should be seen instead as consequences of the positions men and women occupy in social structure and of the various forms of exclusion from social participation that such locations tend to produce. To the minimalists there are few demonstrable patterns of human functioning that are uniquely female or male. The sources of what appear to be sex-specific patterns of action are in the socio-cultural system rather than the actors.

Applied to the discussion of the ministry, commentators with a relatively "maximalist" orientation present highly divergent imagery of masculine and feminine approaches to work. They see the traditional "masculine" ministry style as involving clergy who seek to have power over lay persons, who see themselves as authority figures in the church, are defensive and detached in interaction with church members, place too much emphasis on dogmatic preaching, are excessively concerned with their social status, pay too little attention to social issues, are compulsively rationalistic and highly structured in making decisions, and deal with ethical issues in legalistic terms. By contrast they describe the "feminine" ministry style as seeking to empower the laity, eschewing positions of formal authority, interacting with lay persons in open and approachable terms, playing down the importance of preaching that talks "down" to people, pressing egalitarian values, being highly involved in social issues, using intuitive and integrative logic for making decisions, and promoting flexible ethics of responsibility (see Christ and Plaskow 1979; Ice 1987; Nason-Clark 1987; Weidman 1985; Stevens 1989; Hahn 1991; Ochs 1983; Franklin 1986; Ruether 1983, 1985; and Maitland 1983). The "minimalists," of course, deny the existence of such sex-specific ministry styles, and argue that the defining realities are more cultural than psychological.

Who is right? Can we demonstrate empirically that ministers, in fact, differ in these various aspects of how they approach their work? If so, is there also any evidence that the ministry style labeled as "masculine" is found primarily among men, and that the approach designated as "feminine" mainly characterizes the women?

The Evidence

The study approached those questions using data collected by means of structured interviews with a national sample of 517 female and male clergy in four "mainline" Protestant denominations in the United States—The American Baptist Churches, The Presbyterian Church (USA), The United Church of Christ, and The United Methodist Church. The interviews included questions dealing with a wide variety of assertions about how men and women differ in their ministry style, questions derived from specific statements found in the cultural feminist literature. The ministers also indicated how much time they devoted to selected clergy roles and how important they thought each role was for them personally.

The analysis of the clergy responses indicated clearly that *the ministers were not all alike in their approach to their work as pastors.* Some of them described themselves in basically "feminine" terms, while others presented a more "masculine" picture of their approach to ministry. They differed widely on all possible dimensions of ministry style. However, *as a group* the ministers also tended to manifest relatively *feminine* styles of ministry regardless of sex. There appeared to be a feminine slant in their responses. The main reason for that drift was probably the association of the feminine responses with the socially desirable answers. The traits that cultural feminist literature had identified with a "masculine" orientation were often characteristics that one would not see in the "ideal minister." The supposedly masculine attributes were deviations from the ideal. So it is understandable that as a group the ministers prefered to portray themselves more in line with that ideal than as persons deviating from it. Nevertheless, coming full circle, they did differ in their responses, and some appeared to be more feminine than others. The question, then, is how one explains those differences. Does the sex of the minister account for them?

Sex of Clergy and Ministry Style

What appeared at the outset to be a very simple question turned out to involve a very complicated set of issues. In effect, the maximalists (religious cultural feminists) were neither entirely correct nor entirely incorrect. The same applies, of course, to the counterassertions of the minimalists (religious structural feminists). The world of reality would not accept the "total package" of male/female descriptions offered by either camp. Social and psychological reality surrounding variations in ministry style was far more complicated than either of their arguments could contain.

Do men and women differ in their approach to the pastoral ministry? It depends. The answer depends on (1) what aspect of ministry style one is considering, (2) what type of minister one has in mind, and (3) the type of ministry situation with which one is dealing.

Dimension of Ministry Style

Differences in some dimensions of ministry style appeared to be more sex-specific than others. Male and female clergy differed fairly consistently in their:

> willingness to use power over the congregation,
> desire to empower the congregation to manage its own life,
> preference for rational structure in decision making,
> legalistic tendencies when dealing with ethical issues.

The *men* were more prone than the women to use power, prefer rational structure, and approach ethics legalistically. The *women* were more likely than men to try to give the congregation power over its own affairs. In these instances, the analysis tends to *support* the cultural feminist argument.

On the other hand, there was little evidence to support assertions that men and women differed systematically in their:

> desire for positions of formal authority,
> openness and vulnerability in interpersonal style,
> approach to preaching,
> acceptance of traditional criteria of clergy status,
> involvement in social issues beyond the congregation.

There were few (if any) significant sex differences in these areas. There was also intermittent or inconsistent support for the idea that men and women differed in their typical involvements with social issues. These particular results tend to give credence to the position of the minimalists. *In general, then, whether or not men and women can be said to differ in their approach to pastoral ministry depends on which aspect of ministry style one has in mind.*

Type of Minister

The literature in which possible masculine and feminine approaches to pastoral ministry are discussed tends to deal with ministers of either sex in monolithic terms. "Men" are lumped together as one category, and "women" compose the other. Likewise, the concept of "pastor" tends to be seen in an undifferentiated manner. In one sense that pattern is not surprising, because the literature dealing with the question of sex differences is frequently polemical, and oversimplification of categories is a common device in argumentative discourse involving policy and competing interests.

However, that approach to making comparisons between men and women can mask important distinctions that affect one's view of reality and even one's selection of strategies for social change. *Even in relation to the dimensions of ministry style that appeared initially to be related to sex of clergy, additional distinctions concerning the ministers in question were important analytically.*

Race and Ethnicity The racial/ethnic identity of the pastors was more consistently related to variations in ministry style than was the male/female dichotomy. On all dimensions of approach to ministry but one (approach to preaching), racial/ethnic clergy tended to manifest more "masculine" approaches to ministry than did white clergy. This pattern held regardless of sex, that is, racial/ethnic women had more masculine ministry styles than did white women, and the same pattern appeared among the racial/ethnic and white men. What was initially conceptualized in terms of gender (variations in ministry style) was even more strongly related to racial and ethnic differences than to sex differences. Furthermore, the sex differences in approach to ministry that emerged from the initial bivariate analysis, including involvement in social issues, appeared to hold among white clergy but not the racial/ethnic clergy. These patterns tended to support earlier observations that racial/ethnic churches differ significantly from those of whites (e.g., Lincoln and Mamiya 1990). They also reinforced the argument that the arguments of white feminists do not always apply to the experiences of racial/ethnic women (Grant 1989; and Andolsen 1986). It will be important to examine these racial/ethnic group configurations more closely in future research involving samples more adequately sized than was the case here. The balance of this summary will deal primarily with the white clergy, because there were enough cases in that WASP sample to be able to make further distinctions with sufficient assurance that sampling variation will not get in the way. Such was not the case with the sample of racial/ethnic clergy.

Sex and Dimensions of Difference in Ministry Style

The analysis in chapters 4 and 5 indicated that many factors influence possible linkages between approach to ministry and clergy sex differences. It is simply not a matter of all or nothing-at-all. Reviewing the conditions that appear to determine whether or not sex is predictive of ministry style can help conceptualize the complexity that is involved in relation to each dimension. Sex tended to be predictive of differences in four facets of ministry style under similar sets of conditions. Those four dimensions were use of power over the congregation, seeking to empower the congregation, using rational structures for making decisions, and approaching moral issues legalistically. *The results of the study supported the cultural feminist argument in relation to these dimensions of ministry style.*

Use of Power over Congregation   Given the long history of women's subordination and exclusion from positions of power in both religious and secular life, it is not surprising to find religious feminists concerned about the role power plays in the ministry. Even though the ordination of women has been a reality for many years in each denomination participating in the study, there are still fairly frequent instances of clergywomen experiencing lack of power over their own life and work. Most of the time when that subordination takes place, it is at the hands of one or more men acting either as denominational officials or as members of a lay board of the local congregation. Yet it is more of an institutional sexism than a male conspiracy. Some religious feminists, therefore, argue that the practice of abusing power over others is a peculiarly male phenomenon. Fair enough.

However, the analysis of these data indicated that under certain conditions women were as prone as men to use power to get what they want. Men appeared to use power more than women *primarily if*:

they were members of the white majority, not racial/ethnic groups, they were *not* serving as a copastor of the congregation, they were senior ministers in multiple-staff situations, they had graduated from seminary since 1970, *and* they had been serving their present church for no more than six years.

In the absence of these conditions, there were no significant differences between female and male clergy concerning their stated use of power over the congregation. That includes a large number of male and female clergy.

Congregational Empowerment   In contraposition to the perceived tradition of male clergy dominating the life and work of lay church members, cultural feminists have argued that the role of the pastor is to find ways to give lay church members power over their own lives as individuals and as members of a congregation. Women clergy, they say, will be more prone to *give away power* than to seek power for themselves, because their own experience of powerlessness will have sensitized them to the need of lay members to control their own religious life. As persons who have experienced the consequences of others (men) exercizing power over women in particular and over lay church members in general, female clergy will be more inclined than men to seek to rectify that imbalance. Again the analysis showed that sex differences in congregational empowerment emerged from the analysis only in particular circumstances.

Female ministers were more likely than men to try to empower members of their congregation to manage their own collective and private lives *if:*

> they were in the white majority, not racial/ethnic groups,
> they were not serving as copastor of a congregation,
> they were senior ministers in multiple-staff situations,
> they completed seminary subsequent to 1970, *and*
> they had been serving their present church for no more than six
>   years.

A woman also tended *not* to press for congregational empowerment if her husband was unemployed. There were very few significant sex differences in efforts to empower the congregation in the absence of these conditions.

Rational Structure for Problem Solving   The religious maximalists argue that women and men solve problems and make decisions by means of divergent strategies. The current "rational" approach that characterizes decision making in modern organizations is considered a "masculine" one. It involves preference for structure and organization, application of formal logic, concern for order and efficiency in moving toward solutions, or what some term "science." The feminine approach tends to be the opposite of these traits, that is, making decisions by intuition, free and open discussion (or "process"), and unstructured dialogue. The analysis of these data indicates that such was the case only in particular circumstances. Male clergy tended to approach decision making with more rationality and structure than did the women *if:*

> they were *not* serving as copastors of the congregation,
> they were placed as senior ministers in a multiple staff situation,
>   and

they had completed their theological education since 1970, but regardless of length of tenure in their present position and regardless of their racial/ethnic background.

The picture changes if one considers the occupational involvements of the clergy person's spouse. If a clergy*man* had a wife in a high-status occupation, he tended to show little of these masculine tendencies. If the clergy*woman* had a husband who was not employed, she tended to manifest a more *masculine* approach to problem solving.

Legalistic Tendencies   Much of the feminist literature places considerable emphasis on sex differences in dealing with moral or ethical issues. The most common distinction found there portrays "masculine" ethics as concentrating on "duty" and "rules." According to those discussions, the problem for men is to find "the correct answer" by searching through precedents, moral maxims, rules of conduct, and so forth. Male ethics, then, are legalistic ethics. The "feminine" approach to moral issues, on the other hand, revolves around the concept of 'responsible caring'. Regardless of the "rules," the important thing in the latter approach is to focus on the *process* of making the decision (which ideally involves everybody) and on *responsibly caring about the consequences* the judgment will have for the individuals involved. It is a struggle toward finding the best outcomes for people in the community. However, these sex differences do not always appear. As above, men tended to describe themselves in more legalistic terms than women *primarily if*:

they were members of the white-majority group,
they were not copastors,
they were senior ministers in a multiple-staff situation,
they finished seminary since 1970, and
they had served in their present position for no more than six
   years.

There were few sex differences in the pastors' legalistic tendencies in the absence of these conditions.

Involvement in Social Issues   The cultural feminist argument about sex differences among clergy also asserts that male pastors tend to overlook their responsibilities for dealing with social issues. The maximalists' description of the "masculine" approach portrays male clergy as concerned with building up the membership and financial statistics of the local congregation and seeking to meet the needs of their church members. But they view men as having little interest in social issues beyond the concerns of the local church. By contrast, since women have suffered neglect and discrimination at the hands of the masculine system, they are said to identify with the underdogs of society—the oppressed, impoverished, suffering—and they get more involved than the men in efforts to solve those problems in the community at large. The analysis gave *some* support to those assertions but less than that given to the other four dimensions discussed above. Female clergy tended to be more involved with social issues than male clergy *if*:

they were members of the white majority,
they finished seminary either before 1970 or since 1981,
they had held their present position for up to *two* years.

Female pastors also tended to be highly involved in social issues if they were *not* serving as solo pastors, if they enjoyed a relatively large family income, and if they lived in a large community (e.g., a city).

Dimensions Typically Not *Related to Sex* Contrary to the expectations derived from the cultural feminist argument, there were very few conditions under which sex differences predict variations in the other four dimensions of ministry style, that is, wanting positions of formal authority, interpersonal style, approach to preaching, and criteria of clergy status.

1. Formal Authority. More men than women stated a desire for formal authority only if they were senior ministers in a multiple-staff situation.

2. Interpersonal Style. More women than men manifested an open interpersonal style only among senior ministers of multiple-staff charges and among persons who had completed seminary since 1980. Clergy of *either* sex also demonstrated such openness if they enjoyed a large family income and if they were serving a large congregation. Could it be that the social realities of life in "ordinary" solo pastorates are such that ministers simply cannot afford this kind of interpersonal style? Is the feminine ideal of openness in interpersonal relations something that only prosperous senior ministers in large churches can manage? These patterns would be consistent with that configuration.

3. Approach to Preaching. More *women* than men *may* prefer a "masculine" approach to preaching if they *are* serving as copastor.

4. Criteria of Clergy Status. More *women* than men preferred "masculine" criteria of clergy status *among members of racial and ethnic groups.* For the WASP ministers, more *women* than men

preferred the masculine criteria of status *if they were copastors.* More *men* accepted the masculine criteria of status if they had been serving their present church between three and six years.

Again, the relationships between the male/female dichotomy and these four dimensions of approach to ministry were very tenuous. The coefficients were quite weak, and they emerged from the analysis only in highly specific circumstances. The most appropriate conclusion at this point, therefore, is that *divergences in these four aspects of ministry style had little or no relationship to differences between the sexes, and that the cultural feminist assertions were not supported in relation to these aspects of approach to ministry.* The minimalist argument appeared to apply more to these latter dimensions of ministry style.

Sex Differences and Involvements in Clergy Roles

The results of trying to find sex differences in involvement in various clergy roles were also quite mixed. Cross-tabulations of the male/female dichotomy with variations in hours spent in each role and the degree of importance placed on it indicated that some variations in involvement were associated with sex while others were not. Combining the results of examining both hours in role activities and importance placed on them, only six clergy roles appear to be sex-typed. Men were more involved than women in three roles, and the women were more given to the other three. The role involvements that were mainly characteristic of the *male* ministers were:

> preparation and delivery of sermons,
> teaching formal classes, and
> visiting church members and prospects.

The role activities that appeared to involve more women than men were:

> dealing with funerals,
> working in church structures beyond the congregation, and
> dealing with social justice issues.

The male-dominated activities involved roles in which the minister could exercise dominance, authority, and identity as the local leader. By contrast the female-dominated roles were those entailing compassion and caring in the case of funerals and social justice issues. Greater female activity in church structures outside of the local congregation could reflect a greater felt need by women to be involved in denominational programs in order to enhance their visibility in more inclusive church circles. There is also a widely shared perception at various levels of denominational structure that women tend to be *invited* to participate on denominational committees, boards, and task forces more often than men, because women clergy still constitute a minority of clergy (in absolute numbers), and denominational "affirmative action" policies call for them to be represented in official activities. In any case, these patterns tended to fit with common assumptions concerning activities in which one would expect to observe mainly male or female participants.

The clergy role activities in which there seemed to be little or no sex typing were personal counselling, church fellowship activities, local church administration, local community affairs, and personal development and growth.

Conditions Affecting Role Activities

It should be noted, however, that the role activities that tended to involve mainly men or women did not display those characteristics under all circumstances. The various roles were sex-typed *in some conditions but not in others.*

1. The preparation and delivery of sermons primarily involved men if the clergy in question had completed seminary since 1980 and had been in their present position more than two years.

2. Men tended to report heavy involvement in teaching formal classes if they had completed seminary since 1970 and had been in their present position seven years or longer. It also made no difference whether they were serving as copastors or not.

3. Men were the more involved in visitation if they had completed seminary between 1971 and 1980. Males tended to dominate this activity regardless of whether they were long- or short-timers in their present post and whether or not they were copastors.

Other role activities were the provinces of mostly females, but only under certain conditions.

4. Women tended to be the more involved in funerals if they were *not* copastors, if they were appointed as senior ministers in a clergy team, and if they had been in their present position for seven years or longer.

5. Women had more involvements in church structures beyond the local congregation primarily if they were *not* copastors but were senior ministers and if they had completed seminary since 1980. And the women tended to dominate this activity regardless of how long they had been serving their present congregation.

6. Women were more involved in social justice issues than men mainly if they were not copastors but were serving as senior minister in a clergy team. Length of service also did not diminish this relationship.

Corroboration by Lay Church Members

The patterns summarized above derive from an analysis of what the male and female clergy reported about *themselves*—clergy self-perceptions. The study also asked whether those self-reports could be corroborated by the perceptions of members of the churches those ministers served. Did the lay church members perceive their pastor in the same way the pastor perceived him/herself? To pursue that line of inquiry, the project asked two members (one man and one woman) of the congregations involved in the study the same questions about their pastor as had been asked of the ministers themselves. The two parallel data sets then allowed the analysis to make direct comparisons between the clergy and lay responses in a search for agreement.

The lay data tended to corroborate the clergy data. This convergence took several forms. In spite of the fact that the lay members tended to be more generous in their descriptions of their pastor than the ministers were in describing themselves:

1. The sex of the pastor predicted differences in lay members' perceptions of their pastor's ministry style. These relationships between lay perceptions and minister's sex appeared on the same dimensions as observed in the analysis of the clergy data. The laity perceived more male pastors than females as willing to use power over the congregation, as rational and structured in approach to decision making, and as legalistic ethically. Lay members also perceived more female pastors than males as

seeking to empower the congregation and as highly involved in social issues.

2. The sex of the pastor predicted variations in lay members' perceptions of their minister's involvements with various clergy role activities. These lay perceptions included many of the the same role activities as had appeared sex-typed in the analysis of the clergy data. The members perceived male pastors as the more involved in preparation and delivery of sermons, visiting church members and prospects, personal counselling, local church administration, and teaching formal classes. They described women ministers as the more committed to participation in church structures beyond the congregation, personal development and growth, and social justice issues.

3. Directly matching the perceptions of the lay members in specific congregations with the self-reports of their particular minister indicated that the central tendencies of the ministry style scores of the two groups tend to be similar. Comparisons of the matched lay and clergy scores also produce positive correlations of scores on willingness to use power over the congregation, desire for formal authority, interpersonal style, criteria of clergy status, involvement in social issues, and desire for rational structure for decision making.

4. Directly matching the perceptions of the lay members with the self-reports of their particular minister indicate positive correlations on degrees of involvement in virtually all clergy role activities.

The lay members tended to perceive their pastor's approach to ministry in terms quite similar to those reported by the ministers themselves. The correlations were not very strong, but they were notedly consistent. This pattern thus lent indirect support to the cultural feminist argument, but only in relation to the specific facets of ministry style identified above.

Implications of the Specifying Conditions

Three of the above specifying conditions are particularly noteworthy. By "specifying conditions" we mean factors that identify some conditions under which the associations between sex differences and ministry style will vary—which partly determine whether or not such relationships will appear. Those three factors are (1) whether or not the pastor was serving as "copastor" with another person, (2) whether the minister's appointment was as "senior minister" in a team of two or more clergy serving one congregation, and (3) the cohort in which the minister experienced a theological education. These three elements appear to set fairly consistent lines of demarcation between circumstances in which sex of minister is predictive of approach to ministry and when it is not.

Whether or Not Serving as Copastors

Time and again the results of the analysis indicated that there were few (if any) sex differences in ministry style among clergy serving as copastors. The differences between male and female clergy in the use of power, desire to empower, use of rational structure, and ethical legalism showed up instead among ministers who were *not* copastors. There was something about the explicit egalitarianism of the copastor arrangement that suppressed most sex differences in ministry style. What was it that has that effect? Was the key element the fact that most copastors were *married couples* who had been called to serve one congregation together as equals? Did this type of placement *selectively attract* persons who define ministry in androgynous terms? Did the informal negotiating about role responsibilities that goes on when copastors enter a field *promote* consensus about one's ministry style? Is the key something to be found among the *lay members* who recruited and installed couples as their pastors? While we know that the distinction was important in specifying conditions under which sex differences in ministry style emerged, we do not know why. This issue should be addressed in some further investigation involving a more adequate sample of copastors than was available in this undertaking.

Whether or Not Appointed as Senior Minister

The same point applies to clergy having an appointment as senior minister in a team of two or more clergy serving a single congregation. The ministerial staff structure in which one person was defined the "senior pastor," the "minister in charge," the "head of staff," the "first in team," (or similar title) was more common than the copastor arrangement discussed above. Where one person was identified as the "senior" minister, that individual was assumed to be in a position of authority over other clergy on the staff, and those others would typically have had the title of "associate minister" or "assistant minister" or a title specifying a particular function, such as "minister for education" or "minister of music." Generally those other ministers were subordinate to the senior minister. In most instances this type of staff structure was clearly hierarchical in nature. So it was a logical opposite type from the copastor arrangement.

It is interesting to note that occupying the position of senior minister was also related to the opposite pattern of association between sex differences and ministry style. While being a copastor was associated with a pattern of androgynous approaches to the pastorate, *being a senior minister involved some of the clearest instances of sex typing of approach to ministry*. Among senior ministers, sex predicted differences in *more dimensions* of approach to ministry than among persons in other types of appointment, and those correlations tended to be *stronger* than observed with other positions. These patterns among senior ministers provide support for the maximalist's arguments about sex differences.

Furthermore, among *women* (much more than among the men) there were clear differences concerning power, authority, and interpersonal style between senior and solo pastors. Women in senior-minister positions tended to manifest a more "feminine" approach to ministry than women working all alone as pastors. Clearly there was something about being in the superordinate position in a ministry team that predicted differences in the way men and women identified their ministry style. What was that "something"? And why did it make more difference for women than for men?

One is tempted to argue that the pattern simply derives from the structural effects of occupying a superordinate position. The norms associated with being the "senior minister" specify different behaviors from those associated with solo pastorates. Senior ministers typically specialize in some clergy roles, leaving other role activities, for example, religious education, some committee work, visitation, youth work, and music, to other ministers on the staff. Solo pastors rarely have the luxury of such role specialization. The senior-pastor structure allows for unique work patterns.

Perhaps so, but this doesn't really address the findings, because occupying the senior position had *opposite effects for women and men*. Male senior ministers were more "masculine" in their approach to ministry, while female seniors were more "feminine." Yet they both occupied the same type of structural position. And comparisons of the ministry styles of solo pastors with those of senior pastors indicated clear differences among the women but not among the men. Since the structural location is the same for male and female senior ministers, focusing on the structure alone is not satisfactory. The structure is manifestly the *same* for both men and women, and one cannot explain a variable in relation to a constant. Any explanation of the relationships between type of placement, ministry style, and male/female distinctions must deal with the *interaction* of these variables rather than just the effects of the separate factors by themselves.

Note once again that there was no significant correlation between senior and solo appointees among *either* men or women when considering preference for rationality in decision making and the matter of ethical legalism. These two dimensions of ministry style showed sex typing in previous analytical categories but not in this one. Why? Perhaps this difference relates to the fact that mode of decision making and approach to ethics tend to be rather "private" (or "internal") actions for the minister, while matters of power, empowerment, authority, and interactional style involve more *open and public* relationships with the congregation. Perhaps habits of intrapersonal functioning are less likely to be affected by holding appointments of different power and prestige than are tendencies to relate overtly to people in a manner that also assumes superordination and subordination.

Could the patterns associated with the senior pastorate simply be an extension of the ways in which the women and men have "made it" in becoming senior pastors in multiple-staff situations? By traditional criteria of success in clergy careers, they have "arrived." Is it possible that the incumbents then simply continue the same approach to ministry in the senior position as they used in getting there through lesser appointments? For men it would be a traditional "masculine" approach, something that they learned and successfully implemented as their career developed. For women it would be a more "feminine" approach, something that they also have mastered and carried out in their work. But for both of them it would also have to be a matter of executing their approach to ministry in a way that was also acceptable to the congregations involved, of relying upon modes of behavior that would have brought positive response from lay church members to tell the pastor that he/she is doing the job in ways they approve of. The relative security of the senior appointment (allowing for some idiosyncrasy) and the reinforcement of past actions would then encourage the senior pastor to continue the things that seemed to work in the past. The men would continue to carry out their masculine approach, and the women would work within their more feminine style. Perhaps. However, if this "explanation" alone were the case, then one would also expect to see more sex differences among the solo pastors, those who are still on lower rungs of the career ladder—"on the way" if you please.

An alternative hypothesis, and one that is equally plausible, is that the male/female tendencies in ministry style among senior ministers emerged not because of traits or approaches those persons *brought to* the senior appointment but because of what the structural arrangements of senior positions *allowed* the incumbents to do. It is possible that there was a relative *absence* of differences between the men and women ministers *while they were still solo pastors*, the pattern that actually existed among the solo pastors at the time of this study. In this case the differences between men and women would emerge only *after they became senior ministers*. Prior to those senior placements, they could have been just as overloaded, just as vulnerable, just as guarded, and lacking just as much role flexibility as experienced by the solo pastors in this study.

Kleinman's (1984) study of seminary students includes some observations consistent with this interpretation. She says, for example, "Since the female students expect parishioners not only to challenge their nontraditional professional ideology but their claim to the ministerial role as well, they feel an even greater need than men to have a firm sense of professional authority in their future relations with clients. [They]...are placed in a situation where they cannot fully accept the [feminine] rhetoric and ideology lest they diminish the role-model strength needed to survive in a male-dominated field" (82). "In entering the professions as marginal members, malelike behavior is the resource available to women who seek recognition as professionals" (97). "Because the wider public 'lags behind' the [feminine] humanistic rhetoric, some of the female students use that rhetoric in ways circumscribed by old cultural understandings and adjust to that wider context by reverting back to old ways" (99). These patterns are probably more likely to be manifested by solo pastors than by senior ministers with subordinate ministerial staffs.

It is also likely that ministry styles of senior pastors are also matters of interaction between characteristics of minister and congregation. The men with masculine styles and local churches wishing ministerial leadership with masculine modes of work are likely eventually to find each other. Similarly, experienced women with more feminine work patterns and congregations seeking people with more feminine ministry styles most likely will locate each other. The convergence between work environment and approach to ministry encourages the pastors to pursue their unique inclinations. Again, perhaps. Hopefully this matter of the effects of senior placement on ministry style—or the influence of ministry style on the work of senior ministers—can be pursued systematically in the near future. We do not have in this undertaking the requisite longitudinal data needed to pursue such a question.

The Effect of Seminary Cohort

The third specifying condition of the relationship between sex and ministry style is seminary cohort. Ministers who completed their theological education prior to 1971 manifested few sex differences in approach to ministry as indicated in either the "like-me" questions or degree of involvement in clergy roles. However, clergy who graduated from seminary from 1971 onward increasingly indicated approach to ministry in sex-typed ways. In these later cohorts, more men than women were willing to use power over the congregation, took a rational approach to decision making, and were legalistic ethically. More women than men in those cohorts sought to empower their congregation and were involved in social issues. Similar sex differences appeared in the later cohorts concerning hours spent in clergy roles.

These patterns raise some interesting questions. Did the cohort difference stem from changes in the characteristics of the students, of the seminaries, or both?

Selective Recruitment Hypothesis   One possibility is that the cohorts represented different kinds of individuals. Prior to the 1970s the particular women who completed theological seminary could have been of a very different nature from those who came later. Before about 1970 female seminary students would have had to enter seminary knowing that they would complete their courses as part of a "man's world." The curriculum was as it had been for decades before—unquestioned, traditional, not questioning masculine symbols and language. If the women were to succeed, they would have to do it on men's terms. And some did it. After 1970, however, when the feminist movement became more widespread in church circles, women who entered seminary brought with them a different set of assumptions and values from those of their predecessors. As the women-in-ministry movement became more widespread, paralleling the secular women's liberation movement, new seminary students entered with more distinctly feminist presuppositions and agendas, and they brought about changes in the seminary curriculum and subculture, which then carried over into their work as pastors. The change in sex-typing of ministry style in seminary cohorts before and after 1970 would be a result of this pattern of *selective recruitment* into theological education.

Dual Seminary Subculture Hypothesis   An alternate explanation of the change in cohort behavior before and after 1970 deals with differences in the *seminary* rather than the individuals recruited to it. Before about 1970, the seminary curriculum and student subculture was relatively homogeneous. After 1970, however, with the challenges to sexism in the seminary curriculum, faculty hiring practices, sexist language, pre-feminist Biblical exegesis and church history, and so forth, *the seminary itself changed.* Sexist language began to disappear, women's studies courses became part of the curriculum, female faculty joined the staff, women's support groups appeared (some of which became women's social action groups), and feminist religious literature appeared in the campus book store and on course reading lists. However, these additions to seminary life did not appeal equally to male and female students. The new feminist material came to be seen as the "cultural property" of the female students more than the males. The feminist scholarship and polemics appealed more to the women than to the men. The feminist support and action groups included almost exclusively women students. It was mostly the women who enrolled in the feminist courses and soaked up the feminist literature. The women assumed that all of these materials were relevant to their life and work, while most men did not.

As a result the seminary student culture became bifurcated. The traditional "mainstream" seminary world remained the province mainly of men, who tolerated what they perceived as feminist appendages on an otherwise standard curriculum and literature. The "feminist" seminary subculture existed alongside the mainstream structure, appealing to and including mostly women. When these students completed seminary, they entered their pastorates with divergent assumptions of what was important, and their respective masculine and feminine ministry styles flowed from those partly separate seminary experiences.

In the case of the first explanation, pointing to selective recruitment of different types of students before and after about 1970, each cohort becomes simply a grouping of students who pursue preexisting interests in their theological education. The seminary constitutes the ground or the arena within which they selectively shape and develop those interests. The path into the ministry is but a means of realizing their identities, and their subsequent ministry styles are but further flowering of those masculine and feminine work styles that were there all along.

In the case of the second approach, focusing on the new realities in the structure and culture of theological education, each cohort becomes a product of the values and patterns learned in the context of separate male and female worlds existing side-by-side in the universe of seminary life. The women's path to ministry involves encounter with feminist values, assumptions, and objectives that are not adopted until they are enrolled in seminary courses and assimilated into seminary life and its feminist interest groups. The path for men tends to be different. It involves but minimal "exposure" to the feminist structures and subculture but not real immersion in them. Carroll (1992) suggests that this process closely resembles "self-fulfilling prophecy." The seminary subculture takes on postulates that women perform ministry differently from men and that the women who enter that arena develop uniquely feminine ministry styles.

There is one important implication of these patterns that should be given considerable attention in further thought about possible uniquenesses in women's approach to pastoral ministry. The cultural feminist argument makes a great deal of the observation that women's life experiences differ greatly from those of men. A major building block in their argument for a peculiarly feminine style of ministry on the part of women is the idea that these *female life experiences* are the major sources of the sex-specific character of women's ministry. The effects of seminary cohort on the relationship between sex and ministry style raises a question about that assumption. The patterns in these data suggest instead that *the feminine characteristics of some women's approach to ministry result from women's experiences as seminary students as much as—or even more than—their prior experiences as women*—again, the self-fulfilling prophecy.

This pattern is consistent with the findings of Eagly and Johnson (1990) that gender-stereotypic expectations generally were *not* supported in "organizational studies" of sex differences in approach to work. In formal organizations, especially work organizations, male and female leaders tend to go through parallel (if not identical) educational and training programs to prepare them for the work expectations specific to the organization. Those experiences tend to standardize work patterns in general and specifically produce more similarities than differences between men and women and their approach to organizational leadership. In the case of ordinands completing seminary education after 1970, women and men experienced somewhat *different* definitions of appropriate approaches to pastoral ministry—the men the "traditional masculine" style and the women additionally a "feminine" style. The organizational conditions in this case were *not* identical. The female seminarians participated in the "feminine" subculture with greater enthusiasm and intensity than did the males.

Which of these explanations is correct? One? Both? Neither? Kleinman (1984) presents a portrate of seminary life manifesting relatively "feminine" values for everyone—both male and female students. Are other "mainline" Protestant seminaries also shifting in that direction? Again we have identified a need for further inquiry into the interaction of gender, student interests, seminary culture and the mechanisms of its influence on students, and subsequent patterns of approach to the pastoral ministry.

The Strength of the Evidence

The statistical relationships we encountered in the process of the analysis constitute the bases for making these judgments. Most of those correlations were not as strong as one would normally like to see. Only a few of them were even moderately strong. What are we to make of this pattern? There are numerous factors that could lead to what some would characterize as the less-than-ideal analytical outcomes we obtained, results that some observers might be tempted to characterize as having marginal utility.

The Survey Approach

Some individuals interested in the issue of sex differences in ministry style would argue that survey research is not the way to deal with it. After all, in survey research subtle and complex concepts have to be reduced to concrete questions in the process of operationalization. In the effort to measure differences in those constructs, meanings get oversimplified as they are concretized, and the resulting measurement is at best a superficial approximation of the elusive logic embodied in the concept at its higher level of abstraction.

Fair enough. However, if the goal is to be able to compare the approaches to ministry among male and female ministers throughout the religious bodies under study, and if one wishes to be able to make generalizations about all of the men and women in question, then survey research is the way to go, for all practical purposes. There is no body of literature that presents the information we need to make the necessary comparisons. Doing a series of case studies would be so highly selective as to raise questions about the representativeness of the cases covered. Unobtrusive observation of men and women at work would be so time consuming and expensive as to render it practically unworkable. With all of its difficulties, the survey was the appropriate research design.

Gender Bias

It is possible that the results have been tarnished by the fact that the researcher is a male and has approached the issues from a masculine perspective. Yes, this is always a potential problem. However, it is certainly no less likely that gender bias would influence the results if the project had been undertaken by a woman and the resulting feminine perspective. The study incorporated as many safeguards as possible, within the constraints of time and money available for the undertaking. Those steps have been described already in chapter 4. Again, the burden of proof of sex bias in this study rests with the plaintiff.

A more fruitful approach to the matter of less-than-ideal statistical outcomes is to view the results in the light of the realities of exploratory research and the social context of the research problem.

Exploratory Research

The level of precision and validity of measurement one can usually attain in exploratory work is inherently limited. In this case (as in many others), the concepts in question derive from the clamor of a social movement. They typically have a great deal of political meaning, but they are often poorly defined for analytical purposes. The best of measures of those concepts are a bit crude, and the logic of their inter-relationships has not been spelled out clearly. (Developing that logic is precisely one of the things exploratory work is trying to accomplish!) Accordingly, in dealing with subtle and somewhat vague constructs in this undeveloped and exploratory context, it is surprising to some researchers that we ever come up with *any* significant relationships at all! So to find *any* of the measures in hand to be associated with each other beyond what is likely to occur by chance may be bordering on the miraculous in itself. In this study, not only were such associations found, but they were also internally consistent. That is, the same dimensions of ministry style were repeatedly associated with being male or female and under very similar conditions. They also conformed to the expectations of one school of thought. There were some clearly identifiable and repetitive patterns. Those patterns emerged in both the clergy self-descriptions and the lay members' perceptions. So it is quite likely that the relationships observed in the analysis of the data do in fact reflect some aspect of social reality "out there."

The Ideological Context of the Study

Technical matters in conducting research do not exhaust the contextual issues to be considered in assessing the outcome and discovering its implications. Another significant point to bear in mind when reflecting on this study is its ideological context, that is, the fact, first of all, that the expectations of sex differences studied here flow from an *ideological* base, rather than detached, objective discourse. Let's go back to where the discussion started. Women seeking ordination and placement as pastors (and other church-related positions) have experienced prejudice, discrimination, humiliation, and rejection in response to their efforts at expanding their roles in the church. Even in these denominations, where women's ordination is a matter of policy, often even reinforced by quasi–affirmative action plans, women are not always welcome as pastoral candidates, especially at the level of the local congregation. Churches have to be persuaded to "do the right thing."

How do women seeking ordination and placement deal with that? One thing they can do is seek legitimations for their cause. Another possibility is to develop strategies for changing lay members' minds about their resistance. One such strategy—which also constitutes an implicit form of legitimation—is to indicate ways in which accepting women as ordained church leaders will improve the situation in the churches. In this mode, adopting the maximalist stance, one tactic has been to show how women will avoid the mistakes men have made in their ministries, how "women's way" is more consistent with basic Christian values than is the traditional "men's way" and thus how the situation for the churches will be better under the pastoral leadership of women than of men. To word it in the style of a Broadway song, "Anything they can do, we can do better!"

Thus a significant background to these assertions about sex differences in ministry style is the need for a rationale by the women-in-ministry movement for legitimating their demands. Viewed in this light, the source, objectives, and logic underlying the argument takes on a unique character. The impetus for the cultural feminists' assertions of sex differences in the way pastors approach their work was not a rigorous theoretical inquiry into the social psychology of gender. Instead the basis of the propositions was the political agenda associated with the social movement pressing for changes in sexist religious institutions. The basic objectives of the persons proposing sex differences was not a program of study to explain patterns of human functioning. Rather the purpose was to criticise the male-dominated world of religious leadership and to motivate religious decision makers to question their sexist assumptions and open up church structures to broader female participation. The logic in the predictions of sex-specific ministry styles did not derive from a social scientific theory. Instead, the rationale behind those expectations flowed from the political strategy of one branch of the women-in-ministry movement.

And of course the minimalists' agenda qualitatively was no different; they also spoke primarily from rather similar political motives, objectives, and rationale. *Their political objective was the same as that of the maximalists,* that is, expanding women's role in the Church. But their argument was different. Either out of simple disbelief in the descriptions of sex differences in approach to ministry, or from concern that the "women's way" argument would merely serve to further marginalise clergywomen, they argued for perceptions of basic similarity of ministry styles of men and women.

In this sense the statements by cultural religious feminists about male and female clergy are not unlike those made of opponents in the heat of political campaigns and many social movements. They are intended to attain political objectives by castigating one's antagonists, not to present analytically useful descriptions of them. They portray the opponent as the "bad guy." They depict themselves as more closely approximating the "ideal." Whether those contrasting images are accurate representations of reality is not the central question. The focal issue is what will bring about the desired result. This is *not* to say that the maximalists are being deceptive. There is no evidence to suggest anything other than that they firmly believe what they say. Rather it is to suggest that the force of cultural values and social objectives have an almost irresistible power to structure perceptions of reality—a proposition enjoying wide acceptance in social and behavioral science.

Statements by the structural religious feminists participate in some of the same dynamics. Rather than primarily being empirically based statements of reality, the minimalists' discourse is largely political. Its contentions of "no difference" are intended to avoid having women ministers shoot themselves in the foot by stigmatising themselves in the eyes of persons whose acceptance they desire.

The distinctions between these two types of argument can also be characterized in terms proposed by Alfred Schutz (1967). Schutz delineated the difference between political and scientific discourse in terms of "different orders" of concepts. Concepts shared by actors in the concerns of everyday living were called "first-order constructs." These are the typifications of objects and events by which ordinary people make sense out of their experiences. They are the shared constructs of the taken-for-granted culture that pattern people's thoughts and deeds— the "folk concepts." Social science, says Schutz, is concerned with making sense out of those systems of concepts. In that enterprise, scientific discourse creates "second-order constructs," theoretical fabrications designed to explain the first-order constructs, to account for the systems of meaning of everyday life—the folk concepts. Social science is constructs about other constructs. The criterion of validity (or "success") of first-order constructions is simply whether they work for the purpose of organizing individual and social action. The criterion of validity of second-order constructs is whether their theoretical propositions can be supported by replicated empirical research. In these terms making sense out of one's life goals and experiences rests on selective observation and consensual validation, while systematically explaining those ways of making sense out of life rests on formal social-scientific discourse—two quite different enterprises.

To the extent that assertions of sex-specific approaches to pastoral ministry derive from perceptions of useful strategy for broadening women's roles in the church, the arguments are basically *first*-order constructs, the meaning systems of the participants. They are the language of the social actors—political statements. As such their criterion of validity is primarily whether they *work*. The critical question is simply whether they actually serve to open up church structures to broader female participation. It matters little whether they can be confirmed by empirical evidence. And in the end it may make little sense to expect them to conform to the rules of logic and evidence comprising the canons governing second-order constructs in social-scientific research.

However, it is important to remember that in the case of this study, *some of the actors' assertions about sex-specific approaches to ministry were in fact confirmed empirically.* Male and female pastors tended to differ according to measures of willingness to use power over the congregation, desire to empower the congregation, preference for rational decision making, and ethical legalism. Conceptualizations comprising primarily first-order constructs found support in a study typically reserved for analysis of second-order constructs. Yet those sex differences were quite weak, that is, the distributions across the ranges of scores on each of those indexes tended to be quite similar for males and females. And the sex differences were confined to specific conditions associated with ethnicity, type of placement, seminary environment, and length of tenure. Why were they not stronger, more general, or more consistent? The answer may lie in the simple disjuncture between the level of discourse of the argument and the criteria of validity applied to it.

This problem of possibly misinterpreting disagreements over sex differences between participants in the women-in-ministry movement by viewing them out of context appears to be but a specific instance of the perplexities endemic to the broader feminist movement today. Bacchi (1990) points out that feminists have not always divided into two camps, one emphasizing "sameness" and the other focusing on "difference." That kind of split did not occur until after the turn of the century, acccording to the evidence she presents. The divisions that occurred in the movement at that time were primarily a result of divergent perceptions of what strategy could best improve women's situation (Bacchi 1990, 104)—the same kind of objective as we see in the women-in-ministry movement. The debates within feminism along sameness/difference lines arose where there appeared to be only two options for women, joining the male-dominated system on its own terms or remaining outside of it. "The debates dissolve, or never even surface, when it is possible to expect humane living conditions for everyone" (p. 259).

The debates about similarity and difference have not always involved the same substantive issues. There have been at least three distinct questions in the history of the discussions. One issue has been "metaphysical," asking about the fundamental nature of men and women. A second focus has been "functional," where the question has been whether or not men and women should play distinct roles in society. The third question has been "institutional," asking whether women need special institutions or legislation to meet their needs. Proponents of the interests of women have stressed either sameness or difference from men as it has appeared to be useful strategy to bring about arrangements helpful to women in these specific terms, and each type of issue has been dominant in specific historical struggles of women for social participation and change (Bacchi 1990, 2). Translated into these terms, in the arguments about male and female clergy, the question has been whether a "metaphysical" stance would best promote a "functional" objective.

So the feminist debates between maximalists and minimalists at root may not have been primarily about differences between men and women. The fundamental issue has been what kind of argument would be strategically useful to bring about changes in women's lives. The real question has been how to organize social relations. Disputes about differences and similarities between women and men have been disagreements about which kind of polemic would bring about the desired result. They are legitimations.

Bacchi also points out that in fact neither strategy has worked very well for women (1990, xiii). The gains in creating societal structures to allow women (and men) to participate in the economic and political life of the society and still deal adequately with the needs of hearth and home have been small. And whether the pressure for change was based on sex similarity or difference may have had little to do with the eventual outcome. Bacchi says that we need to move beyond the dichotomous debate and focus instead on how society is organized and how we should live, work, and care for our families. "The sameness/difference framework does feminism a disservice since it mystifies these political issues" and distracts us from the real problems associated with contemporary social organization (Bacchi 1990, 265). It derails discussion from a mainline focus on ways to eliminate sex discrimination and sidetracks it on the spur of possibly unproductive arguments about sex differences.

Could the women-in-ministry movement benefit from Bacchi's argument? Could it be that the arguments for a distinctively feminine ministry style brought by women are primarily legitimations for social goals? It is probably too early to tell whether the religious maximalists or minimalists have been more successful in bringing about institutional change in access to the ministry in these denominations. My own prejudice resides with the minimalists. Perhaps the structural alterations that have taken place to date would have happened regardless of whether the pressure for change involved an emphasis on sameness or difference. The differences we discovered in this study were certainly not great, and they tended to appear only in particular circumstances. In the long run of history they may prove to have been important in dealing with religious sexism, or they could turn out to have been irrelevant. Only time will tell. Nevertheless, if there is a chance that the cultural/structural feminist debate on the nature of women clergy is focusing on legitimations that draw attention away from the issue of equal participation in ministry, perhaps the combatants will want to reconsider the importance of the entire discussion. The question of masculine and feminine approaches to pastoral ministry is still wide open.

Ministry Style in Perspective

So what are we to make of the results of the study? The outcome is mixed. The evidence is clear, but it is not as decisive as one would like. The cultural feminists' assertions about sex differences in approach to ministry were partly correct but not entirely. Neither were they entirely incorrect. The minimalist arguments setting forth a basically androgynous ministry style were also partly supported, but they could not be completely accepted either. The patterns in the results of the analysis allow one to say to both camps, "Yes, but...." Yes, there was confirmation of some sex differences in ministry style, *but* only under certain conditions. Yes, there was evidence of similarities in men's and women's approach to ministry, *but* only under particular circumstances.

These outcomes constitute another example of what happens so often when one takes categorical statements about the social world and subjects them to empirical assessment. So often descriptive declarations about the real world that are presented in unqualified form have to be modified when the evidence is in. What typically happens to them is that the unconditional statement gets transformed into a question. In this case, the competing assertions about the nature of men's and women's ministry styles now have to be restated as questions. *The declaration that men and women differ clearly and markedly in their approach to ministry has now become an inquiry into the conditions under which male and female clergy are likely to manifest divergent ministry styles.* This transformation is one of the "secrets" of successful science. It forces us to rethink our assumptions and assertions about the world, and the result is usually at least a slight improvement in our understanding of why things happen as they do.

Under what conditions do clergymen and clergywomen approach their work as pastors in gender-specific modes? We're still not sure. But if we keep working at it—studying their ministry styles as openly as possible, that is, without prejudging the evidence ideologically—perhaps we can come closer to the answers than we are now.

References

Andolsen, Barbara Hilkert. *Daughters of Jefferson, Daughters of Bootblacks: Racism and American Feminism*. Macon, Ga.: Mercer University Press, 1986.

Babbie, Earl. *The Practice of Social Research*. Belmont, Calif.: Wadsworth Publishing Co., 1979.

Bacchi, Carol Lee. *Same Difference: Feminism and Sexual Difference*. Sydney: Allen & Unwin, 1990.

Baer, Hans A. "Bibliography of Social Science Literature on Afro-American Religion in the United States." *Review of Religious Research*, vol. 29, no. 4 (June 1988): 413–30.

Bem, Sandra L. "The Measurement of Psychological Androgyny," *Journal of Consulting and Clinical Psychology*, vol. 42 (1974): 155–62.

Bendix, Reinhard, and Symour Lipset, eds. *Class, Status, and Power*. Glencoe, Ill.: Free Press, 1953.

Blizzard, Samuel W. "The Protestant Parish Minister's Integrating Roles," *Religious Education*, vol. 53 (July): 374–80.

Brehm, J. W., and A. R. Cohen. *Explorations in Cognitive Dissonance*. New York: John Wiley, 1962.

207

Briggs, Sheila. "Women and Religion." In Beth B. Hess and Myra Marx Feree, eds., *Analyzing Gender: A Handbook of Social Science Research*. Newbury Park, Calif.: Sage, 1987.

Cardwell, Sue Webb. "Why Women Fail/Succeed in Ministry: Psychological Factors." *Pastoral Psychology*, vol. 30, no. 4 (Summer 1982): 153–62.

Carpenter, Delores C. "The Professionalization of the Ministry of Women." *Journal of Religious Thought*, vol. 43 (Spring–Summer 1987): 59–75.

Carroll, Jackson W. Personal correspondence, February 28, 1992.

———. Barbara Hargrove, and Adaire T. Lummis. *Women of the Cloth: A New Opportunity for the Churches*. New York: Harper and Row, 1983.

Charlton, Joy C. "Women in Seminary: A Review of Current Social Science Research." *Review of Religious Research*, vol. 28, no. 4 (June 1987): 315–18.

Chodorow, Nancy. *The Reproduction of Mothering*. Berkeley and Los Angeles: University of California Press, 1978.

Christ, Carol P. "The New Feminist Theology: A Review of the Literature." *Religious Studies Review*, vol. 3 no. 4 (October 1977): 203–12.

Christ, Carol P. and Judith Plaskow. *Womanspirit Rising: A Feminist Reader in Religion*. New York: Harper and Row, 1979.

Collins, Shiela. *A Different Heaven and Earth: A Feminist Perspective on Religion*. Valley Forge: Judson Press, 1974.

Cook, Mark. *Perceiving Others: The Psychology of Interpersonal Perception*. London: Methuen & Co., 1979.

Crawford, Mary, and Jeanne Marecek. "Psychology Reconstructs the Female: 1968–1988." *Psychology of Women Quarterly*, vol. 13 (1989): 147–65.

Daly, Mary. *Beyond God the Father: Toward a Philosophy of Women's Liberation*. Boston: Beacon Press, 1973.

———. *The Church and the Second Sex*. New York: Harper and Row, 1975.

———. *Gyn/ecology*. Boston, Beacon Press, 1978.

Eagly, Alice H., and Blair T. Johnson, "Gender and Leadership Style: A Meta-Analysis." *Psychological Bulletin*, vol. 108, no. 2 (1990): 233–56.

Ekhardt, Bonita N., and W. Mack Goldsmith. "Personality Factors of Men and Women Pastoral Candidates." Part 1, "Motivational Profiles." *Journal of Psychology and Theology*, vol.12, no. 2 (1984): 109–18.

Epstein, Cynthia Fuchs, *Deceptive Distinctions: Sex, Gender, and the Social Order*. New York: Russell Sage Foundation, 1988.

Festinger, Leon. *A Theory of Cognitive Dissonance*. New York: Harper and Row, 1957.

Finch, Janet. *Married to the Job: Wives' Incorporation in Men's Work*. London: Allen and Unwin, 1983.

Fiorenza, Elisabeth Schussler. *In Memory of Her*. Wayne, N.J.: Crossroads Press, 1976.

Franklin, Margaret Ann. *The Force of the Feminine*. Sydney: Allen & Unwin, 1986.

Friedman, W. J., A. B. Robinson, and B. L. Friedman, "Sex Differences in Moral Judgements?" *Psychology of Women Quarterly*, vol. 11, no. 1 (1987): 37–46.

Gerth, H. H., and C. Wright Mills, eds. *From Max Weber: Essays in Sociology*. Fair Lawn, N.J.: Oxford University Press, 1946.

Gilkes, Cherly Townsend. Personal correspondence, July, 1992.

Gilligan, Carol. *In a Different Voice: Psychological Theory and Women's Development*. Cambridge, Mass.: Harvard University Press, 1982.

Goldsmith, W. Mack, and Bonita N. Ekhardt. "Personality Factors of Men and Women Pastoral Candidates." Part 2, "Sex Role Preferences." *Journal of Psychology and Theology*, vol. 12, no. 3 (1984): 211–21.

Glock, Charles Y., and Rodney Stark. *Religion and Society in Tension*. Chicago: Rand McNally, 1965.

Grant, Jacqueline. *White Women's Christ and Black Women's Jesus: Feminist Christology and Womanist Response*. Atlanta: Scholars Press, 1989.

Greeno, Catherine, and Eleanor Maccoby, "How Different Is the Different Voice?" *Signs*, vol. 11, no. 2 (1986): 310–16.

Hahn, Celia Allison. *Sexual Paradox: Creative Tensions in Our Lives and in Our Congregations*. New York: Pilgrim Press, 1991.

Hale, Harry, Morton King, and Doris Jones. *New Witnesses: United Methodist Clergywomen*. Nashville: Board of Higher Education and Ministry, 1980.

Hare-Mustin, Rachel T., and Jeanne Marecek. "The Meaning of Difference: Gender Theory, Postmodernism, and Psychology." *American Psychologist*, vol. 43, no. 6, (June 1988): 455–64.

Hargrove, Barbara W. *Reformation of the Holy: A Sociology of Religion*. Philadelphia: F. A. Davis Co., 1971.

Heider, Fritz. *The Psychology of Interpersonal Relations*. New York: John Wiley, 1958.

Ice, Martha Long. *Clergywomen and Their World Views: Calling for a New Age*. New York: Praeger Publishers, 1987.

Jacobs, Janet L. "Women and the Divine: The Reconstruction of God and Spirituality." Paper presented at the annual meeting of the Society for the Scientific Study of Religion, Louisville, Kentucky, October 1988.

Kahn, Robert K., and Elise Boulding. *Power and Conflict in Organizations*. New York: Basic Books, 1964.

Kerlinger, Fred N. *Behavioral Research: A Conceptual Approach*. New York: Holt, Reinhart and Winston, 1979.

Kleinman, Sherryl. *Equals Before God: Seminarians as Humanistic Professionals*. Chicago: University of Chicago Press, 1984.

Kohlberg, Lawrence, and R. Kramer. "Continuities and Discontinuities in Childhood and Adulthood Moral Development." *Human Development*, vol. 12 (1969): 93–120.

Lawless, Elaine J. *Handmaidens of the Lord: Pentecostal Women Preachers and Traditional Religion*. Philadelphia: University of Pennsylvania Press, 1988.

Lehman, Edward C., Jr. "Status Differences Between Types of Ministry: Measurement and Effect." *Research in the Social Scientific Study of Religion*, vol. 2, (March 1990): 95–116.

———. *Women Clergy: Breaking Through Gender Barriers*. New Brunswick, N.J.: Transaction Books, 1985.

Lenski, Gerhard. *Power and Privilege*. New York: McGraw-Hill, 1966.

Lerner, Alan Jay. *The Street Where I Live: The Story of "My Fair Lady," "Gigi," and "Camelot."* Sydney: Hodder and Stoughton, 1978.

Lincoln, C. Eric, and Lawrence H. Mamiya. *The Black Church in the African-American Experience*. Durham, N.C.: Duke University Press, 1990.

Lips, Hilary M. *Women, Men, and Power*. London: Mayfield Publishing Co., 1991.

Maccoby, Eleanor E., and Carol Jacklin. *The Psychology of Sex Differences*. Stanford, Calif.: Stanford University Press, 1974.

Maitland, Sara. *The Map of the New Country: Women and Christianity*. London: Routledge & Kegan Paul, 1983.

McDavid, John W., and Herbert Harari. *Psychology and Social Behavior.* New York: Harper and Row, 1974.

McDougall, William. *Introduction to Social Psychology.* London: Methuen, 1908.

Mead, Margaret. *Sex and Temperament in Three Primitive Societies.* New York: Dell, 1949.

Mednick, Martha T. "On the Politics of Psychological Constructs: Stop the Bandwagon, I Want to Get Off." *American Psychologist,* vol. 44, no. 8 (1989): 1118–23.

Meyers, Eleanor Scott. "Searching for Feminist Ecclesial Forms of Power and Authority: A Sociological Perspective." Paper presented at the annual meeting of the Society for the Scientific Study of Religion, Chicago, October 1988.

Miller, N. E., and J. Dollard. *Social Learning and Imitation.* New Haven: Yale University Press, 1941.

Miller-McLemore, Bonnie J. "Ruth or Orpha: Shall We Return to Our Mother's House?" Paper presented at the annual meeting of the Society for the Scientific Study of Religion, Chicago, October 1988.

Mobley, William H. *Employee Turnover: Causes, Consequences, and Control.* Reading, Mass.: Addison-Wesley, 1982.

Montagna, Paul D. *Occupations and Society: Toward a Sociology of the Labor Market.* New York: John Wiley & Sons, 1977.

Nason-Clark, Nancy. "Are Women Changing the Image of Ministry? A Comparison of British and American Societies." *Review of Religious Research,* vol. 28, no. 4 (June 1987): 331–40.

Neitz, Mary Jo. Remarks made as a panel member at the annual meeting of the Association for the Sociology of Religion, Washington, D.C., August, 1990.

Ochs, Carol. *Women and Spirituality.* Totowa, N.J.: Rowman and Allanheld, 1983.

Osiek, Carolyn. *Beyond Anger — On Being a Feminist in the Church.* New York: Paulist Press, 1986.

Paris, Peter J. *The Social Teachings of the Black Churches.* Minneapolis, Minn.: Augsburg Fortress Publishers, 1985.

Piotrkowski, Chaya S. *Work and the Family System.* New York: Free Press, 1979.

Riley, Maria O. P. *Transforming Feminism.* Kansas City, Mo.: Sheed & Ward, 1989.

Robb, Carol S., ed. *Making the Connections: Essays in Feminist Social Ethics*. Boston: Beacon Press, 1985.

Roof, Wade Clark. *Community and Commitment*. New York: Elsevier, 1978.

Royle, Marjorie H. Personal correspondence, 1991.

———. "Women Pastors: What Happens After Placement?" *Review of Religious Research*, vol. 24, no. 2 (December 1984): 116–26.

Ruether, Rosemary. *Sexism and God Talk: Toward a Feminist Theology*. Boston: Beacon Press, 1983.

———. *Women-Church: Theology and Practice of Feminist Liturgical Communities*. San Fransisco: Harper and Row, 1985.

———, and Eleanor McLaughlin, eds. *Women of Spirit: Female Leadership in the Jewish and Christian Traditions*. New York: Simon and Schuster, 1979.

Russell, Letty. *Human Liberation in a Feminist Perspective*. Philadelphia: Westminster Press, 1974.

Schaller, Lyle. *The Church's War on Poverty*. Nashville: Abingdon Press, 1967.

Schutz, Alfred. *The Phenomenology of the Social World*. Translated by George Walsh and Frederick Lehnert. Evanston, Ill.: Northwestern University Press, 1967.

Skinner, B. F. *Science and Human Behavior*. New York: Macmillan, 1953.

Stevens, Lesley. "Different Voice/Different Voices: Anglican Women in Ministry." *Review of Religious Research*, vol. 30, no. 3 (March 1989): 262–75.

Stump, Roger W. "Regional Variations in the Determinants of Religious Participation." *Review of Religious Research*, vol. 27, no. 3 (March 1986): 208–25.

Tavris, Carol, and Carole Offir. *The Longest War: Sex Differences in Perspective*. New York: Harcourt, Brace, Jovanovich, 1977.

Thibaut, John W., and Harold H. Kelley. *The Social Psychology of Groups*. New York: John Wiley & Sons, 1959.

Thoma, S. "Estimating Gender Differences in the Comprehension and Preferences of Moral Issues." *Developmental Review*, vol. 6 (1986): 165–80.

Verdesi, Elizabeth H. *In But Still Out: Women in the Church*. Philadelphia: Westminster Press, 1976.

Warner, R. Stephen. *Woman's Place, Women's Space*. Manuscript, 1989. Cited with permission.

Weidman, Judith L., ed. *Women Ministers: How Women Are Redefining Traditional Roles*. Rev. ed. New York: Harper and Row, 1985.

Werther, William B., Jr., and Keith Davis. *Personnel Management and Human Resources*. New York: McGraw-Hill, 1985.

White, Leslie. *The Science of Culture*. New York: Farrar & Strauss, 1949.

Winter, Gibson. *The Suburban Captivity of the Churches*. Garden City, N.Y.: Doubleday, 1961.

Appendix

Date: _____   Start time: _____

second call: _____   Stop time: _____

third call: _____   elapsed: _____ minutes

APPROACH TO MINISTRY PROJECT
CLERGY QUESTIONNAIRE

Name: _____ Telephone: _____

Mailing address: _____

---

1. Denomination: (1)__Baptist   (3)__Presbyterian

                         (2)__Methodist   (4)__United Church

2, 3, 4. Clergy I.D. number   _ _ _   5–6. "CLERGY" = 11

7. Interviewer: (1)__Lehman   (4)__Carr

                    (2)__Cummings   (5)__Del Piero

                    (3)__French   (6)__Lowe

8. Respondent's Sex: (1)__male   (2)__female

9. Region: (1)__Northeast   (4)__Southwest
                    (2)__Southeast   (5)__Mountain
                    (3)__Midwest   (6)__Far West

A.   HELLO. MAY I SPEAK WITH (person named above) PLEASE?

   (If person is available, go to "B" below.)

   (If person is not available, find out:
   (1) when to call back   _____
   and/or (2) another number _____

B.   HELLO, MR/MS_____. MY NAME IS_____.
I'M CALLING FROM THE STATE UNIVERSITY OF NEW YORK IN
BEHALF OF DR. EDWARD LEHMAN AND YOUR DENOMINA-
TION. DR. LEHMAN WROTE YOU RECENTLY CONCERNING THE
STUDY OF APPROACHES TO THE PASTORAL MINISTRY. DID
YOU GET THAT LETTER?

        (If "yes," go to "D.")   (If "no," then read "C" below.)

C.   I'M SORRY. IS YOUR MAILING ADDRESS_____(above)?
(Correct if needed.) LET ME EXPLAIN WHAT WE ARE DOING.
YOUR DENOMINATION IS WORKING WITH DR. LEHMAN IN A
SURVEY OF A NATIONAL SAMPLE OF MINISTERS TO DETER-
MINE HOW THEY APPROACH THEIR WORK. YOUR NAME WAS
DRAWN AS PART OF A RANDOM SAMPLE OF CLERGY IN
THOSE CHURCHES—THAT IS HOW WE GOT YOUR NAME. THE
LETTER DESCRIBED THIS TO YOU. WOULD YOU LIKE ME TO
READ THE LETTER? (Read letter if necessary.)

THE LETTER ALSO INDICATED THAT I WOULD BE CALLING
YOU TO ASK YOU SOME SPECIFIC QUESTIONS. THE INTERVIEW
WILL TAKE ABOUT 20 MINUTES, AND YOUR ANSWERS WILL BE
COMBINED WITH THE RESPONSES OF ALL THE OTHERS. YOUR
NAME WILL NOT BE USED IN ANY ANALYSIS OR REPORT.
SINCE I'M CALLING LONG-DISTANCE, COULD WE START
THROUGH THE QUESTIONS NOW?

   (If "yes") "THANK YOU" (Go to Part I.)

   (If "no") Try to resolve the situation. If not possible, thank the
   person for his/her time. Hang up.

D. (if did receive the letter) GOOD! AS THE LETTER STATED, I'M CALLING TO ASK SOME QUESTIONS ABOUT HOW YOU APPROACH YOUR MINISTRY AND SOME DETAILS ABOUT YOURSELF AND YOUR CHURCH. YOUR ANSWERS WILL BE COMBINED WITH THOSE OF OTHER CLERGY, AND YOUR NAME WILL NOT BE USED IN ANY PART OF THE ANALYSIS OR RESEARCH REPORT.

I'M CALLING LONG-DISTANCE, SO MAY WE BEGIN NOW? (Go to Part I.)

Part I. Background Data

FIRST LET ME ASK A FEW THINGS ABOUT YOURSELF AND YOUR CHURCH.

10. About how long have you been serving your present church?

(1)__less than one year (9)__NA

(2)__1–2 years

(3)__3–4 years

(4)__5–6 years

(5)__7–8 years

(6)__9–10 years

(7)__more than 10 years

11. Are you the only salaried minister serving this church?

(1)__yes (2)__no (9)__NA

(if "Yes" skip to #14)

(if "No") 12. How many other salaried ministers are on the staff?

(write in)_____ (9)__NA

13. What is your position there?

(1)__Senior minister (pastor, copastor)

(2)__associate pastor

(3)__assistant pastor

(4)__minister of religious education

(5)__minister for counselling

(6)__minister for youth

(7)__minister for visitation (or hospital)

(8)__(other)_____

(9)__NA

NOTE *IF OTHER THAN "SENIOR MINISTER," "PASTOR," OR "COPASTOR," DISCONTINUE THE INTERVIEW!*

14.   Are you serving as a *copastor* of this congregation?

(1)__yes   (2)__no (Skip to #16.)   (9)__NA
(If yes, to #14.)

15.   Is the other copastor your spouse?

(1)__yes   (2)__no   (9)__NA

16.   About how many people are present in a typical Sunday morning worship service?

(1)__less than 50   (5)__201–250

(2)__51–100   (6)__251–300

(3)__101–150   (7)__301–350

(4)__151–200   (8)__more than 350   (9)__NA

17.   How would you describe the growth of the size of your congregation over the last ten years. Would it be:

(1)__growing faster than the surrounding community

(2)__growing about as fast as the community

(3)__growing, but *not* as fast as the community

(4)__holding its own

(5)__declining a bit

(6)__declining a lot?

(9)__NA

18.   And what type of community is your church located in?

(1)__within a large city (100,000 +)   (4)__in a small town

(2)__within a small city (25,000–100,000)   (5)__in a rural area

(3)__in a suburb to a city   (9)__NA

19. How about the budget? Would you say that your congregation's budget over the last ten years has been:

(1)__growing faster than inflation   (9)__NA

(2)__about keeping pace with inflation

(3)__steady, but not quite keeping up with inflation

(4)__declining

20–21. How old are you now? (As of last birthday.)

(write in)_____   (99)__NA

22. What is the highest level of formal education you obtained?

(1)__less than B.A./B.S.   (5)__D.Min.

(2)__B.A./B.S.   (6)__Th.D.

(3)__M.Div (or B.D.)   (7)__Ph.D.

(4)__Th.M. (or S.T.M., etc.)   (9)__NA

23–24. In what year did you graduate from seminary? (write in_____)

(98__did not graduate)

(99__NA)

25–26. In what year were you ordained? (write in_____)

(98__not ordained)

(99__NA)

27. What is your marital status at present?

(1)__single, never married (skip to #30)

(2)__married, living with spouse (go to #28)

(3)__separated (skip to #30)

(4)__divorced (skip to #30)

(5)__widowed (skip to #30)

(if #2, married)

28. What is the highest level of formal education your spouse attained?

    (1)__less than B.A./B.S.   (5)__M.A./M.S.

    (2)__B.A./B.S.   (6)__D.Min.

    (3)__M.Div (or B.D.)   (7)__Th.D.

    (4)__Th.M. (or S.T.M., etc.) (8)__Ph.D.   (9)__NA

29.   Which of the following categories best describes your spouse's occupation?

    (1)__clergy   (5)__sales or clerical

    (2)__other professional   (6)__skilled manual labor

    (3)__administrative or proprietor (7)__unskilled manual labor

    (4)__technical   (8)__not gainfully employed

                              (9)__NA

30.   How would you describe your own ethnic background? Would it be:

    (1)__Hispanic   (4)__American Indian

    (2)__Afro-American   (5)__White European

    (3)__Asian-American   (9)__NA

31.   Which of the following categories includes your annual family income, including allowances (housing, car, etc.)?

    (1)__less than $20,000   (6)__$40,000–$44,999

    (2)__$20,000–$24,999   (7)__$45,000–$49,999

    (3)__$25,000–$29,999   (8)__$50,000 or more

    (4)__$30,000–$34,999   (9)__NA

    (5)__$35,000–$39,999

Part II. "Like-Me" Questions

THANK YOU FOR THAT INFORMATION. NOW WE GET INTO SOME QUESTIONS DEALING WITH YOUR APPROACH TO THE PASTORAL MINISTRY. I'M GOING TO READ A LIST OF STATEMENTS TO YOU. THEY DEAL WITH VARIOUS FACETS OF PASTORAL WORK, AND THEY ARE IN NO PARTICULAR ORDER.

WHAT I'D LIKE YOU TO TELL ME IS HOW MUCH EACH STATE-
MENT IS *LIKE YOU.* TO DO THAT, LET'S USE A SCALE FROM 0 TO
5: 0 INDICATES THAT THE ITEM IS *NOT LIKE YOU AT ALL,* AND 5
MEANS THAT THE STATEMENT IS *LIKE YOU COMPLETELY.* THE
NUMBERS IN BETWEEN WILL INDICATE VARYING DEGREES OF
SOMETHING BEING "LIKE YOU," SUCH AS:

1 = ONLY THE SLIGHTEST BIT

2 = A BIT MORE

3 = MORE YET

4 = CONSIDERABLY LIKE YOU, BUT NOT COMPLETELY—OK?

THE FIRST STATEMENT—HOW MUCH IS THIS "LIKE YOU"—
0 to 5?

32.__I make my major contribution to my congregation through my
preaching.

33.__I believe that only ordained clergy can properly administer the
Lord's Supper (Holy Communion).

34.__I am uncomfortable when people open up and share their inner-
most feelings with me.

35.__My sermons typically focus on theological beliefs.

36.__As a minister it is important for me to remain somewhat
detached from members of my congregation.

37.__It is hard for me to ignore requests from my congregation even
when I feel overwhelmed with work.

38.__When dealing with difficult decisions in the church, it is usually
my "gut feeling" that serves me best.

39.__My ministry is effective, because God is within me as well as
beyond me.

40.__Of all the things I have to do as a minister, I feel least competent
at financial matters like raising the budget.

41.__My sermons simply involve one believer speaking to another.

42.__I try hard to get my people involved in social issues that affect
their lives.

43.__I encourage my congregation to innovate when dealing with current issues instead of sticking with traditional patterns and programs.

44.__I usually focus my preaching on the concrete concerns of my
people.

45.__I contribute the most to my congregation by sharing in their celebration or their suffering.

46.__There is no substitute for rational, analytical thought for solving
congregational problems.

47.__When I preach, I always try to remember that I speak as a representative of Almighty God.

48.__I find that I must be a skilled and energetic fund raiser to prod
parishioners to give enough money to keep the church alive.

49.__I would really feel successful as a minister if I were serving a
large church.

50.__Sometimes I have to drag my congregation kicking and screaming in the direction I think the church ought to go.

51.__I often will bend church rules if they don't meet the needs of the
congregation.

52.__I think today's church members need to hear the correct position
on ethical issues delivered from the pulpit.

53.__I do not feel free to express my true feelings about things with
anyone in my congregation.

54.__I cannot be the leader I want to be if I do not have authority to
implement my own decisions.

55.__My daily working theology has little to do with my professional
ministry studies.

56.__I know I have my congregation's confidence when they openly
discuss with me their critical assessments of my program proposals.

57.__My primary concern in concrete moral choices is applying the
best rules for conducting human life.

Part III. Relative Importance of Ministry Roles

OK, THANK YOU! NOW LET'S MOVE TO A DIFFERENT TYPE OF
QUESTION—HOW YOU DEAL WITH THINGS YOU ARE CALLED
UPON TO DO. THE ROLE OF "PARISH MINISTER" CAN BE BRO-
KEN DOWN INTO SPECIFIC TYPES OF ACTIVITY, SUCH AS
PREACHING, COUNSELLING, ETC. I'M GOING TO READ A LIST
OF THOSE ROLES TO YOU. AS I READ THEM, *TRY TO RECALL
YOUR ACTIVITIES OVER THE LAST TWO WEEKS.* THEN AFTER I
READ EACH ACTIVITY, PLEASE TELL ME *ABOUT HOW MANY
HOURS YOU SPENT IN THAT SPECIFIC ROLE—OK?*

THE FIRST ONE—IN THE LAST TWO WEEKS, HOW MANY HOURS DID YOU SPEND IN:

58–59.__preparing and delivering sermons   (99__NO ANSWER)

60–61.__funerals

62–63.__teaching formal classes

64–65.__visiting church members and prospective members

66–67.__personal counselling

68–69.__church fellowship activities

70–71.__local church administration

72–73.__involvement in church structures beyond the congregation

74–75.__community-wide activities

76–77.__personal development

78–79.__social justice issues

THANK YOU. NOW LET'S COME AT THAT LIST IN A DIFFERENT WAY. I'M GOING TO READ EACH ROLE AGAIN. THIS TIME AFTER I READ EACH ONE, PLEASE TELL ME *HOW IMPORTANT THAT ROLE IS TO YOU PERSONALLY.* LET'S USE A SCALE OF 0 TO 5 AGAIN.

0 = NOT IMPORTANT TO YOU AT ALL

5 = EXTREMELY IMPORTANT TO YOU

1, 2, 3, AND 4 = GRADATIONS IN IMPORTANCE BETWEEN THE
        TWO EXTREMES—THE CLOSER TO "5," THE GREATER
        THE IMPORTANCE—OK?

ON A SCALE OF 0 TO 5, HOW PERSONALLY IMPORTANT IS THE ROLE OF:

80.__preparing and delivering sermons   (99__NO ANSWER)

81.__conducting funerals

82.__teaching formal classes

83.__visiting church members and prospects

84.__personal counselling

85.__church fellowship activities

86.__local church administration

87.__involvement in church structures beyond the congregation

88.__involvement in community activities

89.__personal development and growth

90.__social justice issues

OK! THANK YOU! *NOW WE'RE ALMOST FINISHED!* LET'S MOVE TO THE LAST PART -A FINAL SET OF STATEMENTS THAT MAY OR MAY NOT BE "LIKE YOU." I'M GOING TO READ ANOTHER LIST OF STATEMENTS. THEY ARE IN NO PARTICULAR ORDER, JUST AS WHEN WE WENT THROUGH THE OTHER SET EARLIER. AS BEFORE, PLEASE TELL ME HOW MUCH EACH STATEMENT IS *LIKE YOU.* LET'S USE THE SAME SCALE FROM 0 TO 5:

0 INDICATES THAT THE ITEM IS *NOT LIKE YOU AT* ALL, AND

5 MEANS THAT THE STATEMENT IS *VERY MUCH LIKE YOU.*

THE NUMBERS IN BETWEEN INDICATING VARYING DEGREES OF SOMETHING BEING "LIKE YOU"—THE CLOSER THE NUMBER IS TO 5, THE MORE THE STATEMENT IS "LIKE YOU"—OK?

Part IV. "Like-Me" Questions

THE FIRST STATEMENT—HOW MUCH IS THIS "LIKE YOU"—
0 to 5?

91.__I believe that lay people, not the clergy, should decide the direction in which the church will go.

92.__My authority as a minister rests primarily on my professional training and ordination.

93.__I prefer to use my professional title in relating to the local community.

94.__I think there is too much talk among ministers about salaries and "promotions."

95.__When I'm really sure about what the congregation should do, I try hard to get them to take my advice.

96.__I think it is more important to do the work of the church efficiently than to have a lot of people involved in it.

97.__I think that democratic decision making is a poor basis for local church policy.

98.__I feel uneasy when members of my congregation touch me in any way physically.

99.__I consider myself accountable primarily to the denominational administrators in my region.

100.__I think ordination to the ministry places too much distance between ministers and lay people.

101.__I don't think congregations can function very well without guidance from the clergy.

102.__I would like to be remembered as a helpful mentor to other ministers.

103.__As a church leader, it is important that I reveal no points of personal weakness to the congregation.

104.__I feel uncomfortable in the absence of clear organizational guidelines for ongoing church programs.

105.__The measure of success of my ministry is my positive influence on the community.

106.__One of my ministry goals is to enhance the power my members have in the mission and operation of their local church.

107.__I prefer that church members address me only by my first name.

108.__My ministry will be most successful if I can lead my congregation to get along without me.

109.__It is more important to me to maintain congregational solidarity than to follow denominational policy.

110.__A collaborative leadership style works best for me in working with the congregation.

111.__One of my goals in ministry is the eradication of social inequalities in the church.

112.__If I have any power in my congregation, it is based simply on the trust I have earned from the people.

THANK YOU! THAT'S THE LAST QUESTION! YOU HAVE BEEN MOST HELPFUL.

ONE LAST ITEM OF BUSINESS—THE NAMES OF TWO LAYMEMBERS. AS OUTLINED IN THE LETTER, WE NEED THE NAME AND ADDRESS OF TWO LAYPERSONS YOU REGARD AS THE LEADERS IN THE CONGREGATION—ONE MAN AND ONE WOMAN. CAN YOU GIVE ME THAT INFORMATION NOW PLEASE? (Fill in lay leader form.)

BEFORE WE HANG UP, IS THERE ANYTHING YOU'D LIKE TO ADD OR COMMENT ON CONCERNING YOUR APPROACH TO THE MINISTRY?

(Take full notes.)

THANK YOU AGAIN! GOODBYE.

Index